ROLLINS COLLEGE
CENTENNIAL HISTORY

For Stacy,
Thank you for your
support

Jack C. Lane

STORY FARM

WINTER PARK · MIAMI · SANTA BARBARA

ROLLINS COLLEGE
CENTENNIAL HISTORY

———

A STORY *of* PERSEVERANCE
1885–1985

JACK C. LANE

WEDDELL PROFESSOR
of AMERICAN HISTORY, EMERITUS
and COLLEGE HISTORIAN
ROLLINS COLLEGE

Rollins College Centennial History:
A Story of Perseverance (1885-1985)

Published in the United States of America by Story Farm, Inc.
www.story-farm.com

Printed in the United States of America by Bang Printing

Library of Congress Cataloging-in-Publication Data
available upon request
ISBN 978-0-9969441-2-0

EDITORIAL DIRECTOR Bob Morris
ART DIRECTOR Jason Farmand
COPY EDITOR Marcela Oliveira
INDEXING Amy Hall
PRODUCTION MANAGEMENT Tina Dahl

10 9 8 7 6 5 4 3 2 1
First edition, June 2017

This book is dedicated to past, present and future Rollins Alumni, whose multifarious lives embody the essence of what it means to earn a Rollins liberal education.

CONTENTS

———

CONTENTS

FOREWORD

———

FOUNDED IN 1885, ROLLINS COLLEGE has a history that intertwines with the political, cultural, and economic history of Florida and of our nation. Rollins has persisted through world wars, economic crises and periods of dramatic social change. All of this has shaped our character to what it is today.

Even before I arrived on campus, Professor Jack Lane was recommended to me as the most knowledgeable and authoritative source on our history. This was good advice. I learned that Professor Lane had a draft manuscript of the history of Rollins College, and that it was available in digital form through our college library. I read it with great eagerness and found it difficult to put down. The story was so rich, the chapters were filled with personalities, crises, bold and inspiring innovations, with a spirit that persisted through all of it. It is this manuscript that became, suitably revised, the book now published.

The story of Rollins told here is a tale of fragility and durability. Through all manner of calamity and existential threat, Rollins has persisted, borne on the backs of many who believed—who still believe—in the importance of our mission. One cannot read this story and not feel inspired by the efforts of so many to realize the original and evolving vision for Rollins and not feel obliged to do all one can to move Rollins forward into its next century.

This is a pivotal moment to show the public the first hundred years of Rollins' remarkable history. Liberal education will need to evolve to meet global challenges in the 21st century; however, any new direction for Rollins must be built upon the college's past. In this time of rapidly shifting changes, one that requires the (re)envisioning of the role of liberal education in a global context, it is critical that present and future Rollins generations embrace the distinctive character of the college that previous Rollins communities strove to build. The awareness of this precious legacy strengthens a college whose identity has become solidly grounded in the praxis of progressive liberal education.

In this sense, the publication of the Rollins' centennial history is probably more critical now than it was thirty years ago. Moreover, the thousands of students who have graduated from Rollins, as well as future graduates, should be given the opportunity to know and appreciate the fascinating history of the college from which they earned their degrees.

Grant H. Cornwell
PRESIDENT

PREFACE

In 1984, I was appointed college historian by
President Thaddeus Seymour and granted a year's sabbat-
ical to write a centennial history of Rollins College. For a
number of reasons, but mainly because I returned to full-
time teaching, the first draft manuscript remained uned-
ited. Now thirty years later, with the earlier issues resolved,
the history deserves to see the light of day. Rollins College
played a critical role in Florida's past as well as in the nation's
higher educational history. The college achieved national
recognition in the 1930s when it adopted John Dewey's theories of progressive education. As a measure of its national
prominence, Sinclair Lewis, in his 1932 Nobel Prize speech,
cited Rollins College as only one of four colleges in the
United States that exhibited high standards of innovation
and intellectual life.

Therefore, given its national significance, I thought it
essential to write a full account that would tell the whole
story. This book depicts a struggling little college on a
sparsely settled Florida frontier slowly building character
from adversity as well as from successes, from failures as
well as from accomplishments and from conflict as well as
from community. I have tried to portray a college guided by
trustees, administrators and faculty who were at times less
than competent and at other times almost heroic. This is a

story of students who were sometimes indifferent learners and at other times agents of change. This is the story of an institution's life whose character was formed by remarkable successes as well as by debilitating adversities.

The readers will also perceive that this account is an institutional history of a college evolving over time. By the nature of such approach, those who were most responsible for shaping the college—the trustees, presidents, administrators and the faculty—occupy most of the story. I do spend time discussing students and their collegiate life in those moments when they helped shape the institution. I have also attempted to place the college in a larger context of changes in higher education and influences of the larger society.

I have chosen perseverance as a theme for my story of the college's first one hundred years. Perseverance may be defined as steadfast commitment to a mission in the face of difficulties and delays in achieving success. The reader will see the college struggling with adversity in almost every administration. However, rather than defeating the college, the many incidences of hardship strengthened it, preparing it to meet the challenges of the future with greater confidence. The college endured these tribulations and thereby secured its liberal education mission for generations to come.

One of Hamilton Holt's most endearing conventions was the way in which he began faculty appointment and reappointment letters. At most other institutions such letters began bureaucratically: "I am pleased to offer you (re)appointment to the faculty for the following academic year." This was not Hamilton Holt's style. His letters began: "I call you to serve for another year on the faculty of Rollins College." What seems today like a quaint expression struck a responsive chord with me. Holt had chosen a word often used in the Victorian era that meant loving an institution or someone enough to make a commitment without a sense of personal gain. Shortly after I arrived in 1963, during the administration of Hugh McKean, I observed a personal attachment to the college among the older faculty I had never experienced in other institutions. My research in the archives revealed that this sentiment had been going on for multiple generations. Within a short time, I too became infected with an incurable affection for Rollins. The opportunity to tell the story of the college's past considerably reinforced that attachment.

Jack C. Lane
ROLLINS COLLEGE
2017

Chapter 1

───────

THE FOUNDING, 1885

THE MINUTES AND hours moved at a maddeningly slow pace for the handful of local inhabitants of Winter Park, Florida, on an April day in 1885. They were awaiting news from Orange City where representatives of the Florida Congregational Association were meeting to select the site for Florida's first institution of higher learning. Confident that their town would be chosen, the residents of Winter Park had prepared for a joyous celebration. They had constructed a miniature altar composed of "fat" pine logs on empty barrels covered with boards and buried in sand at a spot on north Interlachen Avenue. The women had baked cakes and prepared lemonade; speakers had written speeches with appropriate rhetorical flourishes; and a nationally known poet, Emily Huntington Miller, who was wintering in Winter Park, had composed a commemorative poem. The Congregational Association voted in the early morning at Orange City, but it would be well past noon before Winter Park would receive the news. With no direct rail communication between Orange City and their town, Winter Park's representatives had to travel by wagon to the St. Johns River, by boat down to Sanford, and again by wagon to reach the little hamlet on the outskirts of Orlando.[1]

In mid-afternoon, the courier arrived with the expected good news. Winter Park had been selected as the site for the new college. As planned, the bell on the tiny, unfinished Congregational Church pealed the happy tidings of victory. Before a roaring bonfire, several prominent residents made short but enthusiastic speeches. The evening was climaxed by the reading of Miller's poem, which ended with a vision of the future:

> *Lo! Down the years our fancy strays to see*
> *The wondrous picture of the days to be*
> *When her broad foundations wisely laid*
> *Her fair halls clustering in their quiet shade*
> *By the blue lake, our college towers shall rise*
> *And lift their heads to greet the smiling skies.*

Afterwards people "from far and near" gathered at the home of Frederick Lyman for a victory celebration. As eighteenth century Chinese lanterns illuminated Lyman's home on the corner of Interlachen Avenue and the Boulevard, and as dying bonfires glowed in the streets, the celebrants ate cake, drank lemonade, sang songs and listened to more congratulatory speeches. When one orator for the first time spoke of "Rollins College," the term received a loud round of applause. All sensed that a new era had dawned for their little hamlet on the Florida frontier.

The launching of Rollins College in 1885 strongly resembled the founding patterns of other small liberal arts colleges throughout the nineteenth century. During most of the century an indiscriminate college-building mania swept the nation, one that produced over two hundred colleges between 1850 and 1900. This incredible orgy of college founding continued in the latter half of the century, leading one writer to describe America as a "land of colleges.[2] Such casual building promoted, however, a high mortality rate. Colleges rose "like mushrooms in our luxurious soils, are duly lauded and puffed up for a day and then sink to be heard no more," one writer intoned. In most cases survival, not academic attainment, was a major achievement.[3]

In this time period, several forces converged to produce this surge in college building. Three stand out as the most significant: religious denominationalism, community pride and land development. Denominationalism was an initiating factor in this process because Protestant denominations wanted to assure their children a sectarian Christian education. Congregationalists and Presbyterians, with the tradition of Harvard, Yale and Princeton behind them, were most active in college building in the early nineteenth century, They were joined in the mid-century by Lutherans, Dutch Reformed and Unitarians, followed later by Methodists and Baptists. These religious sects accounted directly for the founding of eleven colleges in Kentucky, twenty-one in Illinois, and thirteen in Iowa before 1860. And this represented a fraction of the total.[4]

Community pride, called the "booster spirit," became a second prime mover in college building. Regardless of its size, and some were only two or three houses, pioneers dreamed of turning their hamlet into a "town." A post office, a newspaper and a hotel were thought critical in shaping the destiny of a town. A railroad would guarantee its economic future. But only a college could give the little town a mark of distinction.[5]

Closely tied to this booster spirit was real estate development. Throughout the nineteenth century land speculation provided the most popular and one of the most profitable forms of economic endeavor. Those who owned property in a village, which included almost everyone, perceived the growth of their town in economic terms. As the town grew, so did their property values. Real estate promoters sought to foster their town's growth with various kinds of promotional schemes. The quickest way to make the little village attractive to buyers (in some cases of literally putting it on the map) was to found a college. Colleges inevitably meant increased population and a rise in property values. Thus, village property owners were easily convinced to contribute funds to build an institution of higher learning in their town.

The convergence of these three forces created a college founding pattern repeated many times over. A church denomination sent out a circular letter inviting communities with geographic and economic appeal to submit "inducement" bids. Real estate entrepreneurs then took the leadership in mobilizing financial campaigns in the villages, appealing to community pride and economic gain. Several villages and some towns submitted bids, and as with any other entrepreneurial endeavors, the college went to the highest bidder. As one contemporary wrote: all these forces and more resulted in "a magnetic chain of reciprocal influences, by which light flashes from college to the community, and life streams back again from the community to the college, so that while the college redeems the community from ignorance, the community preserves the college from an undue tendency to monkish corruption and scholastic unprofitableness."[6]

It was precisely this long-established model that led to the founding of Rollins College in 1885. All the traditional elements—the frontier environment, denominationalism, booster spirit and real estate development—were present in the founding of Rollins. In 1885, Florida represented America's last frontier. Since the Civil War, northeastern tourists had been pouring into the state in ever-increasing numbers, and enterprising hotel and land developers followed them. Still, in 1885, much of Florida contained frontier characteristics. Central Florida, still sparsely settled, was dotted here and there with small villages. People the local inhabitants

called 'crackers' worked small pioneer farms, but northern
entrepreneurs were already establishing large-scale orange
groves. As with most frontier regions, communication was
primitive. Transportation consisted of wagons crawling
over crude dirt roads and small steamships plying the St.
Johns River. A major improvement came with the building
in 1884 of a railroad line connecting Sanford and Orlando.
The South Florida Railroad allowed Central Florida to
become a destination for scores of winter tourists from the
North.[7]

Several denominations began to make their way into this
virgin, primitive territory, but none was more active than
the Congregational Church, having established by 1880
thirteen churches in north and central Florida. Considering the poor condition of education in the state at that time
and given the Congregationalism's historic college founding tradition, not surprisingly the first topic discussed in
the initial meeting of the Florida Congregational Association was the need to create a college. Lucy Cross of Daytona
was the first to place the matter before the association. Miss
Cross, a graduate of Oberlin College (one of the Congregational Church's oldest co-educational institutions), had
moved to Daytona, Florida in 1880 where she established
an active, private elementary school. Concerned with the
lack of educational opportunity in the state, "hope sprang
in [her] heart and an idea in [her] mind." Her idea was to
propose at the initial meeting of the General Congregational
Association—to be held (prophetically) in the little hamlet

of Winter Park—that the Congregational Association found a college in Florida. Miss Cross made her appeal to her pastor, C. M. Bingham, a delegate to the Florida Association. At the Winter Park meeting, Bingham took advantage of his position as moderator to read Miss Cross's paper even though the subject of a college was not on the agenda. "I dare not go home and face Miss Cross if I do not read this," he cagily told the assembled members.[8]

In the paper, Miss Cross made an appeal for the founding of a college in Florida so that Floridians could provide their children with a New England education. It seemed foolish, she said, for the Florida families to send their children out of the warm weather of Florida to the cold, sickly climate of the North. The youth of Florida and the sons and daughters of tourists, said Miss Cross, deserved the "soundest moral and religious teaching" that the Congregational Church could provide.

Accepting Miss Cross's suggestion, the association appointed a committee to report at the next annual meeting on the educational conditions in Florida. We have no evidence that the committee ever studied the Florida educational system. But if it had made such a study, the committee's report would not have been encouraging. In 1884, Florida possessed only eight county high schools, ones so meager in their course offerings and in session such a short time the state was forced to support several private secondary academies. Even in these academies conditions were poor. As one investigator observed: schools were "running from two to five months per year with little classification and wholly inadequate facilities." Most of the "crackers or poor whites" could not read; "forty-five of every one hundred voters," he concluded, "are illiterate." Several private secondary school academies were scattered throughout the state. They included a Baptist school at Deland, a Christian Church academy at Starke and Catholic Church academies at St. Augustine, Tampa, Key West and Jacksonville. Florida could claim no institution of higher learning in 1884. These conditions served as a magnet that attracted such committed Congregationalist missionaries as Lucy Cross.[9]

As a way of presenting a report to the association, the committee persuaded a newly arrived minister, the Reverend Edward P. Hooker, pastor of the Winter Park Congregational Church, to prepare a paper for the 1884 annual meeting on the subject of Florida education. The records do not show why Hooker was chosen for this important task, but the choice could not have been more appropriate. He had only recently come to Florida under the auspices of the Home Missionary Society. The fifty-year old Hooker, a pious New England Congregational minister, and a descendant of the famous independent-minded Colonial minister, Thomas Hooker, had received his BA and MA from Middlebury College in Massachusetts. Ordained by Andover Theological Seminary, a leading divinity school in New England, Hooker preached in several Congregational Churches in Massachusetts, and later in his former college town of Middlebury. While at Medford, Massachusetts, Hooker's wife became ill and died. Later he married his second wife, Elizabeth Robbins, the daughter of a missionary, who bore him six children. In 1882 Hooker developed arthritis problems that led him to accept an opportunity for home missionary work in the warmer climate of Florida. He was assigned to work with Reverend S. F. Gale, director of the Florida Home Missionary Society, who sent Hooker to Winter Park to found a Congregational Church.[10]

When he and his large family arrived in Winter Park in 1883, they found no churches at all in the little hamlet. Hooker began holding services in a hall over the village's only store while plans were being laid for building a Congregational church. In addition to preaching services in Winter Park, Hooker spent several Sunday afternoons carrying the gospel to outlying rural areas. These trips on horseback allowed him to become familiar with, in his daughter's words, "the strange pioneer world to which he had come, so different from the long-established order of New England." She recalls his speaking of the crudeness and ignorance prevailing throughout the area and worrying about the role the church should play in "building a wholesome order" in Central Florida.

At this point he received an invitation to speak on Florida education at the forthcoming meeting of the association. Hooker's paper, entitled "The Mission of Congregationalism in Florida," was a forceful articulation of the Congregational Church's historic educational mission and a moving plea for an institution of higher learning in Florida.[12] He began by summarizing what he called "Congregationalism's mission of Christian education," where he documented the historical Congregational college-building tradition. Hooker then turned to the immediate issue: no area of the nation, he proclaimed, was more in need of an institution of higher learning than Florida. Europeans had settled Florida, he observed, fifty years before the Plymouth settlement. Why was Florida educationally so far behind New England? Hooker's answer repeated a traditional New England Puritan self-serving litany: Florida has remained static because its progress was retarded by a Spanish papal and aristocratic legacy that "forced the torch of learning downward." "Has not the time come," Hooker asked the ministers, "to reverse the torch and bid it burn and illumine the forests with the free [Protestant] gospel and the college?"[11]

In a practical vein, Hooker argued that the growth and prosperity of Florida could not be assured simply by planting more orange groves. Prosperity depended just as much on educational institutions because no industry would attract families without educational opportunities for their children. Families of the North, he suggested, were waiting for an answer. Hooker then ended with a final rhetorical flourish: "The outlook is grand and glorious. A few of us stand on these early heights of the new time. We love the State to which we have come; these genial skies, these clear, sparkling lakes, the souls of the people who dwell among the forests. We rejoice at the arrival of those who crowd the steamboats and cars. We are a little before them and we bid them welcome. We rejoice in the privilege of laying foundations for the future. Has not the hour struck for the courage, wisdom and devotion of our Fathers?" He pleaded with them to found a Christian college and announce the decision at the present meeting.[12]

Moved by this powerful exhortation, the association appointed a committee to consider Hooker's stirring proposal. The following day, January 29, 1885, the committee reported that it agreed with Dr. Hooker that the time had come "to take initiatory steps toward the founding of an institution for higher education in the state of Florida." To accomplish this end, the committee recommended that another group be appointed to receive monetary bids for the location of the college and at the appropriate time to present those inducements to a special meeting where the association would then select the "most suitable location." The association accepted the proposal and appointed a committee of five: Dr. Hooker and Frederick W. Lyman of Winter Park, Reverend S. F. Gale of Jacksonville, Reverend C. M. Bingham of Daytona Beach, and Mr. R. C. Tremain of Mount Dora. The initial historical step had been taken; denominationalism had sparked the process of college building on the Florida frontier.[13]

The news that the Congregational Association planned to found a college was initially received with some skepticism throughout the inhabited areas of the state, but within a week newspapers were spreading the word that the association was "in earnest" in its determination to build a "first class college." The Orange County weekly newspaper reported that "assurances have been received" "from northern friends to the undertaking that important pecuniary aid" was forthcoming.[14] The *Florida Times-Union* in Jacksonville, the most widely circulated newspaper in the state, was even more optimistic. The Congregational Association, it declared, "has the means to carry out its plans and the school would doubtless, if located in a center of population and wealth, be a credit to the Association and the state, and a great boon to our young people who cannot afford to go to Yale or Harvard."[15]

These assurances, combined with the news that a committee was asking for inducements, caused an outburst of community booster spirit.. Editors and promoters, religious and secular leaders moved to awaken their communities to the "great advantages to be derived from the presence of such an institution." Reverend Bingham and Lucy Cross spurred Daytona to action; businessmen and land promoters in Mt. Dora began accumulating funds; Dr. Nathan Burrows, later a charter teacher and trustee at the new college, led the activity in Orange City.[16] The *Orange County Reporter* touted Orlando as a railroad, manufacturing and commercial center. "Why not an educational center?" the paper asked.[17]

But Jacksonville, in the state's northeast corner, appeared to lead all other aspirants. With a population of almost eight thousand and a thriving river port, it was a hub of economic activity and the main port of entry into the state. The most prominent churchman in the state, the Reverend S. F. Gale, director of the Florida Home Missionary Society, led its cause. Finally, the state's largest newspaper was published in Jacksonville, and its editor aggressively advocated the site. In an editorial printed in early April, he minced no words in promoting his city: "Here is a chance for our Jacksonville property holders to make a point. They can get this school here if they will do as several places in south and central: give lands and money to the enterprise. If the Congregational Association wants to build up a flourishing and influential school their best plan is to locate it here in Jacksonville where the population is dense. Many of these people have young men and women they are educating. The school will be under the eyes of thousands of wealthy people and doubtless get large volunteer donations for its support. It is utterly useless to locate colleges in out-of-the-way places and in sparsely settled communities. Scholastic studies are no longer pursued in monkish cells or in the solitude of caves and mountain fastnesses."[18]

There was much logic and common sense in the editor's argument, but it was historically flawed. "Sparsely settled, out-of-the-way places" so disparaged by the editor were precisely the location of most liberal arts colleges in the nineteenth century and for very same reasons that in the final analysis Jacksonville would not be chosen. That river port did not depend for its identity on establishing a college. With or without a college Jacksonville would grow and prosper, and its citizens could not be mobilized with cries of desperation. For Jacksonville's competition, however, a college could very well provide the key to their destinies. Daytona was a small village of a few hundred souls huddled along the ocean; and Mt. Dora and Orange City were small inland communities with no distinguishing features. But in terms of size, no community could have been more desperate for an identity than Winter Park.

Despite its small size and lack of population, Winter Park possessed two advantages over the other competitors. Two of its residents, Reverend Hooker and Frederick W. Lyman, as members of the committee chosen to receive inducements, were able to gauge the strength of the competition. Both men had established themselves as outstanding leaders in their community and the state, and both had strong personal reasons for wanting a college in Winter Park. Without even considering his moral commitment to Christian education, Hooker must have understood that his education and background made him a principal candidate for the presidency of the new college. Almost assured of that position if the college was located in his community, he therefore took a more than normal interest in raising subscriptions in his little village.[19]

Hooker's co-worker in this endeavor was developer Frederick W. Lyman, who nurtured an even greater personal and professional stake in locating the college at Winter Park. Lyman proved to be a host unto himself. The son of a New England Presbyterian minister, Lyman moved to Minnesota at the age of twenty-two where he prospered as a wholesale druggist. In his early thirties, his wife's asthma forced him to abandon his successful business in Minneapolis and move to Florida in search of a milder climate. Interest in land development led him to Winter Park, where he soon became involved with two real estate promoters—Loring Chase of Chicago, and Oliver E. Chapman—who had recently bought six hundred acres of land a few miles from Orlando that bordered Lake Osceola and Lake Maitland. Chase and Chapman had purchased the land, a newspaper reported, for the purpose of "creating a first class resort for Northern and Southern men of wealth, where amidst orange groves and beautiful lakes and luxuries that every enterprise and wealth can devise and command, a community of grand winter homes [would arise], a resort second to none in the South."[20]

Before Lyman arrived, the two promoters already had a real estate scheme underway. After platting the town, they constructed a railroad station on the South Florida Railroad line running though their prospective village. Three large lots on Lake Osceola had been set aside as the location of a large resort hotel. They called the little settlement Winter Park and in 1882 took the important step of securing a post office, and Chase had also constructed a two-story building near the railroad station, with the lower floor housing a grocery store. The upper floor was intended to be used for community and church services. In addition, they had given a lot to one A. E. Rogers who had built and was operating a small hotel. By 1885 the little village was beginning to resemble a town.[21]

Lyman, a "natural organizer," as one contemporary saw him, quickly grasped the possibilities in Chase's and Chapman's real estate schemes.[22] He joined the group shortly after arriving in Winter Park, incorporated their efforts into the Winter Park Company with himself as the president, and under Chase's direction, laid out a town along the railroad tracks. Well before the advent of city planning and zoning, they designed an entire town complete with a park, straight and curving avenues, special sites for a business center, for a school and for hotels and villas. As a final step they built a separate "coloreds" residential area, predictably across the railroad tracks, intended to provide "help" for wealthy residents. After devising "an expensive and alluring" advertising campaign, the company in February 1885, began construction of a large hotel designed to entice wealthy easterners and mid-westerners to its new development.[23]

About the time he joined the company, Lyman learned of the Congregational Association's interest in founding a college in Florida. He was struck immediately by an inspiration: a college was precisely what the Winter Park Company needed to complete its resort and real estate plans. Although the evidence is indirect, it seems likely that Lyman was the first to suggest such an idea to Dr. Hooker, who was Lyman's pastor. At any rate, in the persons of Lyman and Hooker, entrepreneurism had joined hands with denominationalism to arouse community spirit.[24]

With refreshing openness, Lyman later recalled how he and his colleagues mobilized the community. Winter Park, he explained, became the center of the most intense activity and a house-to-house canvassing. Everyone was expected (pressured?) to give. Lyman later wrote: "No sum was too large to ask for and none too small to receive. Every loyal Winter Parkite felt that no place in the state could offer natural advantages comparable to here. Day by day the roll of honor lengthened as signature followed signature on the subscription list, till eight figures became necessary to express the total pledge in dollars and cents. The whole amount subscribed was kept a profound secret, as it was feared that should other places learn what Winter Park would offer they would redouble their efforts and the prize therefore [would be] lost." Lyman's greatest contribution came when he persuaded winter resident Alonzo Rollins to offer land for the location of the college and to donate two large orange groves (one on Lake Osceola and one in Palatka) as a part of his initial gift of $50,000. In return for Rollins' critical donation, Lyman agreed to name the college in his honor.[25]

On April 14, 1885, the association held a special meeting in Mt. Dora to receive the inducements. Five towns—Jacksonville, Mt Dora, Daytona, Orange City and Winter Park—submitted proposals. As Lyman suspected, his and Hooker's membership on the proposal committee worked to Winter Park's advantage. They arranged to have their proposal presented last so as to ascertain the strength of the other inducements. The host town, Mt. Dora, presented a substantial initial proposal. It offered a ten-acre wooded lot on Lake Dora, cash, lumber, and over seven hundred acres of land for a total of $35,564. The impressed delegates immediately recessed to tour the location of the proposed site.[26]

Next, Bingham and Lucy Cross presented Daytona's proposal of $11,500, a sum that fell woefully short of Mt. Dora's. Sullivan F. Gale represented Jacksonville, but he could offer only $13,000. Most of his time was spent pressing the advantages of locating the college in a population center. To Lyman's relief, the last town, Orange City, submitted a smaller amount than Mt. Dora. Lyman later described the drama of the meeting when Winter Park made known its inducement: "As one proposal after another was read it became evident to [me] who alone knew what its subscription was, that other towns were hopelessly distanced, and [I] was resoundingly elated, but managed to maintain a calm exterior, perhaps even to assume an aspect of gloom, which was misleading." When his turn came and he presented the pledge from Winter Park, "there was consternation and deep despair on many faces." Winter Park had offered $114,180, a sum that easily eclipsed other bids. Included were an attractive high-ground site on the shores of Lake Virginia, pledges for cash, stock in the Winter Park Company and finally the generous gift of $50,000 from Alonzo Rollins. Stone-faced, Lyman had held his cards close to his vest, playing them like a master poker player to achieve an overwhelming moment of drama.[27]

The size of Winter Park's proposal stunned the delegates, particularly those from Mt. Dora, who had been overly confident of their bid. As one participant noted: "The discussion grew hot and bitter and full of suspicion of misrepresentation." Several representatives claimed that the college site offered by Winter Park was covered by water most of the year. Lyman vehemently denied this accusation, but the concerned delegates postponed a final decision until they could visit both the Winter Park site and also that of the third highest bidder, Orange City. They journeyed to the village the following day. As Lucy Cross described the trip: "The ride from Mt. Dora to Winter Park, a distance of twenty-five miles was, as far as Apopka, through hilly country full of small lakes; beyond Apopka, it was quite level until we reached the vicinity of Winter Park. We were given a pleasant ride through the town and out to the proposed site of the college; this rises fifty feet above Lake Virginia, across which some Pleasant looking residences and grounds were in sight, giving a pretty view. The college site is a handsome piece of property valued at $23,000 and overlooks Lake Virginia."[28]

The delegates then proceeded to Orange City where the town residents turned out a large welcome. "Young ladies greeted us with wavy handkerchiefs," Lucy Cross wrote, "and led us into the midst of a joyous social where an excellent supper was served." The efforts of Orange City citizens were to no avail. On April 17 the association met in session for a formal vote. The results were: Mt. Dora, 2; Orange

City, 9; and Winter Park, 13. A motion was then made to unanimously declare Winter Park as the location of the new college. The motion passed without dissent.[29]

The representatives from Winter Park had pulled off an incredible feat. In their imaginations they could see a group of stately buildings clustered around Lake Virginia, forming a beautiful addition to their bucolic little town. What they did not visualize was the strain and stress, the burden of anxiety and debt, the days and nights of struggle that lay ahead. When the euphoria of college founding had worn off, the awful weight of college building descended. Lyman later captured the morning-after reality: "What a simple thing it seemed to build a college. At that time we did not think of the sorrow and travail of the years ahead." But that stark reality was months away.[30]

The unanimous vote of the association did not satisfy everyone by any means. Some were skeptical of Winter Park's ability to raise the promised money. Others still considered that Winter Park was an unsuitable location. With obvious bitterness the *South Florida Times* of Orange City adamantly maintained that the college's chosen site was "surrounded by swamps and about nine months out of the year the hooting owls hoot to the few families that will forever be the only inhabitants."[31] The *Florida Times-Union* admitted that the site was probably acceptable but still argued that large sums of money would be thrown away "in building a schoolhouse where there are not enough pupils to fill it,"[32] Orlando's *Orange County Reporter*, as might be expected, was lyrical in its approval. "The moral atmosphere [of Winter Park]," it said, "is as pure as the breezes from the crystal lakes and the scenery of the sort to assist in the development of the moral and good in the nature of the pupils."[33] The *Sanford Herald* carried a stinging rebuttal to the attackers: Jacksonville and its editor had no right to complain, because, in a fair competitive bidding, Florida's largest city could not raise as much as a single citizen did in Winter Park. "A magnificent bid of over $100,000," the paper declared, "is not to be weighed against the pitiful offer of Jacksonville with a sum of money in just about a sufficient amount to buy a bell." No one, the article continued, had reason to complain when "a more enterprising community captures an influential institution by reason of its superior public spirit and liberality." As the editor so pointedly suggested, Jacksonville and the other communities were simply "out-boostered" by a little frontier village.[34] But Winter Park citizens were much too busy celebrating to be concerned with the envious criticism.

At the April 17 meeting in Orange City, the delegates also elected eighteen (later increased to twenty-one) charter trustees for the college. Lyman, who took responsibility for formal incorporation, issued a call to form "a corporate body for the purpose of establishing a Christian College at Winter Park, Orange County, Florida, to meet in the Directors' Room of the Lyman Bank in Sanford, Florida on Tuesday, the 28th day of April, AD 1885 at 9 o'clock in the morning."[35]

The adopted constitution or charter provided that the

corporation name be Rollins College and that it would be located in Winter Park, Florida. It then stated the college's purpose: "Its object, which shall never be changed, shall be the Christian education of youth and to this end it proposes to provide for its students the best educational facilities possible and throw about them those Christian influences, which will be adopted to restrain them from evil and prepare them for a virtuous, happy and useful life."[36] To fulfill this purpose the trustees proposed to establish preparatory, industrial, normal and collegiate departments and any professional or graduate education "as present or future exigencies may require." The charter also vested the government and management of the college in five offices: President, Vice-president, Secretary, Treasurer and Auditor. The by-laws created a five-member Executive Committee and authorized it to "transact any ordinary business during the interval between the regular meetings" of the trustees. The by-laws further established a faculty composed of professors, tutors and a president. The faculty, headed by the president, was made responsible for governing the institution, for determining admission standards and for creating a curriculum embodying "a classical course which [gives] extensive attention to the liberal arts." In addition, the faculty was to be responsible for rules and regulations governing of student conduct and "for promoting in the highest degrees their health and decorum, their mental, moral and spiritual welfare, giving the institution, as far as possible, a parental influence and the atmosphere of a Christian home." Finally, the by-laws required that members of both the trustees and the faculty proclaim connection with some evangelical church.[37]

The incorporators then elected the following officers: F. W. Lyman, President, C. M. Bingham, vice-president; A. W. Rollins, treasurer; Nathan Barrows, auditor; S. D. Smith, secretary and Reverend Edward Hooker, president of the faculty. They authorized Hooker "to engage such professors and teachers for the ensuing year as, in his judgment may seem best." Hooker, Lyman, Francis Knowles and Franklin Fairbanks formed a building committee with powers to erect the necessary structures for the new college. Although the minutes are silent on the matter, apparently the executive committee decided to open the college in the coming fall of 1885.[38]

The day following incorporation the local newspaper reported that Dr. Hooker and others would be going north to raise funds, to seek students and to hire "the best faculty that can be found."[39] The announcement was revealing for several reasons. These northern Congregationalists viewed the founding of the college as serving not only the people of Florida but also contributing to the larger national purposes of instilling northern values in the former Confederacy. Hooker perfectly expressed this sense of mission in a letter to Noah Porter, president of Yale University: "We intend that Rollins College shall be such that you might step into any department of it and think you were in New England. The teacher standards, the methods, are all to be Northern.

Rollins College will be a sample of New England educational institutions in the South. How can we, as lovers of country, make this land one without changing the civilization of the South and making it in education like the North? Florida will be the first Southern State to become Northern in its civilization, and the College will be the right hand of this true progress."[41]

The *Boston Herald*, noting Hooker's initial visit to the Northeast, echoed Hooker's sentiment: "New England has taken Florida captive as a pleasure and health resort, and the question [is], why cannot a New England college be planted in the heart of the state?" The editor saw no reason why, and predicted that Hooker would make a successful fund-raising effort because "those who know the importance of giving southern youth a New England education are emphatic in commending Dr. Hooker's mission."[42]

From the outset the college's basic resources—students, teachers and finances—came largely from the Northeast, or from northerners who wintered in Florida. Few financial resources were available to the college in Florida's frontier agricultural economy and local schools could not prepare students for the college's rigorous curriculum. Only colleges outside the South could provide professors. For many, many decades after the founding, presidents, therefore, turned to the Northeast, particularly New England, to fulfill the college's financial and academic needs. As a result, the college gained the reputation of being a New England college located in Florida, which proved to be both a blessing and a problem.

On his trip north Hooker did realize success on his first call. One of the trustees, Francis B. Knowles, a wealthy Massachusetts industrialist, had earlier indicated a special interest in helping to open the college. During the founding campaign he pledged one thousand dollars and promised four thousand more if the college was located in Winter Park. In March, he suggested that Hooker come to Massachusetts and "beg" for money among Knowles' friends in his home-town of Worcester. Hooker had little luck with Knowles' friends, but the generous industrialist himself added five thousand dollars to his original pledge, for a total of $10,000 for the purpose of building a classroom. The assurance of a classroom building, destined to be named in honor of the donor, finally made the college a reality. Within a few weeks, Hooker collected enough pledges to begin construction of a dormitory.[43]

With money pledged and with Hooker and Lyman in the North seeking more funds, trustee Loring Chase assumed responsibility for getting construction underway. Fortune continued to smile on the undertaking for a while at least, as George Rand, a Boston architect residing in Winter Park, volunteered to design the new buildings and George Rollins, son of Alonzo, who was building the Seminole Hotel, agreed to oversee the project. Work began in mid-summer, but even under the best of circumstances they had a very short period to construct a building in time for an October opening.[44]

Meanwhile, Hooker and the executive committee faced the daunting task of creating a college from scratch. In a period of six months they planned to construct buildings, enroll students, find or build quarters for the students, locate and hire teachers, order textbooks from distant places, publicize the college, and, most urgently, raise funds to support these requirements. Fortunately, the executive committee found a sufficient number of qualified faculty living in Florida. On August 12, they announced the first members of the charter faculty: Dr. Nathan Barrows, professor of mathematics and physics, and Annie Morton, instructor in history and, later, principal of the training department. A few weeks later, they hired William M. Lloyd, professor of ancient languages and principal of the preparatory school, and Louise Abbot, assistant principal of the Training Department. Others would be added during the year, but this little band of teachers would greet the students on opening day.[45] Decades later, Lloyd, who came from Chicago, left a bleak picture of what this intrepid band of instructors faced: From Jacksonville, Lloyd traveled "up the St. Johns River on the steamboat by night, the search light thrown from side to side on the black, pitchy waters hemmed in by forests of water oaks and pines." He disembarked at Sanford and boarded a train. When he "stepped off the train in Winter Park, he seemed to be set down in a forest of telegraph poles in a sandy desert" dotted with a scattering of a few wooden buildings. A few blocks away he received another surprise when he viewed what was supposed to be a college campus. "The non-existence of the college buildings shown on the prospectus of Winter Park was a chilling shock. The Ladies' Cottage, though not complete, proved to be an actuality, and Knowles Hall was under construction, but the rest of the buildings were as yet but noble fantasies. This was much worse than expected . . ."

As opening day approached, the realization dawned that the new classroom would not be ready. Hooker therefore advanced the planned October opening date to November 4. On October 6, Barrows arrived to relieve Chase of the preliminary work of opening the college, just as students began registering in surprisingly large numbers. Chase wrote to Lyman that Orlando was sending a "big delegation almost every day." But as late as the middle of October the college officers still had no place to house or teach students. Chase reported that George Rollins had the money to pay only ten men to work on the classroom building and none on the dormitory. "If we had funds," he lamented, "we would put on more men on the college building, and it is a great pity [because] if we had been ready I think we should have had 150 pupils." Under the circumstances only seventy students had registered.[46]

The college had no place to accommodate even this number of students. Chase later acknowledged that as the day of opening drew near he and Hooker were at their "wits' end." The weeks before opening found Hooker and Chase scurrying around Winter Park, arranging for rooms and trying to locate classrooms. On the evening before opening day, Chase wrote Lyman with some relief that things were "fairly fixed," meaning that they had secured White's Hall above the Ergood Grocery store for classroom space, the Larrabee house at Morse Boulevard and New York Avenue for the boys' dormitory, and had rented the Ward cottage for girls located on Osceola Street. At the eleventh hour yet another serious complication arose: the plastered partitions of White's Hall completed at the last moment were not dry. Chase deemed the room unsafe. At that point, he realized that the unfinished Congregational Church might serve as a temporary classroom, even though the sanctuary was without seating. The congregation was using boards set on small barrels. "Tonight as I write (10 p.m.)," Chase described the scene, "our whole force of carpenters is there setting up desks and partitions." Sometime in the late evening hours they made the spare little carpenter gothic building ready for Rollins' first classes.[47]

Opening day on November 4, 1885, according to the *Orange County Reporter*, proved to be a "typical Florida fall day, with sunny skies and mild temperatures." The weather may have been pleasant, but panic seized William Lloyd, the new classics professor, when he arrived at the Congregational Church an hour before classes were scheduled to begin. As he later recalled: "At 8 o'clock the church door was still locked. Pupils and parents began to arrive, and stood waiting on the steps." Once inside, after retrieving the keys, he found the room bare. The newly ordered school desks were still sitting in a freight car several blocks away. Lloyd quickly organized a crew of young men, moved the church pews to the sidewalls, and unloaded the desks, just in time for the arrival of the first students.

Promptly at 9 a.m. the Congregational Church bell pealed the beginning of a new era. In addition to the sixty-six students and five teachers, twenty friends of the institution had gathered to launch the new enterprise. The program was a simple one: the audience sang a hymn to open the convocation program, and a prayer followed. President Hooker and Reverend Sullivan F. Gale, destined to be an indefatigable worker for the new college, gave "interesting addresses," at the conclusion of which Hooker called the roll of students, and formally announced the beginning of classes. The *South Florida Sentinel* bannered a sentiment common to all who gathered in the little Congregational Church on that fall day in 1885: "Joy to the Park, the school's begun!"[48]

1. The following narrative is constructed from sources in the Rollins Archives, including Frederick Lyman, "Early Days at Rollins," *Rollins College Bulletin V* (October 1911); Kitchell Diary, *South Florida Sentinel*, April 18, 1885; *Orange County Reporter*, April 18, 1885.

By 1885, when she wrote the poem commemorating Rollins' founding, Emily Miller had achieved national renown as a novelist, poet and hymnodist. She also served as editor of The Little Corporal, a children's magazine and as associate editor Ladies Home Journal. In 1891 she was appointed Dean of Women at Northwestern University. The records do not reveal why she was in the little village of Winter Park.

2. Donald Tewksbury, *The Founding of American Colleges and Universities Before the Civil War* (l962), 4-8; Frederick Rudolph, *The American College and University* (l962), 48-50.

3. Quoted in Tewksbury, *Founding*, 24.

4. Rudolph, *American Colleges*, 49.

5. Daniel Boorstin, *The Americans: The National Experience* (Vintage edition, l967), 152-160.

6. Quoted in *ibid*.

7. Maurice O'Sullivan and Jack C. Lane, "Introduction," *The Florida Reader*: (1991).

South Florida Railroad began running between Sanford and Orlando in 1880. Henry B. Plant purchased the railway in 1883 and extended the line to Port Tampa where he planned a resort hotel to rival that of Henry Flager's Ponce de Leon in St Augustine. For decades after South Florida was the only mode of transportation into the Florida interior.

8. Lucy Cross, "The Beginning of Rollins College," Manuscript, Rollins Archives; Minutes of the Annual Meeting of the General Congregational Association of Florida, l883. (Hereafter cited as Minutes, GCAF).

Cross was born in New York in 1839, the fourth of seven children of a Congregational minister. After graduating from Oberlin College in 1868, she taught high school in Iowa. She came to Dayton in 1879 for health reasons and afterward decided to make Daytona Beach her permanent home. She started the Daytona Institute, a school for sons and daughters of winter visitors. She continued to operate the school until 1904 when she retired. Cross was killed in a automobile accident in 1927. With the possibility that the college would be built in Daytona, we may assume that an entrepreneurial motive had sprung into her heart as well.

Rollins built a hall in 1937 dedicated to Lucy Cross. It was originally intended as a "hall of science," but was used exclusively as a girls's dormitory. In 1935, the Florida DAR placed a stone honoring Lucy Cross on the Walk of Fame.

9. George Cary Bush, *History of Education in Florida* (1899). 50-54; Edward Hooker to Noah Porter, September 1, 1885. Hooker Papers.

10. Minutes, *GCAF*, 1884; "Biographical Sketch of Edward Hooker," in

Hooker Papers.

Most of the early pioneers of Winter Park were Congregationalists. They built the first church in the little village, a little wooden carpenter Gothic structure located on the corner of Interlachen and New England where the present neocolonial church stands today. The wooden church was demolished in the 1930s.

11. Elizabeth Hooker, "Edward Hooker." Manuscript in Rollins Archives.

12. Copy in Hooker Papers.

13. Minutes, *GCAF*, 1884.

14. *Orange County Reporter*, February l9, 1885.

15. *Florida Times-Union*, April 5, 1885.

16. *Ibid*, April 9, 1885.

17. February l9, 1885.

18. *Florida Times-Union*, April 9, 1885.

19. For a hint of Hooker's ambitions see Elizabeth, "Hooker."

20. *South Florida Journal*, September 8, 1881. Copy in Chase Scrapbook.

21. William F. Blackman, *History of Orange County Florida* (1927), 167-71.

22. William O'Neal, "Recollections," Manuscript, Rollins Archives.

23. Blackman, History, 172; Frederick Lyman, "Early Days of Rollins," *Rollins College Bulletin*, V (October 1911).

24. *Ibid*.

25. *Ibid*.

26. Minutes, *GCAF*, 1885.

27. Lyman, "Early Days."

28. Cross, "Beginnings of Rollins."

29. *Ibid*.

30. Lyman, "Early Days."

30. Minutes, *GCAF*, 1885.

31. April 22, 1885.

32. April 21, 1885.

33. April 23, 1885.

34. April 27, 1885.

35. Lyman, "Early Days."

36. Minutes of the Rollins College Board of Trustees, April 27, 1885. (Hereafter cited as Trustee Minutes).

37. *Ibid*., April 28, 1885.

38. *Ibid*. Francis Knowles, a wealthy New England textile magnate and Franklin Fairbanks, president of historic Franklin Scales Company, were two of the first investors in the Chase and Comstock Land Company. Fairbanks and Knowles were the chief investors in the Seminole Hotel. Both were charter members of Rollins' Board of Trustees. It was Fairbanks who introduced Charles Hosmer Morse to Winter Park and Rollins College. The Knowles family remained firmly attached to Rollins through the 1930s. Francis's daughter, Frances, provided the funds for Knowles Chapel in 1932.

39. *Ibid*.

41. Hooker to Porter, September, 1, 1885. Hooker Papers.

42. *Boston Herald*, June 21, 1885. Copy in Hooker Papers.

43. Knowles to Lyman, March 27, 1885. *Chase Scrapbook*.

44. *Orange County Reporter*, July 30, 1885.

46. *Ibid*.

47. *Ibid*. At the same time, Chase was supervising the construction on Winter Park Company's Seminole Hotel. "I am overwhelmed with work and get no such thing as rest," he wrote Lyman, who was in the northeast trying to raise funds for the college.

Rand was born on May 24, 1833 in Vermont. He studied architecture and in 1881 partnered with Bertrand Taylor. He is known for Queen Anne style which was characterized steeply pitched rooflines and turned columns.
At Rollins College he designed Knowles Hall (1886), Pinehurst Cottage (1886), Lakeside Cottage (1886), and Lyman Gymnasium (1890). One of his most well-known building is the town hall in Winchester, Massachusetts.

48. *Ibid*.; *Orange County Reporter*, November 5, 1885.

Chapter 2

FROM CONVOCATION
TO CRISIS, 1885–1893

IN 1892, THE editor of the *Orange County Reporter* wrote an article explaining why a liberal education earned at Rollins College made an essential contribution to American society. The writer cogently summarized a common 19th century Victorian sentiment. The true purpose of liberal education, the editor declared, was not to prepare students for a profession but to enlarge the "mind and character" of young people. Such an education provided future leaders of this nation with "a mind to understand difficult things, able to appreciate finest things; a character simple, pure and strong—these are the results of [a liberal] education. It puts the youth on a high plane of thinking and of living."[1]

Rollins College was founded in the "Age of the College," when such views were taken quite seriously. By the late 19th century, the term "college" encompassed the social, the academic and even the religious setting where students lived and studied. The "collegiate way" included a rigidly prescribed curriculum and special methods of teaching. It also embraced the belief that these alone did not make a college. The college way of life also included "an adherence to the residential scheme of things" in a "quiet, rural setting," a dependence on dormitories and dining halls and a sense of nurturing captured in the phrase *in loco parentis*. The college community was often referred to as a family because residential colleges literally served as parents to its young charges. Moreover, the college was seen as an ideal place for young people to experience a rite of passage from adolescence to adulthood. Dormitories, according to the" collegiate way," were more than places to sleep; they represented opportunities for young men (and young women in a few colleges) to share communal living, to learn virtues of common decency and to respect the well-being of others. In this sense, the dining halls were appropriately called the "commons," a place where the collegiate family (including the president and many of the faculty) shared its meals. Permeating and undergirding the collegiate way, therefore, was a protective paternalism that made the college responsible for the total welfare of the students--their studies, their discipline, their problems, their successes.[2]

Perhaps the most striking characteristic of the collegiate way was its classical curriculum. Inherited from Europe and modified slightly to fit American conditions and needs, the classical curriculum became by mid-19th century the keystone of a college education. As the editor of *Orange County Reporter* argued, the classical curriculum proposed to do more than impart knowledge. It sought also to build character and to produce a cultured, refined person. These goals could be achieved, it was argued, through studies in mathematics, Greek and Latin grammar and literature. These subjects had the added value, according to the proponents of the classical curriculum, of sharpening the students' mental faculties. The famous Yale Report of 1828 declared that these fields of study provided "the discipline and the furniture of the mind; expanding its power, and storing it with knowledge. A commanding object, therefore, in a collegiate course should be to call into daily and vigorous exercise the faculties of the student." In American colleges, natural philosophy (physics and chemistry) and natural history (geology and biology) were added later in the century. The senior course on moral philosophy, taught by the President, sought to draw together four years of learning.[3]

Recitation, a pedagogy that required students to memorize and then to recite passages from an assigned text, represented the standard teaching method. The philosophical rationale behind this pedagogical method known as faculty psychology argued that the mind was a muscle requiring daily exercise, that intellectual acumen came from training, habit, routine and hard work. As one contemporary stated, recitation and study of the classics "improve the memory, strengthen the judgment, refine the taste, give discrimination and point to the discerning mind, [and] confers habits of attention, reasoning and analysis—in short, they exercise and cultivate all the intellectual powers."[4]

In the first half of the 19th century such beliefs solidified into orthodoxy and became firmly cemented into the college curriculum. No reputable college would dare deviate from the norm historically set by Ivy League colleges. Yale particularly became a kind of universal model. When many colleges (including Rollins) advertised that they were built on the Yale model, they meant that they had reproduced Yale's classical curriculum and were emphasizing the recitation method. This imitative process valuably produced unity and continuity in American higher education that lasted throughout most of the 19th century. It also created a static, elitist institution in the midst of a democratic society undergoing dynamic change.

A society involved in the practical progress of modern industrialization, urbanization and professionalization had difficulty seeing the relevancy of the classical curriculum with its emphasis on ancient (dead) languages and literature and with its rigidly prescribed courses. Practical American society began pressuring institutions of higher learning to offer courses such as English, history, politics and applied sciences, which seemed more connected to real life. Emerging state universities responded to this pressure by offering a greater variety of courses and also granting a variety of degrees, from Bachelor of Science to Bachelor of Agriculture. Liberal arts colleges resisted these changes, but even traditional institutions like Yale, headed by conservative Noah Porter, conceded to a scientific course of study, although they placed it in a secondary position along side the classical curriculum. In this way purists kept the BA degree unsullied. Other colleges followed Yale's lead and began to diversify courses of study.[5]

President Hooker and the charter professors, therefore,

inherited a course of study from which no respectable liberal arts college could deviate. A classical curriculum anchored the program, but founders also included some moderately bold responses to the practical needs of Florida's frontier conditions. The first prospectus proclaimed that, because Rollins College was dedicated to meeting "the great and diversified educational needs of Florida," its program of study would include four departments:

1. The Collegiate Department, with its course of highest standard in the ancient classics, in modern languages, in mathematics and in physics.
2. The Preparatory Department, which must do important work for the present, at least, in fitting students for the college.
3. The Training Department for teachers, which will instruct those who would teach in public schools and elsewhere. To this end, children will be received into this Department and placed under the instruction of Normal students.
4. The Industrial Training Department, in which the young ladies and gentlemen of other Departments can choose some useful line of practical industry and, while the mind is cultivated, can acquire knowledge and skill in the industrial arts.[6]

The Collegiate Department curriculum, drafted in longhand by classics professor William Lloyd, provided for the prescribed classical curriculum. A "scientific" course of study resembled the classical curriculum in almost every respect, except for a slight reduction in ancient languages.

In the freshman and sophomore years, students in this course of study could substitute an English history course, a history of the English language and a history of civilization course in place of three Latin courses. Otherwise, the two programs were precisely the same. They included three years of Latin, two of Greek, four of mathematics and one of Moral Philosophy. Thus, in an effort to achieve immediate respectability, the college advertised its curriculum as based "on the Yale Model."

In keeping with the standards of other liberal arts colleges, the Collegiate Department admissions requirements were exceptionally high. Only a listing can do justice to the level of prior work required by students entering the collegiate department:[7]

> Latin Grammar, Four Books of Caesar, Six Orations of Cicero, Six Books of Virgil's Aeneid, Jones' Latin Prose Composition, Translation of Latin at Sight, Three Books of Anabasis, Three Books of Homer's Iliad, Herodotus, Greek Prose Composition, Translation of Greek at Sight, Chardenal's 1st and 2nd Courses in French, Corneille's Le Cid and Victor Hugo's Hernani, Arithmetic, Metric System, Wentworth's Complete Algebra, Wentworth's Plane Geometry, Physical Geography, Elementary Rhetoric, United States History, Roman and Greek History, Life and Mythology, and Ancient and Modern Geography.

By reserving the bachelor's degree solely for the Collegiate Department, the college maintained the prestige of a liberal arts education. But it almost certainly guaranteed a low enrollment. With no high schools or private academies in the immediate area, and with very few even in the state, not many students could meet such high requirements, and those who could very likely resided in the Northeast, where many old established colleges were readily available. Such stringent requirements and prescribed courses created a serious dilemma: few local students could meet the requirements, but the college could not reduce those requisites to meet local needs for fear of being considered a substandard institution. The college attempted to resolve this problem in two ways: first, it attached a preparatory department to the college structure and frankly proclaimed that its purpose was to prepare students to enter the liberal arts college; second, it made an appeal to northeastern students who wanted college preparation but whose health required them to spend "a considerable portion of the year in a more genial climate to pursue their studies, and at the same time confirm their health." If this scheme had produced the desired results—it did not—Rollins might have become a college of convalescents.

The Preparatory Department's curriculum corresponded to the Collegiate Department's classical and scientific course of study. The college admitted students graduating from the preparatory school directly without further preparation. The preparatory curriculum stressed Latin and Greek grammar, but it also emphasized the essentials of English grammar, composition and penmanship. In 1888, the college added an "Academic Department" to the preparatory school for those who were uninterested in further study or for those who could not complete the classical or scientific course of study. The Academic Department curriculum contained no Latin or Greek but still included heavy doses of mathematics, science, English literature and history. In fact, it greatly resembled the curriculum that would emerge in the late 1890s when more colleges, including Rollins, abandoned the classical curriculum.[8]

Rollins made a pragmatic bow to local conditions by including a "normal" school and vocational courses. The Training (Teaching) Department allowed the college to broaden its purposes and meet the demand for teachers in the state. It also offered a primary or sub-preparatory education for students in the normal (education) school. Requirements for enrolling in the normal school were much less stringent than those of either the collegiate or preparatory departments. Candidates were required only to pass an examination in reading, spelling, geography, United States history, language, arithmetic and elementary algebra. In addition, they had to present "satisfactory testimony as to moral character and general scholarship." The three-year program included "two recitations daily and constant drill in practical pedagogics." The department expected students to spend two hours each day teaching primary classes under the direction of the Normal School's principal. Upon completion of the Normal program, students received a certificate of graduation.

The Industrial Training Department was considered an appendage to the college. All students could take courses in the department, although no list of courses ever appeared. The by-laws even provided for a director, but no one ever held that position. In fact, by 1895, the department simply disappeared from college literature apparently without ever coming into existence.

In 1890, the college added the Music Department which, although in accord with a liberal arts program, still served somewhat the same purpose as the moribund industrial department: it gave students an opportunity to work on a BA degree and a professional certificate at the same time. The program, providing for instruction in piano, voice and music theory in groups and on an individual basis, was such a success that in 1896 the college turned it into a separate school and allowed it to offer a Bachelor of Music diploma.[9]

For obvious reasons, the Board of Trustees set the cost of education at Rollins at the lowest possible level. The 1886 catalogue established rates for a 12-week term as follows:

Tuition in Collegiate Department $18.00
Tuition in the Preparatory Department . . . $12.00
Tuition in Training Department. $9.00
Board $48.00
Furnished room, with lights $12.00

Each student was required to bring two pairs of sheets for a single bed, two pillowcases, two blankets, a comforter, towels and table napkins. The annual cost for a boarding college student totaled $231 and for boarding preparatory and sub-preparatory students a trifle less.

Characteristic of colleges everywhere, these charges fell far below the cost of running the institution. The trustees met the bulk of college expenses by private donations but these were almost never adequate. Under such conditions, the trustees had two alternatives: they could charge the students the difference or they could cut expenses. Given the problems of enrollment, the board established tuition at the lowest possible level, and to make up the difference between income and costs, it offered charter faculty members salaries significantly lower than any of their contemporary professionals. From the over $20,000 collected in student fees during the first year, less than one-fifth went to faculty salaries. Only President Hooker was paid as much as $1,000 per year.[10]

Of the original 60 students, only two, Clara Louise Guild and Ida May Misseldine, entered the Collegiate Department. The others were enrolled in the preparatory and sub-preparatory departments. These enrollments are revealing because they indicate the disparity between the collegiate way and Florida's educational needs and resources. The Congregational Church had created a liberal arts college while the community urgently needed quality public schools. Not surprisingly, for almost four decades after the founding of the college, the appendages prospered while the college barely limped along with only a few students. Ten years after its founding, the liberal arts college claimed a total of 34 students while the other departments reported 139. This ratio in 1895 was one of the highest in the college's first decade. Significantly, the preparatory departments carried the college during its infancy and years of growth until in the mid-1920s.[11]

The founders of the college believed that the institution would appeal to a national constituency, but in the first decade it remained primarily a local college. Students from outside the state enrolled, but the great majority listed their residences in Florida, and even in this group most were from

Central Florida.[12] Many were within walking distance of the college, but a significant number used the South Florida Railroad for transportation to and from classes. In September 1886, the college agreed to allow the railroad to build the "Dinky Line" through the campus, along Lake Virginia. In return the company issued "school tickets" allowing children attending Rollins to ride at a reduced rate: under 12 miles, one-half cent per mile; over 12 miles, one cent per mile. The charge for a round-trip from Sanford on the South Florida Railroad was 24 cents, a reasonable rate, but riding the train made for a long day. It ran from Sanford to Orlando only twice a day, arriving in Orlando at 7:00 a.m. and leaving for Sanford for a return trip at 6:00 p.m. Moreover, this schedule applied only when the train was on time, which, according to the students, was a rare occasion.[13]

By March 1886, the contractors had finished Knowles Hall, the first classroom building, and Pinehurst, the girls' dormitory. Finally the college was given a sense of substance and roots. The two-story Knowles classroom building contained space for recitation and a hall capable of seating 300 for chapel services, exhibitions and entertainments. Realizing the significance of the college's first structure, Hooker and the trustees planned an elaborate ceremony. The Florida Superintendent of Schools, A.J. Russell, was invited to be the principal speaker. Dedication exercises included music, prayers and orations, followed by Russell's laudatory comments. President of the Rollins corporation Frederick Lyman again displayed his flair for dramatics. After formally presenting the keys of Knowles Hall to President Hooker, Lyman seized the occasion to seek sorely needed funds. The trustees, he said, had spent many hours puzzling how to finance a boys' dormitory and to furnish the girls' cottage with appropriate furniture. Lyman told the captive audience that just before the dedication ceremonies, he had been handed a note from Mr. Francis Knowles, stating that if sufficient funds were subscribed at this meeting to furnish the 34 rooms of the ladies' cottage at $60 per room, Mr. Knowles promised he would finance the men's dormitory. Incredibly, the funds were raised within 15 minutes. The audience then praised "God From Whom All Blessings Flow," but clearly Lyman's ingenuity played no small role.[15]

Knowles Hall immediately became the college landmark and center of campus activity. The large hall was used for recitations, assembly and daily chapel services. A large veranda served as a central gathering place for students between and after classes and also as the preferred backdrop of annual class pictures. But it was the bell tower that gave Knowles its greatest distinction. Purchased from Cincinnati in June 1886, the bell served as the college timepiece, awakening the students in the morning, sending them to bed at night and, in between, marking their class and meal times. One contemporary remembered it as "the finest and most melodious toll bell ever bought." With a good east wind and a bright sunny day, Orlando residents could hear its peal five miles away.[16]

Pinehurst, located beside Knowles, was the college's first dormitory. The administration emphasized the "cottage" concept of boarding because it wanted to replicate the personal characteristics of a home. The cottage system, claimed the college brochure, provided students with the opportunity to develop strong characters and habits. A "house mother" or a member of the faculty lived in the cottage in order to closely supervise students. "Social relations between ladies and gentlemen," the college literature emphasized, would be supervised by the matrons who would make certain that the "inmates" studied properly and engaged in "wholesome recreation." In essence, the college promised that the cottage system would provide a benevolent paternalism, one that would "surround the student with the influences of a cheerful, well-ordered Christian home."[14]

By the end of the first school year, two more buildings had been constructed on the campus: Lakeside Cottage, the men's dormitory which was finished in time for the 1886-1887 school year, and the Dining Hall, another gift from Francis Knowles. Until the completion of the dining hall, boarding students took their meals in two bedrooms beside a small lean-to kitchen attached to the South end of Pinehurst. Now they had a "bright and cheerful" place to take their meals. The college used the former kitchen space as its first library.[17]

By 1887, four imposing buildings stood on the East side of the horseshoe shaped commons. In 1891, President Hooker had raised sufficient funds to construct another and larger women's hall. Although called a "cottage," Cloverleaf was an impressive three-story, ninety room, three-winged structure that resembled a large dormitory. Even though it violated the cottage concept, Hooker and the trustees discovered that a single, large building was less expensive than several smaller ones. Men were now housed in Pinehurst, which, along with Lakeside, gave the college two male dormitories. Finally, with money donated by Frederick Lyman, the college constructed a physical education building. Lyman Gymnasium contained a 50-by-70 exercise room and an inside gallery guarded by an ornately decorated balustrade. With the construction of Lyman Hall, the college completed its initial building phase. A graphic drawing in the 1892 catalogue, although somewhat misleading in its placement of the buildings on the campus, correctly gave the feeling of permanence to the fledgling little college.[18]

Academic life in the early years at Rollins very much conformed to late Victorian views of education. As one of the early students later recalled, the "gay nineties" hardly described the "sober and sedate" life of college students.[19] Most teachers were remembered as "strong disciplinarians," not a surprising characterization for a pedagogy that assumed the mind had to be disciplined in order to absorb knowledge. Learning was considered a matter of hard work. Like physical training, academic endeavor required vigorous exertion that few would describe as pleasurable. Because recitation was seen as the most effective pedagogical method for exercising the mind, most Rollins professors almost invariably employed it in their classrooms. Recitation, classicist L.A. Lloyd wrote in the college catalogue, "is an excellent discipline for the mental faculties" because it demands "accuracy in thinking." The study of Greek, declared Professor John Ford, who replaced Lloyd, gave students skill in forming "such mental habits as exact observation and generalization and will be of value to him in all intellectual work." The "topical method of recitation" was employed in history courses while literature would be "read and committed to memory."[20]

Science courses offered a welcome relief from the routine of recitation. The instructor Eva J. Root, required some recitation from textbooks in botany, zoology, physiology and astronomy, but she also encouraged "hands-on" work. These included dissection, work with manikins and charts. She had use of a microscope and a telescope, a gift to the college from George Rollins, the brother of Alonzo. As Professor Root noted in the catalogue, she always gave students "the advantages of practical work." One of Root's students later praised her for opening the "scientific world of plants and animals that most of us had known only superficially."[21]

Perhaps the most innovative practitioner of the hands-on method was Dr. Thomas R. Baker, who came in 1891. Although retired from the Pennsylvania State University, Baker, at 53, was still an exciting teacher. If not for its location (Baker came to Florida for his health), Rollins would not have attracted such an outstanding educator and scholar. Baker had published a science textbook and had an established national reputation as a teacher of the experimental method in the classroom. The object of the method, Baker wrote in the catalogue, was "not only to fix in the minds of pupils the facts that are presented them, but to teach them how to use this method to the best advantage." He introduced a course entitled "Practical Chemistry," which was designed to give students "a more practical knowledge of chemistry than can be gained by merely studying the theory of the subject." Despite Baker's innovative efforts, years would pass before the Rollins catalogue showed any significant changes in pedagogical methods.[22]

A central purpose of small 19th century colleges, which served as extensions of the prevailing Victorian concepts of family life, was socialization. An enormous amount of energy was expended in regulating active young people's lives. The administration and faculty assumed full responsibility for developing students' character as long as they remained in the institution. Rollins' rigid code of behavior for all students left no doubt about its socialization function: "The object of the school's discipline is to protect the student from temptations and bad habits, to secure the proper improvement in behavior and produce a well-ordered life. Those who cannot give a willing and cheerful assent to the regulations of the school should not seek admission to its privileges."[23]

In December 1885, the faculty published a detailed list of student regulations and conventions. Rules for religious observances headed the list. As one student observed: "What the institution lacked in material means, it made up in religious fervor: faculty and students alike prayed without provocation." With no exceptions, students were required to attend Sunday church services "at the church of their choice." However, in reality, during the early years their choices in Winter Park were limited to the Congregational, the Episcopal, and the Methodist churches. Students were also confined to their rooms on Sunday mornings for the purpose of studying Sunday school lessons. Daily morning devotionals were mandatory for all students.[24]

The faculty considered study-time a vital part of

academic life and they set study hours at any non-class time from 8:30 a.m. to 12 p.m., from 1:30 p.m. to 4:30 p.m. and in the evening from 7:00 p.m. to 9:00 p.m. During these periods, they prohibited students from visiting each other's rooms, although after nine o'clock in the evening students were allowed 30 minutes for socializing before lights were out at 10:00 p.m.. Between study hours on Friday evenings, gentlemen were permitted to make calls in the parlor rooms of the ladies' cottage for two hours, and they were given the opportunity to escort young ladies to church on Sunday, provided they returned directly to campus immediately afterward. After much debate, the faculty in 1889 agreed that both boys and girls might perform gymnastics in the same building. Otherwise, this Victorian generation anxiously attempted to subvert temptation by separating the sexes. Male students were convinced that the threat of temptation dictated dormitory policy as well. They reckoned that the Cloverleaf cottage was divisible by three sections: the college "put all the pretty girls on the third floor--out of reach of the boys, all the middling-looking girls on the second floor, and on the first floor it placed girls "whose faces protected them."[25]

Several "vices" were absolutely forbidden. Alcohol was the greatest of all these evils. Students were prohibited from possessing or using liquor either on campus or in the vicinity. The college faced an early moral dilemma on this matter after Winter Park Company built the Seminole Hotel. The hostelry sold liquor, and the college held stock in the company. One trustee persistently pointed out this moral inconsistency until finally the trustees corrected the problem: they retired the complaining trustee.[26] Other vices received almost equal attention. The college prohibited the use of tobacco "on campus, on the streets or in the vicinity" of the college. After long debate, the faculty decided to prohibit card playing on the grounds that it was a "sedentary game unsuitable for students and tending toward immorality." It further forbade other acts including loitering at the railway station on Sunday, throwing water on beds, stealing, keeping firearms, using profanity and keeping a dirty room.[27]

The college issued demerits for an infraction of these rules and weighed them according to the seriousness of the transgression. Absence from Sunday services and from class drew two demerits each; missing Sunday school, study hours and tardiness drew one demerit each. Eight demerits in one term resulted in a reprimand; 12 resulted in a letter to the parents; 15 demerits led to dismissal. Although all these rules and regulations succeeded in small ways, they achieved much less success in large matters. Young people who ordinarily would have lived under the watchful eyes of parents now sought a limited kind of freedom in college despite the faculty's intentions. They discovered innumerable ways of breaking institutional rules. At almost every faculty meeting students appeared to explain violations, the most common being the use of profanity in some form. Faculty minutes abound with notations: "dismissed on account of licentious talk." Many infractions, of course, went undetected. Frederick Lewton, later a prominent botanist in the United States Agriculture Department and curator of textiles in the Smithsonian Institution, recalled how one night he slipped out of his room in order to observe the constellation Leo, visible only after 1:00 a.m. He burst to share his observances with someone but held it all inside for fear of receiving demerits for breaking the 10 o'clock curfew.[28]

Innumerable infractions occurred because undoubtedly the regulations were too confining for irrepressibly energetic youth. Such was the case of Rex Beach, later to become a popular novelist and one of Rollins' most famous and loyal alumni. Beach, an authentic free spirit, refused to be bound by restrictive Victorian mores. Much more interested in athletics than academics, he took a more casual approach to academic life than Victorian academicians were willing to accept. Beach, who viewed college as a place for good companionship and fun, regarded regulations not as restrictions but as challenges. One Sunday, Beech and four other boys were seen sailing on Lake Virginia, violating the colleges prohibition against frivolous activity on the Sabbath. They were brought before the faculty for explanation and later "personally admonished" by the president. Ten o'clock curfew was also a challenge for Beach. As he readily admitted, most buildings did not offer many escape routes: "It took a trapeze performer to get out [of Pinehurst] and a post-graduate course in porch climbing to get back in." The athletic Beach apparently managed the feat quite often, because in March 1893, he was suspended "for open defiance" of the curfew rule. Two weeks later, after a letter of apology, the faculty allowed him to return. Despite such leniencies Beach never graduated. In fact, he posed a mystery to the Victorian faculty who thought he lacked the qualities of a serious scholar. Most doubted that he would ever amount to much, and later expressed surprise that Beach could write novels.[29]

To manage and instruct these sometimes unruly youngsters, the college hired an unusually talented group of educators. Because the remote little college could hardly expect to attract noted teachers, Hooker used the institution's favorable environment as an inducement for securing qualified teachers. Few of the early instructors came to the area specifically to teach at Rollins. Almost all were already in Florida for reasons unrelated to teaching. Nathan Barrows, a Phi Beta Kappa graduate of Western Reserve, had been a physician for years in Cleveland when he decided to embark upon a new career in citrus, and, therefore, he had been living in Orange City before the founding of Rollins. As the college's most outstanding charter faculty member, the tall, powerfully built doctor with white hair and a full, flowing white beard made an impressive appearance. Even at middle age, he was an active, energetic man, a great proponent of physical exercise and a lover of nature. Free hours found him walking for miles in the woods or rowing long distances on the chain of lakes. He rowed across Lake Virginia to Rollins every day. In addition to teaching mathematics, Barrows also served on the Board of Trustees. He was the only person ever to hold a position in the faculty and on the board at the same time.[30]

The other original faculty members—Louise Abbott, William Lloyd, and Annie Morton—were in retirement in Florida when Hooker hired them. As with so many Victorians, Morton had come south with the forlorn hope that warmer weather would help cure a chronic illness. However, she died of cancer only six years after she arrived at Rollins. In the second term of the first year, Lewis Austin, a former classmate of Dr. Hooker, joined the faculty to teach Greek and Latin. After a short time, he gave up teaching to travel through Italy and Greece. During its second year, the college added instructors in natural sciences, English literature, music and art, as well as instructors in the Normal School, amounting to a total of 13 faculty members. Two of these appointments proved fortuitous. John H. Ford, a Phi Beta Kappa graduate of Oberlin, replaced Lloyd as a professor of Greek. Ford, whose wife was the sister of Illinois Peter Altgeld (a progressive Illinois governor), had sought the warmer Florida cliamte in the hope of relieving what he thought was tuberculosis. Because he lived on campus, in a home directly behind Knowles Hall, Ford assumed an unusually active role in the college's community life, entertaining students and even holding classes on his front porch. Later he would serve twice as interim president.[31]

Eva J. Root also joined the faculty in the second year as the college's first instructor in natural science. Root, a perfect example of the versatility demanded of college teachers, served first as principal of the sub-preparatory department. After two years, the college hired her to teach botany, zoology, biology and comparative anatomy in the preparatory department as well as physiology and astronomy in the liberal arts college. In addition, she taught French in both the preparatory and collegiate departments. As a part of her responsibilities, she was matron for Pinehurst after it became a boys' cottage.[32]

Two PhDs came to the faculty in 1890 and 1891. The first was Dr. Carl Hartman, a native of Germany hired to teach German and Spanish, which later proved to be a disaster. A few weeks after school opened in 1890, Hooker admitted that Hartman was "an unfortunate appointment." He possessed an acerbic, thoroughly disagreeable disposition that immediately unsettled faculty harmony and school routine. Hartman alienated most of the college community, in particular several members of the faculty, whose lives, according to Hooker, "were beyond reproach." His harsh and even violent manner brought on several serious incidents. The climax came at the end of the year when, during an argument with two male students, Hartman pushed both down the stairs of Knowles Hall, slightly injuring one. At the faculty meeting convened to discuss the matter, the irate professor lashed out at everyone, including Hooker. He was not asked to return the following year.[33]

Hartman's dismissal opened the way for the appointment of one of the early college's legendary professors, Dr. Thomas Rakestraw Baker, PhD from University of Goettingen. Baker provided freshness to the study of science by employing what he called the "natural method." Baker who remained at the college for over two decades, proved to be a scholarly inspiration for the college. His impressive shock of white hair and Lincolnesque beard gave him a deceptively sober manner. In the classroom or in student groups, his wit, his infectious sense of humor and willingness to try new methods brought unusual vitality into the traditionally somber, sometimes lifeless, Victorian educational process.[34]

The leader and animating influence for this band of

pioneer educators was President Hooker, who, from the beginning, became deeply involved in both the academic and the administrative aspects of the college. Although somewhat stiff in appearance—his dress invariably included a black Prince Albert coat, white tie and silk hat—the kindness of Hooker's voice and eyes softened an otherwise formal exterior bearing. He had the appearance, one student remembered, of "an other-worldly religious leader, almost a living beatitude." Many spoke of Hooker's gentleness and his love for all living things. The family cat followed him each morning down Interlachen as he walked from the Congregational parsonage to the college. By example and by direction he infused a spirit of dedicated service into the early college community. He loved working with students, making ministerial visits, promoting prayer groups, counseling those with problems, even at times taking into his own large family students who found it difficult to adjust to life away from home. His letter book is filled with notes to parents assuring them that their children were doing well. "Your son is homesick," he wrote in a typical letter, "but is getting over it. Stand by the authority of the school in your letters and we shall be able to help you make your son a noble man."[35]

Without deans or assistants to help deal with the countless administrative matters, the president relied on the faculty to help manage the college. Academic decisions, such as requirements, courses and teaching loads, as well as student affairs—everything from dormitory regulations to granting permission for special student activities--fell within direct faculty responsibilities. Through weekly committee meetings the faculty ruled on such varied matters such as course schedules, demerit assignments and commencement programs, student dismissals and absences. By 1887, the little democratic faculty meetings had apparently become quite lively, forcing the president to invoke new rules of order. He allotted faculty members three minutes each to make his or her case until everyone had been heard. Yet, except for the Hartman affair, little dissension among the faculty developed during Hooker's presidency.[36]

Hooker's most troublesome problem was not administering the college, but finding funds to keep the educational endeavor functioning properly. In this area, he relied on the Board of Trustees, particularly the executive committee. Frederick Lyman provided much of the financial leadership in the early years. Because most of its assets were in land and stocks, and most of its initial cash went into buildings, the first academic year found the college in debt. Lyman borrowed over $2,500 in his own name during the summer of 1886 and told Hooker that the college needed $4,000 more before it opened in October 1886. "I do not like to do this," Lyman wrote to Hooker. "I do not feel that I should be expected to, but I cannot see the work stop as it would otherwise."[36] In October 1886, Lyman borrowed $4,000 from his cousin, which he thought would carry the college until it could sell some of its orange grove property. But during the fall term, the college drifted further into debt, probably owing as much as $8,000. The executive committee sold the college-owned orange grove in Palatka (donated originally by Alonzo Rollins), which provided only temporary relief. Within a year, Hooker was again without money to pay college expenses. Lyman, who was in New England at the time, borrowed a sum from a New York bank but (unnecessarily) warned Hooker to be cautious with expenditures: "I do not know where we can get another dollar."[37]

Despite Lyman's pessimism, the college did receive sufficient funds to stay afloat. Professor John Ford agreed, for a small stipend, to raise money in the state during the summer months, and Hooker went north each summer for the same purpose. Periodic grants from the Congregational Educational Society totaling more than $74,000 proved to be the margin between survival and collapse.

Thus, President Hooker discovered early what a succession of presidents would come to realize—funding and administering a little rural provincial college would be no easy task. Each day, month and year brought a new crisis. Some problems were self-inflicted others were beyond his control. Perceptive students such as Rex Beach clearly saw the financial conditions of the college. In his recollections he wrote: "Florida was pretty poor, many a family went without everything except bare necessities in order to give their sons and daughters an opportunity to better themselves. Rollins itself was starving. There was no running water in any dormitory, a hot bath was unheard of. The teachers were underpaid and no president ever succeeded in wrangling enough money out of philanthropic sources to make both ends meet."[38]

Trouble on the Board of Trustees exacerbated the college's problems. For some time, dissension had been brewing between the ministers, who were led by Sullivan Gale and the businessmen, headed by Lyman. However grateful for Lyman's and his colleagues' contribution to the college, the ministers were not happy with their methods in two respects. They deplored the use of the college in the Winter Park Company's land development schemes, and they decried the college's advertising brochure as lacking in dignity. At the February 1887 meeting, the ministers secured an assurance from the executive committee that "the newspaper advertising of the college [would] be confined to a simple statement in regard to the college."[39]

At the commencement trustee meeting in 1888, the ministers brought the matter to a head. After two lengthy discussions, Lyman and two other trustees resigned from the board. These resignations opened the way for a new set of by-laws that combined the office of President of the Corporation and the office of President of the Faculty into one: President of the College. The trustees named Hooker to the new office. Bruised feelings notwithstanding, Lyman departed with no animosity, issuing a characteristically generous statement. "Having the interest of the college at heart," he noted in his statement of resignation, "and thinking that those interests may be advanced at this time by such actions, I hereby tender my resignation as president of the corporation."[40] Lyman moved to California shortly afterward, but he continued his loyal support of the college. In February 1890, he contributed funds for the construction of a gymnasium, which was completed the following year. The college had no truer friend than Frederick Lyman. More than any single person, he was responsible for its founding and with indefatigable effort he guided the college through its first few years. The gift of the gymnasium after he left showed the real character of the man.[41]

If the internal political struggle of these early years had little financial repercussions, two natural catastrophes had immediate effect. In 1887 and again in 1888, yellow fever epidemics ravaged the state of Florida. The dreaded disease, its cause not yet discovered, struck both Key West and Tampa in May 1887. Although the epidemic never reached Central Florida, people viewed it as a threatening plague and left the state in large numbers. Enrollment at Rollins dropped, though only moderately. But the following year a more serious outbreak occurred in Jacksonville, a debarkation port for northerners arriving in Florida. Authorities citing over 5,000 cases and 400 deaths, quarantined the city, and halted travel in or out of the area. The college sent out 10,000 brochures claiming "no locality was more healthful than Winter Park," but under the circumstances the words sounded hollow. In September, the college postponed its 1888 opening until October. Doomsayers on the Board of Trustees predicted the end.[42]

Nevertheless, the college did open, albeit with reduced enrollment. During the year, registration for 1889-1890 academic year showed an encouraging increase, leading Hooker to project even more registrations than the college could accommodate with its two dormitories. Reluctant to turn away qualified students, the trustees agreed to the expensive practice of housing the overflow of students off-campus. Moreover, to meet what appeared to be a dramatic increase in college enrollments, they voted to construct a new dormitory, a fateful decision because construction began as the nation's declining economy led to the depression of 1893. The trustees had counted heavily on local money, but they soon learned that frontier communities feel the effects of an economic downturn sooner than other areas. They found it almost impossible to borrow funds locally.[43]

Banks in the Northeast provided some money, but not sufficient enough to pull the college out of what Hooker called its "hard place." The president pleaded unsuccessfully with the Congregational Educational Society for a loan and desperately tried to sell another college grove, but to no avail.[44] By July 1891, the college was so deeply in debt that it could not complete the construction of the new dormitory. Hooker gloomily wrote to a friend: "The college treasury is empty of funds for ordinary running expenses. We are spending heavily for buildings and furniture, and we shall have all we can do this summer to open the college."[45]

The college did open in 1891, but its financial situation worsened. Hooker became more despondent. Florida was a poor country, he wrote to a colleague, where most of the people just kept their heads above water and could not be solicited for another subscription. "It is a critical time with us," he wrote, but with stubborn optimism he continued: "the darkest hour is before the morning and faith and success are apt to go together." Eventually even his sanguine homilies could not sustain him. In December, he told a friend that the "burdens of the college in its present stage of growth are so heavy that I sometimes regret that I did not resign the College Presidency instead of the Pastorate."[46] At the February 1892 trustee meeting, Hooker submitted his resignation. College building had overtaxed his strength.

The restored health he sought in Florida was failing again. The trustees accepted his resignation with "thankfulness to Divine Providence for the invaluable service he had rendered the college as one of its chief founders and its first president."[47]

1. November 10, 1892.

2. Frederick Rudolph, *The American College and University* (New York, 1962), 88.

3. Ibid, lo8-109.

4. For a good discussion of the classical curriculum see Frederick Rudolph, *Curriculum: A History of American Undergraduate Study* (1977). For an analysis of the Yale Report see Jack C. Lane, "The Yale Report of 1828 and Liberal Education," History of Education Journal, (27) Fall 1987, 325-338.

5. Rudolph, *Curriculum*, 68-73.

6. Rollins College Catalogue, l885. (Hereinafter cited as Catalogue).

7. *Ibid*.

8. *Ibid.*, 1888.

9. *Ibid.*, 1890, 1896.

10. Trustee Minutes, 1887.

11. Catalog, 1895.

12. Other places included Alabama, Illinois, Indiana, Kentucky, Massachusetts, Minnesota, Wisconsin, New York, Ohio, South Carolina, Vermont, Virginia. Catalog, 1890.

13. Trustee Minutes, 1886; *South Florida Sentinel*, September, l5, 1885; Walter Howe, "Recollections," Manuscript, Rollins Archives.

14. Catalogue, 1891.

15. I have reconstructed the ceremony from *Orange County Reporter*, November 11, 1886; Chase Scrapbook, Rollins Library; "Address" by William O'Neal, 1935, Rollins Archives.

16. Elizabeth Hooker, "Edward Hooker," Manuscript, Rollins Archives; Frederick Lewton, "Autobiography," Manuscript, Rollins Archives

17. Lewton, "Autobiography."

18. Trustee Minutes, 1889, 1890, 1891; Catalog, 1893.

19. Lois Parker Meyers," Recollections," Manscript, Rollins Archives.

20. Catalogue, 1892.

21. Lewton, Autobiography."

22. Catalogue, 1892. Baker was also quite active in the Winter Park community. An article in the January 4, 1917 issue of the *Winter Park Post* made the following announcement: "Dr Thomas Baker, for many years Professor of Natural Science at Rollins College, will succeed William Chase Temple as Mayor of Winter Park. Dr. Baker was made sole nominee for this office when one of there largest bodies of voters ever assembled in Winter Park took a standing vote at the caucus held in the Town Hall."

The famous temple orange, a hybrid of the tangerine and orange, was named for Baker's mayoral predecessor. The parent tree stood in an orange off Temple Grove Circle.

23. Jencks and Reisman, *Academic Revolution*, 28; Catalog, 1894.

24. Faculty Minutes, 1886. Rollins Archives; Hooker to Martha Weld July 19, 1891. Hooker Papers. Rollins Archives. Rex Beach, *Personal Exposures*, 19 (1940)

25. Henry Mowbray, "Recollections," Manuscript. Rollins Archives; Faculty Minutes, 1889.

26. Trustee Minutes, May, 1889.

27. Faculty Minutes, 1890.

28. *Ibid.*, 1889; Lewton, "Autobiography."
Other than Rex Beach, Frederick Lewton was perhaps the college's most successful early student. After finishing at Rollins in 1890, he studied chemistry at Drexel University. He later taught chemistry there and published works on the composition of resins. Later he worked as a botanist for the US Department of Agriculture and as curator of Textiles at the National Museum. He returned to Rollins in 1954 and served a the library's archivist where he collected over 80,00 pieces for the library. He also left behind a valuable account of his experiences as a Rollins student.

29. Rex Beach, "Recollections," Manuscript, Rollins Archives; Faculty Minutes, 1890; Emma Root Van Buskirk, "An Appreciation of Miss Eva Root," *Alumni Record* (June, 1931).

30. For a description and evaluation of the charter faculty see Lewton "Autobiography"; *Chase Scrapbook*; Thomas Baker,"Twenty Years at Rollins" Manuscript, Rollins Archives

31. Chase to Lyman, November 7, 1885, *Chase Scrapbook*; Trustee Minutes, February, 1893.

32. Van Buskirk, "Eva Root". Archives

33. Hooker to E.K. Forte, October 17, 1890. Hooker Papers; Faculty Minutes, December 1890.

34. Marjorie Blackman Wallace, "Recollections," Manuscript, Rollins Archives; Baker, "Twenty Years".

35. For example see Hooker to E. V. October 15, 1889. Hooker Papers.

36. Faculty Minutes, October 1887.

37. Lyman to Hooker, October 7, 1886; December 7, 1887; For early financial problems see Lyman to Alonzo Rollins, October 5, 1886; and Hooker to Lyman, September 10, 1886. Hooker Papers.

38. Trustee Minutes, February and May 1888. Beach, *Exposures*, 20.

39. *Ibid.*, February 1889' O'Neal, "Recollections," Manuscript, Rollins Archives.

40. *Ibid.*, May 1889.

41. *Ibid.*, May 1890.

42. O'Neal, "Recollections"; *Orange County Reporter*, September 21, 1888; *LochmedeL*, September 1888; Faculty Minutes, October 1888.
The outbreak of the yellow fever virus reached epidemic proportions in Jacksonville in 1888. Because its river port was only debarkation point, the epidemic paralyzed the interior as well.

43. Hooker to C.M. Hutchins, December 18, 1891. Hooker Papers.

44. Hooker to Reverend Maile, October 28, 1891. IBID.

45. Hooker to Katy Beck, July 24, 1891.

46. *Ibid.*, December 5, 1891.

47. Trustee Minutes, February 7, 1892.
Over the years Rollins Archivists have collected many fascinating recollections from former students. For a summary of some of these see Darla Moore, "Where to Find the Freshest Memoires," http://wp.me/p3fXva-uq.

Chapter 3

___

THE STRUGGLE FOR SURVIVAL, 1892–1903
(HOPES AND FRUSTRATIONS)

FOLLOWING PRESIDENT HOOKER'S resignation, Rollins experienced three decades of instability caused by a host of problems, some of which came from sources beyond its control. In the mid-1890s, a severe national economic depression made it extremely difficult to raise funds in the Northeast. Then came a natural disaster. Below freezing temperatures crippled the state's citrus crop, devastated the area's economy and sent large numbers of Rollins students home for an indefinite period. The freeze also destroyed orange groves owned by the college, wiping out a significant portion of the institution's projected income.

Faced with these unexpected calamities, the trustees tried desperately to find a president who could guide the college through what seemed to be an impending disaster. After Hooker's resignation in February 1892, the trustees appointed Professor John Ford as acting president while they searched for a new leader. In an attempt to deal with the financial problem that had precipitated Hooker's resignation, they called a special meeting of the trustees on March 22, 1892, "to consider the financial condition of the college and take such action as may seem wise." After debating the problem all day, the board decided to take a well-worn path: Acting President Ford and Lyman would "solicit subscriptions in Winter Park and the vicinity to carry the institution through the current year." Hooker had already rejected this idea because his office had only recently canvassed Winter Park for support of new a dormitory, and many pledges still remained outstanding. The trustees surely were grasping for straws, and yet, with startling optimism, they instructed the Executive Committee to use any surplus funds raised in the proposed campaign to reduce the current debt. The board then authorized the executive committee "to mortgage or sell any portion of the property now owned or claimed by Rollins College on such terms and for such price as to them may seem advisable." Additionally, the trustees authorized the executive committee "to employ a financial agent for the college on such terms, and under such instructions as said committee may decide upon." The trustees had finally proposed a long-range, systematic approach to college financial management. Unfortunately, they never found an effective professional fundraiser to fill the position.[1]

John Ford accepted the temporary position of acting president with some misgivings. Satisfied with his role as a professor of Latin, he was apprehensive about the pressures inherent in the office of the president. Still, he shouldered his new responsibilities with a stoicism possibly derived from years of teaching Greek civilization. Despite the temporary nature of his appointment, he acted aggressively and positively to improve college life.

To deal with the immediate need of funds for operating expenses, Ford and the executive committee achieved some economies through administration reorganization. They replaced housemothers in the dormitories with female teachers and when the principal of the Ladies Department retired because of ill health, Ford assumed the duties of that office. The executive committee made further savings by reducing each faculty member's annual salary by $100.[5] Ford noted in his first annual report that these personnel reductions, along with the $5,000 given each year by the Congregational Educational Society of the Home Missionary Association, would allow the college to get through the 1892-1893 school year without adding to its debt.[2]

Despite Ford's courageous efforts, the college desperately needed a permanent officer at the helm. By October 1893, the executive committee was able to identify a prospect: they found George F. Fairchild, the president of Kansas State A&M College in Manhattan, Kansas. After extensive investigation by the executive committee, the Board of Trustees voted unanimously at a special meeting in April 1893 to offer Fairchild the presidency. But Fairchild, apparently aghast at the financial state of the college, withdrew his name despite the trustees' effort "to impress on him the importance of the Rollins presidency."[3]

Following this depressing outcome, friends of the college in Chicago put forth the name of Charles Fairchild, the nephew of the previous candidate. Formerly a science professor at both Berea and Oberlin Colleges, Charles Fairchild came from a family steeped in higher education. His father had been president of Berea College, and his two uncles served as presidents of Oberlin and Kansas State Colleges. Charles Fairchild taught science at Berea and Oberlin and also had served as part-time financial agent at both colleges. He was particularly successful at Oberlin where he tripled the endowment in nine years and obtained funds for six major building projects. Such fundraising successes undoubtedly made him very attractive to the Rollins trustees.

On September 20, 1893, the executive committee issued a call for a meeting of the Board of Trustees, urging everyone to attend. The committee announced, "it now seems possible to elect a new president." As a measure of the college's fundamental problems, the call for a critical meeting scheduled for October 4 did not produce a quorum. The executive committee managed to gather the required number for a meeting the following day, and the Board of Trustees elected Charles Fairchild to the presidency. Fairchild was in town to accept the offer, but his business interests in Chicago prevented him from assuming office until the New Year. In the meantime, Ford stayed on as acting president.[4]

Fairchild's inauguration in February 1893 seemed to presage a brighter financial future for the college. The new president, the executive committee noted, was a "man of large acquaintances in both the East and the West," and was judged capable of using those acquaintances to good benefit for colleges." But as Fairchild would soon learn, seeking funds for a college with an established reputation and dedicated alumni such as Oberlin was one thing; the chore of rescuing a small isolated institution from the brink of financial ruin was another.

At Fairchild's inauguration, Acting President Ford precisely voiced the college's desperate hope for the new chief's success. "You have been engaged in the financial part of college work, having raised several hundred dollars for colleges. You have planned college buildings, you have had opportunities to study and compare different colleges and acquaint yourself with the economies and details of college management. We have reason to believe that in you, a man of affairs, we have a president this young institution needs at this hour."[5]

In his inaugural address, Fairchild identified the college's most persistent problem: Northerners, he noted, perceived Rollins as located in a climate where little learning could take place. They imagined Florida as located in the "land of perpetual afternoon." In the mind of Northerners, this meant an "afternoon sense of languor" that did not lend itself to serious study. Leaving the biting airs of the North, Fairchild continued, Northerners expected to find "in latitudes rarely visited by frost that which soothes and enervates and predisposes to dreams of romance. A most valuable education is thought to come from the stern struggle with the long winters of snow and ice, and this education must of course be wanting when genial and equable airs give perpetual summer." This sentiment, noted Fairchild, was nonsense. Florida rested on the same global parallel as the ancient civilizations of Egypt, Greece and Rome, which, he asserted, proved there was no special relationship between "latitude and lassitude." Still, he admitted, the college had to deal with perceptions.[6]

Despite the subdued tenor of Fairchild's address, the college community clearly expected impressive results from him, waiting anxiously in the first few months of his presidency for signs of a forthcoming miracle. The new president's first fund raising trip to the north in March 1894 proved unproductive, dampening some anxious hopes.[7] In an effort to prod him along, the executive committee voted "that the President be requested to take up the financial task for the college in such a way and in such places as to him may seem wise." Apparently concerned about Fairchild's lack of success, the Board of Trustees endorsed the executive committee's demand that the president "push aggressively the financial work of the college during vacation."[8] The record fails to document the nature of Fairchild's efforts in the summer and fall of 1894, although the executive committee minutes do indicate that he was absent from the campus all of November and part of December. The results were disappointing. The Treasurer's report for the fiscal year ending December 1894 listed a large debt increase over the previous year. Under Fairchild, the college was not only failing to show a lack of progress financially, it was falling even further behind.[9]

In December 1894, nature dealt the college a severe blow. Following an unusually benign winter, a severe cold front dipped down into Central Florida four days after Christmas. Temperatures plunged to 20 degrees around midnight, dropped to 18 around 4:00 a.m. and remained there until mid-morning. For two additional days, the killing frosts and freezing temperatures persisted. By the time the cold front had passed, virtually the entire Florida citrus crop lay rotting on the ground. One observer left the following description of the landscape after three days of frost: "The whole country looked as if swept by fire. The orange trees were black, the fruit, lumps of yellow ice. As for pineapples, bananas, mangoes and other tropical plants, they were all dead. The frozen oranges began to fall. In one grove I saw as many as four thousand boxes of magnificent fruit on the ground. Groves, for which a week earlier two thousand dollars had been asked could now be bought for twenty."[10]

Still, there was a "ray of hope in this hour of gloom." Although the freeze had destroyed the fruit crop and the leaf growth, the trees themselves remained unharmed. When warm weather returned, sap flowed into the outer layer of bark, and the denuded trees put forth new growth. Then, on February 7, barely a month after the December freeze, an even more severe cold front settled on the peninsula. When temperatures plummeted to 14 degrees, the recently flowing sap turned to ice, expanded, ruptured the bark and virtually exploded from the trees. A later resident, who interviewed witnesses, graphically described the scene in his history of Orange County: "The trees stood bare, gaunt, pathetic; the ground beneath was already covered with fallen fruit in layers and the air was laden with the stench of decaying oranges; the people were shocked, disheartened, bankrupt, and helpless." Overnight the primary source of income in Florida had been wiped out. Hundreds of people simply packed their belongings and left the state as banks failed and business came to a virtual standstill. Mrs. Fairchild wrote a friend that all the college's orange trees had been destroyed. "If there had been a death in every family in the state, we could not be more depressed," she lamented.[11]

Most civic institutions lay paralyzed by the economic calamity, but none more so than a privately funded college with tuition-paying students. Shortly after the freeze, Rollins students began leaving in large numbers, the exodus continuing throughout the school year. The financial condition of the college rapidly deteriorated. When bills for the month of January went unpaid, several businesses threatened to sue the institution. In desperation, Fairchild, along with Treasurer William O'Neal, hurried to New York seeking a note from friends of the college. They returned with a loan, which eased the immediate problem but merely added to the college's indebtedness in the long run. In New York, the College and Educational Society of the Congregational Association offered assurances that funds would be forthcoming, but the Northeast itself was in the grip of a deep economic depression, and the Society failed to keep its promise.[12]

In the midst of the financial crisis, Fairchild was forced to deal with a controversy within the college community. Shortly after arriving from Oberlin College (which before the Civil War was a hotbed of abolitionism), Fairchild made it clear that should a Negro apply to Rollins, he would judge the applicant on his qualifications, not on his color. This statement incensed several trustees, particularly Frederick Lyman, who warned Fairchild that he (Lyman) would withdraw his support for the college if it ever admitted a "colored" person. The incident left lingering hard feelings. If this was not enough stress, Fairchild had personal financial problems. With nine children to support, he often complained to the trustees that his salary barely allowed his family to make ends meet.

On March 18, 1895, overwhelmed by the mounting pressure, Fairchild suddenly resigned his office. The "stress from various directions but preeminently in the financial field" had become more than he could bear. "I have not aided you as yet," he explained, "and I do not see how I can aid you in the near future." He asked that his resignation become effective on March 31. What had begun as an administration filled with high hopes and cheery optimism had ended, in less than two years, in a grievous disappointment. With his proven fund-raiding abilities, Fairchild had seemed a perfect candidate for a college in deep financial trouble. But he proved unable to translate his successes at two other colleges into achievements in a young frontier institution. The freeze did not cause Fairchild's failure; it simply provided the coup de grace to an already failing effort. The national depression of the early 1890s, the devastating freezes, the college's poor financial foundation, its relative obscure and misunderstood location and perhaps Fairchild's own personality, all combined to make his tenure as president one of the briefest in Rollins history.[13]

The executive committee once more turned to John Ford, asking him to assume again the post of acting president until a new executive could be found. He and the committee immediately turned their attention to the crisis brought on by the freeze. With no funds available to meet teacher's salaries for the month of April, the committee persuaded each instructor to accept a 12-month college note at eight percent interest in lieu of the April and May salary payments. Contracts for the 1895-1896 school year were a second urgent problem, because teaching responsibilities and salary promises were traditionally negotiated in April. On April 5, the executive committee made severe salary reductions; all faculty members, including Ford, suffered cuts in their salaries. In its most drastic action, the committee proposed not to "reengage" four faculty members, including the very popular Thomas R. Baker.[14]

In a further effort to forestall bankruptcy, the executive committee sold the college grove and borrowed $6,000 from trustee F. E. Nettleton of Lake Helen. The two actions, plus the postponement of salary payments to instructors, allowed the college to carry on through the spring term. Not surprisingly, by May, rumors abounded that when the college closed its doors for the summer, it would never open them again. But at the last chapel exercise just prior to commencement, Acting President Ford announced to a relieved audience that "the trustees had voted unanimously to open as usual in October."[15]

True to their word, the trustees welcomed students in October 1896, but the college had sustained a 50 percent decline in enrollment. Ford wrote a frank, graphic depiction of this malaise in his February 1896 annual report. The litany of problems was becoming all too familiar:

> The last school year closed in gloom. Both the internal and external conditions of the institution conspired to produce a situation almost utterly

hopeless. The going out of the President with his family and some special friends from the school had a disrupting effect. The fact that some members of the faculty were not to return and salaries of others were cut down was dispiriting to the faculty themselves and ominous to the public. There were persistent rumors that all the faculty would leave and that the institution would close.

Out in the field of our Florida constituency, the people were beginning to realize the sudden poverty that had come upon them from the freeze the preceding February. We received notification from some of our patrons regretting their inability to send their children another year. In addition to these troubles, it was the misfortune of the institution to be under more burdensome debt than before.[16]

SUCH A GLOOMY picture brought desperate suggestions from the trustees. One wanted to suspend instruction in the Collegiate Department for the 1896-1897 academic year. Despite his pessimistic assessment, Ford demurred. He warned that such an effort would be "dispiriting to all departments—to our entire educational cause." Because the temporary nature of his appointment prevented him from taking no more then stopgap efforts to halt the downward slide, Ford urged the trustees to make haste in finding a permanent president. Since the resignation of Fairchild, the executive committee had been busy with the search. By February 1896, the name of George Morgan Ward, a recent graduate of Andover Theological Seminary, had surfaced as the most probable choice. After a trip by the still loyal Frederick Lyman to Boston to interview Ward, the trustees offered him the appointment. When he accepted, Rollins had its third president and many thought its sole hope for the future.

George Morgan Ward came to Rollins with little educational experience, but he did arrive with some administrative background and a reputation for energetic, dedicated work. Although only 43 years of age, Ward had already accumulated a rich and varied background. After graduating from high school in Lowell, Massachusetts, he entered Harvard University in 1879. He later transferred to Dartmouth College, where he graduated Phi Beta Kappa in 1882. While reading law with a Boston judge, he accepted a position as general secretary of the United Society of Christian Endeavor, an evangelical organization dedicated to religious service. He also served as the editor of the society's publication, *The Golden Rule*. After resigning this position because of ill health, he entered the mercantile business in Lowell, Massachusetts. Later he resumed his work in Christian service before attending Andover Theological Seminary, one of the leading theological schools of the Northeast. He accepted the Rollins offer just prior to receiving his Bachelor of Divinity from Andover. Ward's mind must have been spinning from the whirlwind of circumstances descended on him in those few short weeks. Within a month, he had received a BD from a prominent theological seminary, was ordained a Congregational minister, offered the Rollins presidency and, just before leaving for Florida, he married Emma Sprague, daughter of a Massachusetts Congregational minister.

Although a novice to college administration, the young Ward did bring to Rollins a wide and varied experience. While Secretary of the Christian Endeavor he had shown he could raise money for worthy causes. The trustees hoped the contacts he had made in that organization and in New England would serve him and the college well. Above all, Ward was blessed with a magnetic, compelling personality and a commanding appearance. At medium height, with a full head of hair and a curling mustache, both turning steel gray, Ward had the rugged good looks that one of his acquaintances described as "the Gibson type," a very high compliment in the late Victorian era. Many spoke of what one admirer called his "flashing eyes," which could both burn an opponent and melt a friend.[28] In the colorful academic gown he often wore, Ward appeared almost regal. He effortlessly captivated audiences with his deep, resonant and appealing voice, while his youthful good looks made him an idol for the students. In his first address to the college community, he promised to serve them openly and personally, a pledge he made good in the following years. "Grow old with me," he told the students affectionately, "the best is yet to come, the last of life for which the first was made."[17]

Students reciprocated with adoration most vividly manifested in the custom of meeting the new president and his wife at the train station. When the Wards returned from official trips, several college men invariably met their train, waited until they were comfortably seated in their carriage, and then quickly removed the horses and proceeded to pull the vehicle themselves to Pinehurst (which the couple shared with boarding men students) with "rousing hurrahs" from the students along the way.[18]

Although the trustees may have left out a few details, Ward admitted he came to Rollins with no illusions. "They told me in the North," he wrote later, "that Rollins College did not owe any money. Well, I reckon it didn't. But the Trustees owed $5,000." This led Ward in his acceptance letter to warn the Board of Trustees unequivocally he intended to be a college president, not an absentee fund-raiser. He would accept the position of president only with the "full understanding" that if he needed help in raising funds, the trustees would provide him with a financial assistant. "I am not called upon," he bluntly informed them, "to neglect or abrogate the executive duties of the presidency or to delegate the matters of administration and management in order that my own time may be devoted to fund-raising." The trustees assented to these terms, knowing full well what Ward would soon learn: his view of the presidency was idealistically naive because the college's survival depended on annual subscriptions, and only the president could raise the necessary funds. Even when the trustees provided him with a financial agent as they had promised, Ward did most of the fund raising himself.[18]

Ward approached the immediate financial crisis from a much broader perspective than simply as a matter of raising funds. To the new president, underlying financial woes lay in an academic problem brought on by the classical curriculum. Whatever its perceived educational values, (Ward even doubted those), the ancient languages and mathematics requirements barred otherwise well-qualified students from attending Rollins. Rural public schools, he argued, simply could not prepare its students for Rollins' classical curriculum. Those who attended the Academy were not pursuing the classical course of study in large enough numbers to fill the college's needs. Moreover, as he pointed out, those who pursued the classical course of study in the Preparatory Department often did not enter the liberal arts program at Rollins, opting instead to attend colleges in the Northeast. Additional numbers of students would not resolve all of Rollins' financial issues, but an increase in student tuition would be a major step forward. Ward firmly believed that an expanded student body could be achieved only if the college changed its course of study.[19]

The new president laid the groundwork for such a risky curriculum revision in his 1896 commencement address, his first major speech to the college community. He spoke on specialization, approaching the topic not in the circuitous manner so typical of liberal arts presidential addresses, but in direct words considered anathema to supporters of the classical curriculum. "Life is too diverse in its varied interests," he proclaimed, "for any person to have a working knowledge of sufficient breadth, to enable him to be of real assistance to the world in more than one department." In addition to a broad course of study, he proclaimed, colleges ought to give students the opportunity to become specialists in a special field of endeavor.

Ward's remarks clearly foreshadowed a major change in the course of study, because under no circumstances could the classical prescribed curriculum embody such views. After working with a group of faculty in the summer of 1896,

Ward announced a major curriculum revision for the next academic year. In place of the rigidly prescriptive classical curriculum that required all students to take the same course of study, the revision introduced the concept of electives, a program that allowed "pupils to choose their own courses in order that their education may be designed to their tastes and chosen vocations." Thus, whereas the classical curriculum had divided the course of study according to class year and prescribed the courses students would take in each of the years, the new curriculum separated the course of study into four divisions. These new categories included General Courses, Special Groups, Thesis and Additional Electives. General Courses included the fields of English, moral and political sciences and modern languages. Students would be required to take at least one course in each of the areas, but since several courses were offered in each area, they were given the opportunity to exercise the elective principle. The same options were open to the Special Groups, where students could select one of the eight courses and devote an entire year (spread over four years) to the subject. Another requirement included a written thesis "on some subject connected with the Special Group and embodying the results of original investigation." As a way of further emphasizing freedom of choice, the students were allowed to select almost one-third of their courses as electives with "no restrictions whatsoever on the selection."[20]

Rollins College had cast aside the hoary classical curriculum, replacing it with a general framework within which students were encouraged to determine their own course of study. The ancient languages no longer occupied a central role in the college's academic life. Latin was still taught but was not required. Graduates could now receive a Bachelor of Arts degree without a single course in Latin. Greek was relegated to near obscurity and soon disappeared altogether. Entrance requirements, revised drastically to coincide with the new curriculum, replaced a long list of Greek and Latin works with new requirements that emphasized English, modern languages, science and history. Ward announced the new changes in November 1896. He stated in no uncertain terms the demise of the classical course of study: "We have eliminated the old idea that the promoting of higher education must necessarily be the application of some years of Greek, Latin and higher Mathematics. While we are prepared to teach these courses, we do not require study in them as requisite to a degree of Bachelor of Arts."[21] The writers of the Yale Report of 1828 were surely whirling in protest from their graves.

Rollins had made a radical shift in its approach to education. Rather than clinging to conventional wisdom of what constituted a liberal education, the Ward administration decided to redefine that conventional wisdom. In part, the changes were driven by desperation. By employing the classical curriculum, the college had created a chasm between Florida rural educational conditions and the requirements of that course of study. For years Rollins officials were reluctant to abandon the "Yale Model" for fear of being stigmatized as academically substandard. In a sense, it came down to a choice between change and possible survival or no change and certain demise.

From another perspective, new developments sweeping the country gave Ward the courage to fly in the face of conventional educational wisdom. By the turn of the century classical education was crumbling everywhere. Following the example of Harvard University led by President Charles Eliot, many colleges were in the process of replacing the classical curriculum with precisely the kind of elective course of study devised by Rollins. New forces in the late 19th century—increase in the number of students in college, industrialization and urbanization, the growth and democratization of public high schools and universities, the rise of new professions and, finally, the emergence of completely new areas of knowledge such as the natural sciences and social sciences—all placed unbearable strains on the old, prescribed classical curriculum with its elitist reputation. By 1897, Harvard University abandoned Greek and Latin languages for entrance requirements, and Yale, the bastion of classical education, had reduced its requirements in ancient languages by over one-third and mathematics by one-half. Even so most colleges introduced the elective process piecemeal; few undertook the wholesale revision Rollins made in 1896. In hindsight, it is clear that Ward's decision left the college with a permanent legacy: curriculum change, even when risky, or perhaps because of its risk, would become a part of the Rollins tradition to be repeated in almost every generation.[22]

The Ward revsions made a fundamental shift in another way. Gone was the moral thrust of the old classical curriculum, whose stated purpose was to shape character and to direct young people toward a life of service. The Ward administration chose instead to emphasize individual choice through electives and specialization. In its literature the college stressed how the "practical" side of the program would "fit students for earning a living." Many students, it proclaimed "are anxious to attend school but have only a limited time for such a privilege and wish to make their studies count toward a livelihood." For all such interests, the announcement proclaimed, "practical courses are arranged." Accordingly, and this time with conviction, the college revived its business and teachers' education programs. The Normal School provided for a course of study that included a Model School where prospective teachers received experience in practical teaching. Upon completion of the education program, the college awarded the graduate not merely a certificate (as had been the case with the original Normal School) but with a somewhat more prestigious Bachelor of Pedagogy.[23]

The Business School, a revival of the aborted earlier plan for an Industrial Training Department and a barely veiled move toward vocationalism, was perhaps the college's most drastic departure from the ideals of liberal education. It included courses in bookkeeping, commercial law, banking, shorthand, typewriting and letter writing. Several rooms in Pinehurst were equipped with "modern appliances" devoted exclusively to the use of the Business School. In these courses, "the air of the counting room and office rather than the classroom" prevailed. Students who completed the prescribed courses received a diploma in business.

Ward's attempt to open the college to a wider population of tuition-paying students was a mixed success. Total college enrollment did increase during this period from a low of about 50 students immediately after the 1896 freeze to almost 200 by 1900. Undoubtedly, most of the increase can be attributed to the new curriculum's relaxed requirements. It also was helped along by general improvement in the economy as Central Florida began to recover from the freeze, and as the nation moved forward from an economic depression. The new programs in education and business did attract more students, but only in moderate numbers. Students taking business courses averaged between 15 and 20 in this period, while Normal School enrollment reached 18 and then dropped drastically after 1898.[24]

However, the new curriculum, with its less restrictive entrance and course requirements, did result in a modestly higher enrollment rate in the Liberal Arts College. Between 1896 and 1902, students in the college numbered between 15 and 20, which was not a significant increase compared to 11 in 1894, the year before the freeze. Because of the growth of public schools, the number of students in the Preparatory Department never reached the level of the 1894 enrollment of 100 students. However, the college recovered from the catastrophe of 1895, and the highly touted curriculum revision did play a role in that recovery.

Above all, the revision gave the college a psychological boost. Without students, without leadership, and with a serious shortage of funds, the college saw clouds of defeatism settle upon its community after the freeze. Many feared that the institution was doomed to extinction. The youthful, energetic Ward and his reforms dispelled those clouds and brought a breath of fresh buoyancy to the campus. The revised curriculum became a symbol of a new birth for the college.

It revealed an institution not merely managing existence, but vitally alive, and even a bit ahead of national academic trends. For years the young college had proclaimed adherence to the "Yale Model." Now it advertised itself as following in the wake of Harvard, thereby allowing it to discard the traditional course of study without a loss of prestige.[25]

Ward soon directed his energies toward improving a physical plant which was deteriorating from years of neglect. The interiors of buildings were renovated, the exteriors painted and the campus grounds were extensively landscaped. New physics and chemistry laboratories were installed in Knowles Hall, and the library was moved from Knowles to four connecting rooms in Pinehurst.[26] These improvements, plus the new president's contacts and engaging personality helped attract new donors to the college. No new friend was more significant than Frances Knowles, daughter of Rollins' greatest benefactor. The Knowles family had lost contact with Rollins after the death of Francis, but Ward renewed the relationship in a rather dramatic fashion.

During his first year, Ward's work on the curriculum revision left him little time for fund-raising. He paid many of the college's bills with his personal funds, but this source was exhaustible. Just before Christmas of 1896 he learned that much of his personal income had been lost through the failure of his investment firm. As his wife described the calamity: Ward came home to Pinehurst on Christmas Eve lamenting that he was at the end of his rope. "My money is gone and there is nothing in the college treasury to meet the bills which come due on Monday. I have prayed over this matter continually. If this is God's college and he wants me to stay He must make it manifest in some way. You can pack our trunks and we will go north." Emma persuaded him to wait a few days before making the final decision.[32] She gave him wise advice. A few days earlier, Frances Knowles, apprised of the college's financial problems, had placed a generous contribution in the mail. When Ward opened his mail the day after the news of his financial disaster, a check for $5,000 fell out on the desk. The donation marked the revival of a long and fruitful relationship between the Knowles family and Rollins College.[27]

The Knowles windfall was a turning point in Ward's quest to stabilize the college's finances. In 1897, the college not only met its annual expenses but it also started to reduce the size of its burdensome debt. The following year, the college treasurer made one of the first optimistic financial reports that trustees had heard in several years. "The institution's financial condition is excellent," William O'Neal proudly declared, "with all expenses paid up to date, and every provision made for next year." By the end of Ward's administration in 1902, the college had not only satisfied that deficit, but it was also showing a small surplus.[34] At almost every meeting, the trustees voted some accolade to Ward, as typified by the 1899 commencement meeting. "On the motion of Rev. S. F. Gale, it was unanimously voted that it is the sense of the Board that the President brings to the College that energy, vision and judgment, which is raising up a larger number of friends than has ever been known in its history; is placing the institution on that high plain which merits the support of all persons interested in education; that we, by this vote, express our full confidence in and approval of his management of its affairs."[28]

The changes and improvements were intended to present the college to the public as a vibrant, growing institution. But these efforts had not been achieved without some traumatic perturbations within the college community. Not all the faculty agreed with Ward's curriculum revisions. His public claim that he wanted to breathe new academic life into the college carried the implication that present professors were somewhat lifeless and irrelevant. Ward often told others he inherited a failing institution that was in debt and burdened "with a collection of run-down, unpainted buildings." In an observation he did not mean as a compliment, he added that he had also inherited "a faculty composed largely of professors of classics, mathematics and history."[29] Ward determined that a rejuvenated college required a change of personnel and that many of those presently employed at the college were inadequate for the new regime. The cook and the matron of the dining hall were the first to go, followed by the matrons of the women's and men's dormitories. By 1898, several of the original faculty members—Nathan Barrows, Eva Root and Lloyd Austin—had resigned. Only Thomas Baker, who had returned in 1893, Caroline Abbott and John Ford, remained.[30]

Ford presented a special problem for Ward. As professor of Greek, he seemed to be out of place in the new curriculum. According to William O'Neal, Ward took an immediate dislike to the aging professor, probably because he was uncomfortable with a former acting president critically looking over his shoulder. Ford's loyal service when the college was without leadership kept him on the faculty for a while. Otherwise, Ward would have removed him earlier. Ford alienated the new president because he understandably showed little enthusiasm for the new curriculum that devalued Latin and virtually eliminated Greek.[37] In May 1900, at a trustee meeting, the executive committee seriously considered Ford's non-reappointment as professor of Greek, but stopped short of dismissal. "Our difficulty," the committee wrote Ford, "consists in our inability to convince ourselves of your willingness to give the school the hearty support which we must require of all those connected with Rollins College." The committee left Ford's future to the president, who agreed to reappointment. However, Ward wrote Ford that, "because of the undue expenditure of the Department of Greek," his annual salary would be reduced from $800 to $500. Surely Ford's days were numbered. On April 10, 1901, a terse statement without comment appeared in the trustee minutes: "Voted that Prof. J. H. Ford be not reengaged."[31]

It was a sad ending for someone who had been so selflessly dedicated and loyal to the college. Ford had served the institution twice as acting president without an increase in salary or a decrease in teaching load. He had spent his summers, while others were on vacation, traveling the state searching for students and funds. Unfortunately for him, the academic world that he knew and loved was fading. Any change that demoted the classics to obscurity was bound to affect the old professor. Still, one wonders whether he could have been treated more compassionately and whether he could have received more recognition for his long and dedicated service. Surely John Ford deserved accolades for faithfully serving during perilous times when the institution's very survival was at stake. Perhaps President Ward and the trustees could have paid a bit more attention to the college's boast that a liberal education teaches humane behavior.

Ward's relationship with the rest of the faculty was mixed. He admired and respected Baker from the beginning. The college had released Baker in 1892, but rehired him a year later when he agreed to return at a considerably reduced salary. Ward raised it immediately to equal that of the other professors. Baker, who fit well in the new course of study, later had high praise for the Ward administration. The president's relationship with other faculty was less clear. Ward was not comfortable with the Hooker and Fairchild practice of governing through the faculty. Following the curriculum revision, he discontinued faculty meetings without reviving them until 1898. Faculty meetings, he told O'Neal, only produced friction. Even after reinstating them, he rarely chaired the meetings. Other than Baker's cheery attitude, there is no estimate of Ward by other faculty, but the record suggests that his relationship with them was merely professional.[32]

Despite the obvious successes of the Ward presidency, the trustees began to hear unsettling rumors that he may leave. In February 1902, their worst fears came to fruition. Without prior warning Ward submitted his resignation. He told the board that for some years Henry Flagler, the Florida railroad and hotel tycoon, had been offering Ward the summer pastorate at his chapel in the Royal Poinciana Hotel in Palm Beach, a plush resort for wealthy winter residents.

Ward had resisted, telling Flagler that he did not relish preaching "warm cream puff sermons to the idle rich." Flagler persisted (despite Ward's "sassy letter"), promising that he would also help Ward's college. As a further inducement Flagler offered to pay the president's salary that year. The possibility of tying Flagler money to the college assuaged the initial disappointment of losing one of its most effective presidents. Later, they would be sadly disappointed. Other than the initial contribution of Ward's salary Flagler never gave another cent to the college.[33]

At the 1902 commencement meeting, the Board of Trustees characteristically heaped effusive praise on Ward and his presidency. He had worked with "unflagging zeal, and by his great wisdom and diplomacy," they enthused, "he had obliterated practically all the college's indebtedness; interested new and wealthy friends and established the institution upon a substantive basis."[40] The acclaim was not overstated. It verified Ward's success in infusing new life into the college, allowing it to face the future with considerably more optimism than when he arrived six years earlier. Ward was gone but was by no means finished with Rollins College.[34]

1. Trustee Minutes, March, 1893. Treasure's Report in *Ibid.*, December, 1892.

2. *Ibid.* Income from the orange groves averaged about $1,000 per year, but had reached $2,000 in 1891. Hooker to Hutchins, October 10, 1891. Ford to Classmates, May 10, 1893. Ford Papers.

3. Trustee Minutes, April 17, 1893; April 26, 1893; O'Neal, "Recollections."

4. Trustee Minutes, September, 1893; October, 1893.

5. Copy of Speech in Ford Papers.

6. Fairchild Papers. Rollins Archives.

7. The Executive Committee Minutes show that Fairchild was on campus from January through May 1894. See an article in *Orange County Reporter*, March 15, 1894 for a discussion of Fairchild's trip north.

8. Trustee Minutes, May 1894.

9. Treasurer's Report, Trustee Minutes, December, 1894.

10. Herbert Webber, "The Two Freezes in Florida, 1894-1895. *Yearbook*, Department of Agriculture, 1895.

11. William F. Blackman, History (1927), 77-89. Rollins Bulletin, 1895.

12. O'Neal, "Recollections"; Thomas Baker, "Recollections." Manuscript, Rollins Archives.

13. For the controversy over racial policy see O'Neal, "Recollections." For Fairchild's resignation see Trustee Minutes, March, 1895.

14. Trustee Minutes, April, 1896.. Ford Papers.

15. Ford Papers.

16. Trustee Minutes, February 1896.

17. For background on Ward I have used William Shaw, *The Evolution of the Christian Endeavor* (1924); Thomas Baker, "George Morgan Ward," *Alumni Record*, IV (December, 1925); and various biographical pieces in the Ward Papers.

18. Interview with T.W. Lewton by Kay Lehman, July 31, 1956. Ward Papers. On student deception see Baker, "Ward."

19. Ward Speech, February 1930. Ward Papers. Ironically it may have been the college's financial plight that attracted Ward to Rollins rather than to Washburn College. If the college went under Ward could argue that it was unsalvageable; if the college's financial situation improved, he would be seen as a savior. He later candidly admitted as much: "I could do Rollins no harm; I could not hurt the situation." Ward to Brown, June 5, 1896.

20. "Change at Rollins College." Supplement to the Catalogue of 1896. The "special groups" were: Moral and Political Sciences; History of the English Language, the Latin and the Greeks; and Natural Sciences.

21. *Ibid.*

22. Frederick Rudolph, *Curriculum*, 191.

23. Catalogue, 1897,1898.

24. *Ibid.*, 1900.

25. Ward Speech, February, 1930; Emma Ward to Fred Hanna, 1938. Copy in Ward Papers.

26. Trustee Minutes, February 1898; May 1899.

27. Trustee Minutes, February 1903.

28. Trustee Minutes,

29. Ward Speech, 1930.

30. O'Neal, "Recollections."

31. Trustee Minutes, 190l.

32. O'Neal, "Recollections"; Faculty Minutes, 1901;1902.

33. Flagler to Ward, August l2, 1902; Emma Ward to Fred Hanna, March 21, 1938. Ward Papers; Trustee Minutes,. February, 1902.

Even more annoying to the Trustees was the news that Flagler, a confirmed Baptist, had give thousands of dollars to Stetson University in Deland.

34. Trustee Minutes, 1902. The following is a description of Ward's pastorate at Flager's Palm Beach Chapel

"Dr. Ward started at a salary of $1,500 for the season (December 1 to Easter) plus room and board for him and Emma, his wife. The Chapel was essentially 'a religious filling station' for the winter guests, but Dr. Ward made it an exciting weekly event. At age forty-one the young preacher quickly expanded to two services, filling the building and the lawns with close to nine hundred worshipers at each service. He was a tall handsome man, athletic, with blue eyes and a booming voice, with the ability to make instant and inspired friendships. His sermons were beautifully structured, but fashioned of simple words, the products of a master storyteller. Dr. Ward said, 'I am no theologian; my beliefs are few and simple.' He led the Chapel from 1900 to 1931, suffered a heart attack in the pulpit on Palm Sunday, and died before Easter." "Our Story: The Royal Poinciana Chapel." royalpoincianachapel.org.

Chapter 4

THE SEARCH FOR
STABILITY, 1903–1923

THE SEARCH FOR George Morgan Ward's successor was unexpectedly brief. Prior to Ward's resignation, a wealthy supporter put forward the name of William Freemont Blackman, a professor of Sociology at Yale University. The executive committee investigated his background, found him interested in the position, and recommended him to the Board of Trustees in January 1903. The following month, the board appointed Blackman as the fourth president of Rollins with a salary of $2,500 per year.[1]

Although lacking in fundraising and administrative experience, Blackman brought to Rollins a quality educational background, an academic record, a scholarly reputation and a brilliant mind. He held a Bachelor of Arts from Oberlin College (1877) and after receiving a Bachelor of Divinity from Yale University in 1880, he served for 10 years as a Congregational minister in Ohio, Connecticut and New York. While he was pastor of the Congregational Church in Ithaca, New York, he worked on a doctorate at Cornell University, where, in 1893, he graduated with a PhD in sociology. Following a year of study in Germany and France, he accepted a position as professor of Christian ethics in the Yale Divinity School. In 1901, Yale Graduate School appointed him lecturer in social philosophy and ethics, a position Blackman held when Rollins called him to serve as president.[2]

In addition to his intellect and solid educational background, Blackman brought an active and engaging family. In time, they would leave an indelible stamp on the college and on Winter Park. His wife, Lucy Worthington Blackman, whom he met and married while a pastor in Stubenville, Ohio, was a woman of varied talents. She was educated in private schools and, afterwards, traveled widely in the United States and Europe. Her gracious touch transformed the president's house into a cultural center both for the college and for the community. She was a superb hostess whose tea parties and dinners were memorable social events in Winter Park. The Blackman home became a place where educated and artistic folk gathered frequently for teas, receptions and musical recitals. She was active in college life as well. She created a domestic science course that trained students in the management of the household and taught the credit course herself until funds became available for a full-time professor. She formed the Ladies Auxiliary of Rollins College, the forerunner of the Rollins Women's Association, which provided faculty wives a way of participating in college life. In one campaign, the association raised several thousand dollars for the college endowment fund. Mrs. Blackman served on the executive committee of the Florida Audubon Society, acted as vice-president of the Winter Park Woman's Club and, in good Victorian fashion, devoted a large portion of her time serving her husband "with selfless devotion," as her daughter wrote.[3]

The Blackmans brought with them three young children: Berkley, 17, Worthington ("Win"), 15, and Marjorie, 12. With just five years separating the oldest and the youngest, the three were close companions. They were also gregarious children who made friends easily outside the family circle. At New Haven, their home had been a center for all children of the neighborhood, and this tradition changed little in Winter Park. The president's house in Winter Park became a beehive of perpetual activity as friends of all three children moved freely in and out. Still, the close-knit family made time for themselves. In the mornings and almost every evening, the family gathered around the piano to sing hymns and other favorites, with the president playing while Lucy and the children formed a vocal quartet. The Blackman quartet became an institution in the Winter Park community as well. Lucy sang soprano, Marjorie, alto, Win tenor and Berkley bass. During the summer months they sang for funerals. "I wish I had a dollar," Marjorie wrote later, "for every time we stood at a yawning grave and sang Sleep Thy Last Sleep Free From Care and Sorrow."[4]

With its large, spacious rooms, and its rambling veranda, along with its cooling shade trees, the president's home (the former Frederick Lyman house at the corner of

Interlachen and Morse Boulevard) was an ideal setting for entertainment and relaxation. Lucy, queenly and gracious, and President Blackman, dignified and scholarly, endowed the home with an atmosphere of gentile cordiality. One visitor described the home as "not prim but orderly. There were large easy chairs, piano open with music on it, books lying about, not books on display, but books to be read and reread. It was a home of a cultured American family."[5] The *Sandspur* depicted a student's view of the home shortly after the Blackmans arrived: "The hospitality of Dr. and Mrs. Blackman adds greatly to the social life of the college." The editor singled out one special evening of entertainment: "Japanese lanterns illuminated the veranda and the visitors enjoyed the spacious grounds sloping to Lake Osceola where launches were waiting for boat-loving guests."[6]

Given Blackman's lack of college administrative experience, one could reasonably assume that the trustees had been attracted to the new president because of his scholarly and educational background. They saw in him the opportunity to raise the academic prestige and quality of the institution. Either the trustees told him, or he and his family assumed (the records are not clear on this point) fundraising would not be his primary concern. According to his daughter, he was led to believe that "he would devote his brilliant mind, his fine education, his forceful personality to administrative duties, to lecturing about Rollins through the state, to increasing the number of students, and especially to improving scholastic standards."[7] Ward had come with similar assumptions, leaving a lingering suspicion that at least some trustees, anxious to secure a president, dared not discourage such an assumption. Blackman's vision of himself as simply a college administrator and as a scholarly spokesman, left him with a rude awakening before he had time to properly assume office. On the morning prior to his inauguration (scheduled for the afternoon of April 2, 1903), the trustees, at the request of a wealthy physician and eccentric philanthropist named Daniel K. Pearsons, called a special session of the board. At that meeting, Pearsons presented the board with a stunning proposal: "I will give you $50,000 if you will raise $150,000. I will give you one year to raise the money. This money is for a permanent endowment, only the income can ever be used. The original sum of $200,000 must be kept intact forever for the use and benefit of Rollins College."[8]

After a brief discussion, the trustees unanimously accepted Pearson's offer. Along with the acceptance statement, the board offered this stirring homily to Blackman: "Rollins College has vindicated its right to existence by noble history: its field of usefulness is rapidly extending, and the need for it is more imperative than ever." Characteristically the board shifted the incredible burden of raising $150,000 (more than 2 million in today's dollars) in one year to the shoulders of the new president. So much for Blackman's belief that he would not spend his time as a fundraiser. He reluctantly accepted the challenge, but he probably had no other choice. The gift did indeed seem to offer a golden opportunity to establish a much-needed endowment. In the end it proved to be a burdensome mixed blessing. Trying to meet the terms of the gift probably damaged Blackman's health. Former presidents had struggled mightily to raise as much as $20,000 a year. Blackman was expected to find over seven times that amount in the same period of time. True, the original gift from Pearson could act as a spur for a matching gift campaign, but the prospect facing a new president must have seemed overwhelming.

Throughout the following year, Blackman received able assistance from Oliver C. Morse, a fundraiser hired during the Ward administration, and Treasurer William O'Neal, but most of the burden was his. He scarcely had the opportunity to tour the campus before he was "money-grubbing," "in person and by letter, entreating, begging, pleading, exhorting, traveling to knock on hard doors, and harder hearts, wearily sitting in anterooms to talk to the wealth and various foundations, taking disappointment and even humiliation."[9] Through almost constant effort, by February he managed to raise all but $40,000 of the required sum. In his first annual presidential report, he reminded the trustees that the college was still short of the goal, and he also issued a warning: "failure would create a psychological effect that would be fatal to the college." Despite this plea, on the deadline of April 14, 1904, the collected matching funds were still $20,000 short. Morse, O'Neal and Blackman spent the day searching desperately for pledges, and, when the day ended, the entire sum had been collected or previously pledged.[10]

Upon receiving Pearson's check, the president called for a rousing celebration. Classes were dismissed, games and entertainment were organized throughout the day and a celebration dinner concluded the day's activities. At the dinner, President Blackman noted that the trustees contributed half the funds, while the rest came from 73 separate contributors. He then read a letter from Pearson congratulating the college on its success, proposed a toast to Pearson and then led the community in a college yell. With its first endowment the college had taken a giant step toward financial stability. The long-range psychological and economic benefits would be even more impressive.[11]

The benefits of the Pearson gift did not to come without immediate cost. Although Ward had managed to make significant improvements in the college's financial condition, Blackman had nonetheless inherited a $7,000 operating deficit. During his first year, unable to devote his attention to that problem, the college failed to meet day-to-day operating expenses. Consequently, at the end of Blackman's first year, the deficit had doubled to over $15,000. This "perplexing debt," as Blackman described it, would plague his administration from the beginning to the end.

The annual operating deficit was but one of the complications attending the Pearson gift; the Blackman family had to accommodate the additional strain of Pearson himself. The old philanthropist was in the process of disposing of $5 million dollars. Thus, he remained a potential source of income for the college. When, in October 1906, Pearson wrote to the Blackmans hinting that he would like to stay at their home when he next visited Winter Park, they were scarcely in a position to refuse. Blackman wrote in a generous tone that he and Lucy would "welcome no one more heartily than yourself." Pearson having inveigled the invitation announced his further wishes: "I am an old man," he said, "who wants quiet. I do not like a crowd. I seek rest and perfect quiet. I do not wish to get acquainted with anyone. I know more people now than I desire to."[12]

The Blackmans would never forget that winter season when Pearson stayed with them. Lincolnesque in appearance, with a tall spare frame, a granite-like face and a jutting nose, Pearson spoke in a gruff manner that never included the social amenities of "please" and "thank you." Though probably an understatement, "eccentric" was the most common adjective used to describe his personal habits. The Blackmans had constructed a separate bathroom for Pearson but, according to Marjorie, he never used it. Every morning after breakfast he stuffed a handful of toilet tissue in his coat pocket and vanished into the woods behind the president's house. No one heard him taking a bath that entire season nor saw him change his old fashioned black garments, which were, Marjorie noted, "liberally embroidered down the front with a ghost of vanished meals." But no description of Pearson can match Marjorie's account of his most disgusting idiosyncrasy: "Doc had a full set of dentures. After every meal he removed them, dunked them up and down in his water glass, shook them onto the table cloth, and shoved them back into his cavernous mouth. The first time this happened I made a mad rush to the bathroom where I lost my breakfast." As a measure of their Christian character, it is noteworthy that the members of this cultured New England family accepted this bizarre old man with a resolute cheerfulness. Sadly, except for a small gift to help build the library, Pearson never gave the college another cent. In more ways than one, the Blackmans paid a heavy price for that $50,000 gift.[13]

President Blackman found the young college's academic program reasonably sound. The new curriculum earlier inaugurated by Ward retained high academic standards commensurate with New England colleges, and yet was flexible enough to allow for an increase of the number of students in the liberal arts program. The number rose from nine in 1900 to over 30 a decade later. This increase could have been higher, Blackman pointed out, if the state's woefully inadequate public school system could have adequately prepared students for college entrance. The state of Florida still maintained only a few high schools and just a scattering of fully equipped grade schools. Inadequate one-room schools dotted the rural areas. A 1907 Rollins graduate remembered that she could have gotten a teacher's certificate at the age of 14, and she was urged to do so by her well-meaning teacher.[14]

Blackman knew that Rollins had to draw from those areas that did prepare young people for college, namely the Northeast. To attract prospective students from that area, the college needed to establish a national academic reputation. Unfortunately, no commonly acceptable standards for judging academic quality existed. The Rollins president could proclaim loudly the college's high level of admissions and graduation requirements; he could extol the qualifications of its faculty and declare that Rollins students transferred easily into the Northeast's major colleges and universities. But who was listening? The college needed a clear manifestation of this quality, and Blackman thought he had discovered a way to demonstrate publicly Rollins' respectable academic standards. In 1906, Andrew Carnegie startled the world of higher education by announcing the funding of a new philanthropic institution: the Carnegie Foundation for the Advancement of Teaching. The organization proposed several means of advancing teaching, but the proposal that caught Blackman's attention was the Retiring Allowances Fund, which made available pensions for retiring college professors. Because most colleges found it a challenge to afford reasonable salaries, much less provide for retirement funds, these pension grants seemed heaven-sent. When the foundation set high academic standards for the grants, Blackman saw the means of quickly achieving a national reputation and at the same time recording the faculty.

Henry S. Pritchett, the foundation's director, explained in detail the foundation's proposal in an article published in May 1906 in the Outlook magazine. The foundation, he wrote, viewed the pensions as privileges, not as rights; consequently, specific requirements would be established. A college must employ at least six professors giving their entire time to college and university work; must provide a course of four full years in Liberal Arts and Sciences; and must require not less than the four years of academic or high school preparation or its equivalent for admission. Furthermore, pensions would go only to those colleges not under state or religious control. Even further, a participating college could not require its officers to belong to a specific religious sect.[15]

Colleges meeting these requirements would be placed on an accredited list of the Carnegie Foundation, and professors meeting age and time in-service requirements would be automatically eligible for retirement allowances. Professors from institutions not on the accredited list would be dealt with individually by the foundation. The original accredited list included 30 of the leading colleges and universities in the Northeast. Only two southern schools (Tulane and Vanderbilt) made the list.

Two weeks after the article appeared in the Outlook, President Blackman wrote to Pritchett inquiring about application procedures. When the foundation returned a copy of the rules governing retiring allowances, Blackman quickly saw Rollins' problem. Because the college departments were so small, a portion of college faculty teaching load had to include courses in the academy. When Blackman made the application, he sent along a college catalogue and his inaugural address, which, he said, dealt with what he called "the Southern problem, that is, the inability of the Florida public school system to provide adequately qualified students." This condition, he wrote to Pritchett, will "throw light on whether Rollins ought to be placed on the accredited list of the Carnegie Foundation." Later, when the president's son Berkley passed the examination for a Rhodes scholarship, Blackman also rushed this information to the Foundation as further evidence of Rollins' academic quality.[16] It was all to no avail. In March, Blackman received a polite rejection from Pritchett: "I think our only question about the admissions of an institution like Rollins College," he explained, "is that notwithstanding its high standard of admissions, it is for at present mainly a preparatory school with a good but very small college department at the top."[17] Pritchett's insight struck directly at the heart of what had been Rollins' problem since it's founding, and this condition would continue to plague the college for the next two decades.

In the rejection letter Pritchett did imply that the foundation would deal generously with individual applications and, although disappointed with second-best, Blackman applied for a pension for Professor Frances Ellen Lord, a 72-year old Latin teacher who had been at Rollins for 11 years. But even here Rollins ran afoul of the foundation rules: though entirely free from denominational control, the college, in order to guarantee an annual grant, had made an agreement with the Congregational Educational Society to maintain a majority of Congregationalists on the Board of Trustees. Again, Blackman tried to explain away an annoying hurdle. "Rollins is in a rather unfortunate predicament," he complained to Pritchett. "I always advertise her with much emphasis as an undenominational college--and thus offend the sectarians. On the other hand, the Carnegie Foundation treats her as a denominational college and cuts her off from help." In order to qualify for the Carnegie grant, Blackman convinced the Board of Trustees to seek release from the Congregational Educational Society. The Society agreed but it also cancelled a $10,000 endowment grant earmarked for the college. "Thus we are martyrs in a good cause," Blackman dejectedly wrote Pritchett. The break with the Congregational Association allowed the Carnegie Foundation to consider individual Rollins professors. Between 1908 and 1921, four of them--Frances Lord, Susan Longwell, Thomas Baker and James Hoyt--received Carnegie pension grants. By the time Rollins qualified for the accredited list, the original pension program had been replaced by another retirement organization (Teacher's Insurance and Annuity Association) that required no special membership qualifications.[18]

Even though the Carnegie Foundation refused Rollins' initial request for acceptance to the accredited list, the possibility of receiving a future grant continued to exert considerable influence on the college's academic development. The Ward administration had introduced pre-professional programs in music, arts and business. Blackman not only had accepted these diversions from traditional liberal arts, but he had also encouraged others. Lucy Blackman's Department of Domestic and Industrial Arts included courses in cooking, basket weaving, sewing and dressmaking. Such programs were necessary, Blackman explained, for Rollins "to fulfill the vocational needs in Florida." In addition to encouraging vocational education, the administration also slightly relaxed its admissions requirements. Heretofore, those entering the college were required to have a certificate from the Rollins Academy or to pass an examination on subjects selected by the college. In 1905, acknowledging the improvement in public education, the college began allowing students who had successfully completed the "standard course of study for the public high schools of Florida" to enter without taking an examination.[19]

The Carnegie Foundation's requirements for membership, however, changed this trend. The pre-professional programs continued, but the administration began to publicize more the liberal arts course of study. In a speech to the college later distributed to the newspapers, Blackman implored students to avoid over-specialization. Instead they should set their faces "like a flint to becoming an educated man, to knowing something of everything." A more explicit and official statement appeared in the 1910 catalogue under the heading, "Note With Reference to Technical and Professional Studies." It stated: "Rollins is a college, as distinguished from the university or the professional, the technical or the agricultural school. Its mission is to provide for those who come to it for a liberal education, a generous culture and a thorough training in the physical, intellectual and moral nature. It believes in the value of a full college course as a preliminary to technical studies and it is opposed to all shortcuts into the professions." In 1908, the college dropped its automatic admission waivers to Florida high school graduates and restored the examination requirement. None of these additional efforts succeeded in getting Rollins on the Carnegie accredited list, but the prospects of being accepted had led the college to increase its standards for admission and to reverse the trend toward creating professional courses of study.[20]

During these years the college acquired an international flavor by the arrival of a sizable number of Cubans. Although the college was forced to spend money on special English classes, the increase in full-pay students and the advantage of cosmopolitan diversity more than compensated for the extra expense. However, by the time Blackman became president, the Cuban presence began to jar southern racial sensibilities. When several local parents threatened to withdraw their children, the college bowed to the pressure and imposed a limit on Cuban admissions. Blackman sent a formal letter to all applicants from the island: "Public opinion is such in the South that we cannot accept Cuban students if there is in them any admixture of colored blood and we will be obliged to send him away in case he were to come to us through any misunderstanding." Not for the last time, a Rollins president would experience the dilemma of a liberal college located in a racially conservative region of the country. Nevertheless, Cuban nationals who graduated later expressed the value of their educational experiences at Rollins.[21]

Given the small size of the student body, it was inevitable that the three brilliant Blackman children would stand out. Berkley immediately became a campus leader visibly active in the athletics and in the social and academic life of the campus. Probably the college's brightest student, he also starred as halfback in the football team and was the leading member of both the debating team and the Glee Club. He organized the popular Lakeside Club named for the boys' dormitory. Each year the club presented a variety show that became an anticipated annual event. One member recalled one of the most memorable presentations: "One number was a debate on prohibition [of alcohol.] Ben Shaw as a dude delivered his argument in poetry. Maurice Weldon as Charlie Chaplin acted his in silence. I was a German pleading for beer. Then a quartet, featuring Dean [Arthur] Enyart, Fred Hanna, Ray Green and Erik Palmer, sang a parody arguing against prohibition to [the old gospel] 'Blest Be the Ties That Bind.'" After graduation, Barkley was awarded a Rhodes scholarship—the first given to a graduate of Rollins and the second to a student from Florida. Upon completion of his studies at Queens College Oxford, Berkley returned to Rollins as an instructor in physics and chemistry, and, in 1911, he replaced the retiring Thomas Baker as Professor of Natural Science, a position he held until his father retired in 1915. Berkley Blackman thus ranks high among the outstanding Rollins graduates.[22]

Worthington and Marjorie, also exceptional scholars, were a bit less serious than Berkley. They were often involved in the lighter side of college life. Both were quite mischievous, constantly embarrassing their father with youthful pranks that often set the college and Winter Park community abuzz for weeks. April Fools' Day, from the students' perspective, was a time to strain against Victorian restrictions. Each year the president and the faculty braced themselves for some outrageous prank. They were rarely disappointed. The minutes of the faculty meetings following each April Fools' Day recorded stories of mischief, reprimands and occasional suspensions. In 1905, students removed the college bell from Knowles Hall. It was later found several miles away at Clay Springs. For days the college was without a way of announcing mealtime and recitation periods. Greasing the Dinky Line tracks was a perennial April Fools' prank. Students loudly cheered as the little train spun its wheels in place.

One incident in 1908 gave heart tremors to not a few administrators. As it was related to the faculty: on the night of April 1, Messrs. Walter Frost, Walter Bettis and Hollam Donaldson came across the field, apparently quarreling, much excited and using very unseemly language. As they reached Cloverleaf Cottage, three pistol shots were fired. "Someone is shot," a voice cried. Residents in Cloverleaf then heard groaning as if someone was hurt. When students ran to the lawn to give aid to an apparently injured student, they discovered the April Fools' joke. Although the students later apologized for their "profane language before ladies" and claimed that their joke was without "malicious intent," the faculty voted to suspend them for the rest of the year.

No April Fools' prank, however, caused so much embarrassment to the president and the college community as the one concocted by Worthington and Marjorie Blackman. During the dinner hour, on the eve of April Fools' Day in 1904, Marjorie surreptitiously collected panties from the girls' rooms in Cloverleaf, later passing them along to Worthington. The next morning the faculty awakened to gales of student laughter: there in the middle of the Horseshoe, for all the campus to see, was an assortment of female panties strung neatly on the flagpole, complete with identification tags and flapping proudly in a brisk spring breeze. The following day President Blackman called a special faculty meeting to consider "a serious case of misdemeanors, to wit: the flying from the flagpole on campus of certain articles of personal property." After careful consideration, the faculty deemed that Worthington Blackman and Frank Stodderman were "debarred from participating in all social and athletic activities for the remainder of the year." Marjorie feigned total innocence. Her role in the caper, forever called "Undie Sunday," was not known until years afterward.[23]

The Blackman administration was the first to make organized sport activity an integral part of campus life. While traditional gymnastics remained the main source of physical exercise, tennis, golf and basketball became intramural activities. The college fielded its first intercollegiate football and baseball teams in 1905. The football team lost all its games that first year, and it suffered several losing seasons thereafter. It disappeared altogether as an organized sport in 1912. Baseball, however, remained a major organized activity in the pre-World War I period. But the college had difficulty in fielding a winning team. With no association to enforce recruitment rules, Rollins, as with other Florida institutions of higher learning, openly hired professional athletes to play for them. In 1903, pitcher George Edward "Rube" Waddell appeared on campus ready to play and coach the baseball team. Waddell, who had steered the Philadelphia Athletics to an American League pennant in 1902, claimed to be taking classes at Rollins. Actually, he never saw the inside of a classroom. A professional catcher whom he brought along to Rollins did attend one or two classes in the academy, but soon gave them up as a waste of time. Rollins won all its games with this battery on the diamond, but when Waddell and his catcher left after the Christmas holidays to begin spring training, the team collapsed. While college presidents deplored this sorry state of the professional presence in college athletics, few made any attempt to correct it. Professional players were necessary, stated an editorial in the *Sandspur*, "because in the Darwinian world of baseball it is the case of survival of the fittest."[24]

During the first decade of the 13-year long Blackman administration, the college realized substantial growth in all areas. The total number of students averaged around 170 annually, while the liberal arts college itself hovered around 30 most of the years, a three-fold increase since 1900. The Pearson grant created an initial endowment that rose to over $200,000 by 1912. Most spectacularly, the Blackman administration added three large buildings to the campus.

One of them was Chase Hall, a gift from Loring Chase, who still remained connected to the college. The two-story brick dormitory was dedicated in 1908. Built on the south side of Pinehurst, it was the first non-wooden structure built on the campus. It contained 14 rooms, a large common room and a terrace overlooking Lake Virginia. For over a half century, the building was publicized in the literature as a signature building for emphasizing the unique setting of the college.

One year later, the prominent American philanthropist Andrew Carnegie provided funds for the college's first library. The two-story, sand-lined brick building with a red-tile roof contained an interior richly decorated with stained, carved wood. The first floor housed a reading room and space for bookshelves, while the second floor contained administrative work places, including the president's office. Blackman and the trustees felt that the library should be placed near the center of the campus, and surveying the grounds, they came to the conclusion that Cloverleaf occupied that spot. Cloverleaf was therefore moved, and Carnegie Hall was constructed in its place. The third building came as a result of the fire that destroyed Knowles Hall, leaving the college without recitation rooms. The college replaced the first hall with an additional small gift from Carnegie and with money from the Frances B. Knowles family. Placed on the east side of Cloverleaf, Knowles II contained classrooms, a large chapel and science laboratories.

However, despite (or perhaps because of) this growth in the physical plant, Blackman failed to solve the problem of financial indebtedness that had plagued the college since it had admitted its first students. The Carnegie gift, like the

Pearson bequest, required raising matching funds for the building of the library, which again left the President little time to raise funds for daily expenses. As with the Pearson gift, Blackman came to see the Carnegie grant as another mixed blessing. "After the increasing struggle of the past five years to meet conditional offers of this sort," he stated in his 1909 presidential report, "I feel both depression and elation in the view of the tasks set before us."[41] Thus, the college faced a curious paradox: at the same time as it was growing and its assets were ever increasing, operating expenses were also driving the college deeper and deeper in debt.[25]

The academic year of 1912-1913 brought two further financial disappointments. The first came when the General Education Board of the Rockefeller Foundation rejected a Rollins request for a $50,000 grant. Correspondence between the college and the General Education Board concerning this grant pointed to a perennial conundrum facing the college in these early years. The General Education Board had established a policy of providing aid to southern schools only. For decades Rollins advertised itself as a college built on northern educational standards and traditions. In his application for a grant, Blackman pictured the college as a thoroughly southern institution. The result appeared often comical, but in reality it was quite serious because it revealed a systemic identity problem. Although of northern origin and identity, the college was situated in a southern state and surrounded by southern culture. When seeking northeastern money, the presidents had depicted the college as having northern qualities; when seeking foundation money, they emphasized its southern qualities.

During the period when the board was deliberating the Rollins grant, Blackman inundated the Foundation with evidence of its southern characteristics. In another letter, he appealed to the northern predisposition of seeing the southern peopled as ignorant folk in need of Yankee schooling. The college, Blackman wrote the board, could "take the most ignorant, lazy, unimaginative and unadjustable Florida cracker and make something of him." Blackman cited the story of admitting a "redheaded cracker student whose preacher wanted him to get away from a drunken father, and though he was having trouble adjusting, we are doing our best to make something of him." Blackman pleaded with the board that one of the college's missions was to help solve "the Southern problem," meaning that the college "was making a conscientious effort to penetrate the Southland with those ideas and ideals which have vitalized education in New England."

The board was not moved by Blackman's condescending approach. As one Foundation visitor noted with a kind of backhanded compliment: Rollins "is really a northern school on southern soil. The courses of study are considerably better than is usual in southern colleges and the faculty is quite good. But the influence and patronage for this school is primarily from the North and it is therefore not sufficiently in touch with the people and the educational movement in the State." As if to pour salt on the wound, at the same time the board turned down Rollins' request, it approved a $75,000 grant to the college's rival, Stetson University, a few miles away in Deland. Blackman complained bitterly to a friend, not without some justification, that it paid "to be a Baptist" when one was negotiating with the General Board of Education, meaning that Rockefeller himself was committed to that denomination.[26]

On the heels of the board's rejection came a second financial disappointment. In 1914, Henry Flagler died. Ward had promised once he began preaching in Flagler's Chapel he could convince the old railroad magnate to designate Rollins as a beneficiary. Flagler made no mention of Rollins in his will. To make matters worse, Blackman heard that Rollins was in the will at one time but had been removed. He felt betrayed by Ward who had told him 11 years earlier the college definitely would receive money from the Flagler estate. Again, heaping insult upon injury, the newspapers reported Flagler had given a large gift to Stetson University.[27]

In early 1914, Blackman persuaded the trustees to hire a financial assistant who would bear sole responsibility for raising uncommitted funds. The solicitor was expected to raise funds for the college's current expenses and enough income to cover his own salary. The outbreak of war in Europe in the summer of 1914 effectively destroyed any chance the new campaign would succeed. Male students left for the armed forces and donors faltered in the face of uncertain economic conditions. Blackman wrote his financial assistant a plaintive letter: "I had the most confident anticipation when you decided to join our forces, and that my burden would be lightened. This hope has not been realized though through no fault of yours; we must place the responsibility on the German Kaiser and this frightful war."[28]

As with presidents before him, Blackman had simply

worn himself out mainly in an endless search for the elusive dollar. On February 24, 1915, thoroughly humbled by his failure to improve the college's financial condition, he submitted his letter of resignation. The years of fundraising, the prevailing "disturbed business conditions caused by the war in Europe," he lamented to the trustees, had simply drained him of all his energies. He believed that once economic conditions improved the college could find the funds it needed, but he could no longer "endure the strain of it." Blackman admitted that he was suffering from chronic nausea and a "haunting" insomnia brought on by the worry and strain of the presidency." For several months prior to his resignation he had realized only an "hour or two of sleep at the beginning of each night and then a lighted lamp and wakefulness most of the time until welcome daylight." Marjorie Blackman wrote later that her mother invariably "read him to sleep every night, and as long as he could hear her voice, he slept peacefully. But when from sheer weariness her book fell from her hands and her eyes closed, he was wide awake again, worrying."[29]

Blackman's resignation returned the burden of the college's problems to the Board of Trustees. In a letter to Frederick Lyman, Blackman pointed out the difficulty such a situation created: the board was not financially helpful. He had raised $10,000 during the 1912-1913 academic year, and the members of the board had provided only $2,000 of that. Blackman himself had given $500 for repairs to the president's home and Mrs. Blackman had raised $300 from her social organization. The rest had come from sources outside the board and the Winter Park community. Now that same inactive board was entrusted with the responsibility of keeping the school open while it searched for another president. The prospects did not seem promising. Despite Blackman's early notice that he would be retiring in 1915, the members had made only a token effort to find his replacement. With no one to administer the school when it opened in October 1915, the chore fell by default to Dean of the College Arthur Enyart and Treasurer William O'Neal, who served as co-acting administrators. In the meantime, the trustees were begging George Morgan Ward to return to the institution.[30]

Ward refused at first, but when the trustees persisted, he agreed to return for one year, but only if the board would accept some stringent conditions.[31] He asked for a trustee promise to pay off the $64,000 debt so that he could devote time to providing for new expenses, reorganizing the college and searching for a permanent leader. Thus, he lectured the members, if he was willing "to mortgage the next year of his life," he expected them to show good faith by meeting his conditions. The trustees agreed to these harsh terms and appointed Ward as acting president. As he promised, Ward had the college back on its financial feet within the year. The trustees retired the debt and the accumulated unpaid bills of 1915-1916 were paid. The college closed the year without a deficit for the first time in 10 years. (Blackman may have justifiably asked "where were they when *he* need them?") Having assured the college of "its continuance during distressing times throughout the world," Ward resigned his position in June 1917. At the same time the trustees appointed a permanent president, Dr. Calvin Henry French.[32]

French came to Rollins with encouraging qualifications. Between 1898 and 1913, he had served as president of Huron College in South Dakota, where he built the institution virtually from scratch, constructing several buildings and raising a $500,000 endowment. In the early months after his Rollins appointment, French spent a large portion of his time developing a plan to "save the college." In February 1919, he presented a shocking proposal to the Board of Trustees: he would turn the college into a major university with a three million-dollar endowment. French was not just casting about for ideas. He tied his presidency to this plan, informing the trustees that if they could not accept it, he would resign. The board was astounded. Raising funds simply to meet current expenses in the wake of the European war was a major undertaking. In the face of these uncertain conditions, French wanted the board to approve a multi-million dollar campaign to transform the college into a university. With heads still reeling from hearing such a plan, the members of the board flatly rejected French's plan. True to his word French resigned. He had served less than two years. Ward, who had been serving as chairman of the board, again became acting president while the trustees looked for another chief executive.[33]

Ward spent the remainder of the academic year at Rollins but, because of commitments to his Palm Beach church, he persuaded the trustees to hire James Brooks as his assistant. Brooks, given the title Chancellor of the College, came to Rollins in the summer of 1919 to assist (in his words) "in the rehabilitation of the college after the somewhat disastrous effects of the World War," a chore, he thought, that involved "the establishment of an improved morale on the campus, expulsion of some unruly elements, and measures to increase attendance." With the help of Ward, and also with the approval and encouragement of the Board of Trustees, Brooks undertook a one million dollar endowment campaign. As a way of giving the effort an initial boost, Charles Morse, a prominent local figure and a Rollins trustee, pledged $100,000 if the board would raise $400,000 by October 1, 1920. On October 1, even with the help of a $168,000 gift from the George Rollins estate, the college was $60,000 short at the deadline date. At that point Morse withdrew all conditions and gave the $100,000 "as an expression of his appreciation of the generous response of the people of Florida." The campaign had increased the endowment by over several thousand dollars.[34]

While this surprisingly successful effort significantly improved the endowed investment, the college simply could not raise enough operating funds to prevent further indebtedness. This ubiquitous downward slide led Ward for a third and last time to resign from the presidency, complaining he was "no longer able to spare the nervous energy necessary to carry the responsibility for the institution." The trustees offered the position to Chancellor Brooks, and when he declined, they turned to the recently appointed Dean of the College Robert Sprague.[35]

The appointment of Sprague was an act of pure desperation, for the trustees could hardly expect the new president to do what Ward and Brooks had failed to accomplish. The college's options were becoming fewer and fewer. Some trustees suggested that the college should become a preparatory school arguing that the Academy Department had realized far more success over the decades than the college. Such a move would mean abandoning the founders' dream and sacrificing the labor of four decades. Led by William O'Neal, the trustees pulled back from that drastic decision. In fact, because of the competition provided by the state's growing public school system, the trustees decided to drop its preparatory schooling altogether. The last academy class graduated in 1923, ending what had been a happy and even necessary marriage between the Preparatory Department and the liberal arts college. But now for better or for worse, the liberal arts college would have to stand or fall on its own merits.

Another option for the college in the immediate post-World War I era was to search for what Sprague called a "super-president." That was hardly helpful because the trustees had been searching of this ideal person for several decades. In their visions such a president would know rich friends who would gladly and generously fill the college coffers. He would be an astute administrator who would direct the college's academic future, and he would be a scholar who would give the college the academic prestige that in turn would attract qualified students and faculty. Such an educational utopia would relieve trustees of responsibility for the college's well-being. They could then vacation in Winter Park, Florida, once or twice a year, listen to this super-president extol the college's wonderful prosperity, enjoy the lavish entertainment and then return home to bask in the prestige of being a trustee of a flourishing educational institution. Why such an outstanding educator would wish to come to a failing college, no one tried to explain, especially in view of the fact that the Rollins presidency had been passed around so casually that the office had become, in Sprague's words, "something of a joke." Because it would have been the simplest solution to a complex problem, and again would have allowed them prestige without responsibility, the trustees never abandoned hope that such a person could be found.[36]

Acting President Sprague provided a more sensible option the trustees ultimately pursued: he proposed to join with the southern Presbyterians who seemed determined to build a college in central Florida. According to the plan, Florida Presbyterians would promise to add half a million dollars to Rollins' endowment and to build several new buildings. In return, Rollins would agree to elect one-half of its members to the Board of Trustees from the Presbyterian assembly. When the Florida Congregational Association protested this drastic shift from the college's historic Congregational tradition, Sprague countered with a proposal for a Rollins Union governed jointly by the Presbyterians and the Congregational churches. Such a union, Sprague argued, would make Rollins "one of the great centers of Christian liberal education in the South." The Congregational Association consented to the union, but at the last moment the Presbyterians balked. Despite extensive campaigning by Sprague, their final decision was against the combination.[37]

The failure of the union plan left the college in far worse condition than before. Many of its old friends had opposed the change. Most significantly, when he learned that the trustees intended to change "the character of the college," George Morgan Ward threatened to resign from the board.

He opposed, he said, changing the college from "a free, independent, Christian college with a self-perpetuating Board of Trustees, the ideal of its founders, to a denominational institution governed by a denominationally appointed Board of Trustees."[64] Many others who opposed the union refused to fulfill their pledges for contributions. Thus, as long as the proposal remained active the financial situation of the college continued to deteriorate at an alarming rate. At several consecutive trustee meetings the board authorized the treasurer to negotiate a loan with some bank. The college struggled simply to meet expenses one day at a time, as indicated by a query from the treasurer to Sprague: "Next week the faculty pay-roll amounting to $2,513 comes due. How are we going to meet it?"[38]

Because the failure of the union plan made Sprague's position untenable, the board appointed another presidential search committee, which, between May and July 1924, presented three names to the board. All were offered the Rollins presidency, and all turned it down. Finally, a candidate was found who was willing to take on the work. The records do not show how William C. Weir came to the attention of the committee or who recommended him. William Clarence Weir had worked at the Bellingham, Washington Normal School, had also been active in the Red Cross during World War I and had served in the Foundation for Education of the Congregational Churches of America. He had recently resigned as president of Pacific College, a Congregational school in Oregon. Except for his apparently undistinguished work at Pacific, he had little to recommend him for the serious task awaiting him at Rollins. But obviously, the trustees were in no position to be selective.[39]

Weir seems to have surprised everyone with his administrative qualities and his capacity for strong leadership. He immediately laid plans to meet the college's financial and academic problems, encouraging many to believe that he might lead the college out of its malaise. He pursued new contributions energetically. He restored discipline in the student body, while lifting morale among the faculty.[40] Suddenly and inexplicably, his presidency ended. A cryptic note in the trustee minutes on May 22, 1925, declared Weir the victim of a "serious illness." Four days later the board announced that he would be incapacitated for a long period of time. Two days later, on March 28, the executive committee sent a terse, curt memo to Weir: "To Dr. W.C. Weir, President: The executive committee in conference with the trustees of Rollins College deem it for the best interest of the college that you resign."[41] Weir quietly left the campus.

The trustees reappointed Sprague acting president and once again began what had become by now the seemingly unending occupation of a presidential search. For the past five years, the college had experienced three presidents and four acting presidents. Now the trustees were forced to organize another effort at securing a permanent leader. Fortunately for the future of the college it was to be the last presidential search for over 20 years. The trustees finally found that super-president who could stabilize the presidency, halt the slide into academic oblivion and set the college on a course that would lead it to the top of American academia. The trustees discovered Hamilton Holt.

1. Trustee Minutes, January 12, 1903; February 18, 1903.

2. The preceding and following biographical history of the Blackman family is reconstructed from short biographical manuscript sketches in the Blackman papers.

Blackman's dissertation—"The Making of Hawaii: A Study in Social Evolution", a model turn-of-the-century sociological study in what today would be called a third world nation, was published by Macmillan in 1899.

3. Lucy Blackman was essential to her husband's success, but her most notable role was her work with the clubwomen movement that began in the late 19th Century as women became active in seeking remedies to societal ills. Blackman was a member of a number of women's groups, including the Woman's Club of Winter Park, which she helped found in 1915, the League of Women Voters, and the Business and Professional Women's Club. Lucy served as president of the Florida Federation of Women's Clubs from 1923-26, the statewide umbrella for women's groups around the state that pressed for legislation on a number of fronts, from conservation to prison reform to child welfare. The following two years she chaired the education department of the General Federation of Women's Clubs, the national organization that carried great political clout in the United States.

Her service with women from across the state inspired Blackman to write a two-volume history, entitled *The Women of Florida*, published in 1940. "It is high time that this were done," Lucy wrote, noting that many local and state histories "deal in the main with men only; their authors seem to have been oblivious to the fact that in all these years there have been women in Florida." The history provided biographies of women active in different state organizations. "In view of the changes taking place in the social, political, industrial, and financial institutions in our country," she wrote, "it seems a propitious and an appropriate time to make inquiry into the value of the part women can claim in the making of the commonwealth, and in particular the period during the past half-century covering their 'awakening' and the use of their reluctantly bestowed citizenship."

4. Marjorie Blackman, "Whom God Has Joined: The Story of William and Lucy Blackman," Manuscript, R.C. Archives.

5. Speech by Hamilton Holt at Lucy Blackman's Memorial Service, 1942. Holt Presidential Papers.

6. *Sandspur*, 1903.

7. Blackman, "Whom God Has Joined."

8. Trustee Minutes, April, 1903. Pearson graduated from a medical school in Vermont, moved to Chicago and made a fortune in selling real estate. Influenced by the way he was supported at college, he began giving away his fortune to several financially strapped small colleges. It is not clear what he was doing in to Winter Park or how he learned Rollins' needs. The restrictions on the Rollins award was typical of his college gifts. He wrote a popular book entitled *A Guide to Practical Philanthropy* (1898) In the book, he

was refreshingly blunt about his philanthropic purposes: "I do not pose as a benevolent man. I have no benevolence in me—not a particle. I worked hard and laid up a lot of money [and I decided] I wanted to help boys and girls of wage earners get a liberal education." He also called himself as an "economical, close-fisted old man. You can see it in my face," an admission with which the Blackmans would surely concur. Pearson died virtually penniless in 1912.

9. .Blackman, "Whom God Has Joined."; President's Annual Report, 1904.

10. *Orlando Star*, April 29, 1904.

11. *Ibid.*

12. Pearson to Blackman, October 3, 1904; Blackman to Pearson, October 29, 1904; Pearson to Blackman, November 19,1904.

13.Blackman, "Whom God Has Joined."

14.Patty Howe, "Rollins Twenty-five Years Ago," *Alumni Record*, 5 (1928).

15.Henry S. Pritchett, "Mr. Carnegie's Gift to the Teachers," *Outlook*, 83 (MAY 4, 1906), 120-125.

16. Blackman to Pritchett, May 22, 1906. August 2,1906; February 28, 1907. Copy of Blackman's inaugural address in Blackman Papers.

17.Pritchett to Blackman, March 15, 1907.

18. Blackman to Pritchett, April 9, 1908.TIAA remained the Rollins retirement program until 2014.

19. President's Annual Report, 1904; Catalogue, 1905.

20. Blackman' Speech, October, 1906; Catalogue, 1907,1908,1910.

21. Faculty Minutes, October, 1901; Blackman to Dr. S.J. Cuervo, October 22, 1906; "Memoirs of Dewitt Taylor," Archives. For a longer discussion of the Cuban-Rollins relationship see "Cuba: The Roots of Rollins' Global Citizenship," *Rollins 360, September 19, 2015*.

22. Faculty Minutes, April, 1908.

23. *Ibid.*, April, 1904; Marjorie Blackman, "Recollections"; Anthony Morse, "Recollections," Manuscripts, in Blackman Papers.

24. Information on sports has come mostly from the weekly *Sandspur*.

Waddell was a remarkably dominant strikeout pitcher in an era when batters mostly slapped at the ball to get singles. He had an excellent fastball, a sharp-breaking curve, and superb control (his strikeout-to-walk ratio was almost 3-to-1). He led the major leagues in strikeouts for two seasons.

25. See President's and Treasurer's Annual Reports for this period.

26. Fred Ensminger to General Board, January 2,1902; Blackman to General Board, October 20,1905; General Board to William Baldwin, November 7, 1903. Rockefeller Foundation Archives. Copies of extensive correspondence between the Blackman administration and the General Board in the Rollins Archives.

27. Blackman to Morse, June, 1903; Morse to Blackman, June 9, 1913; Blackman to Frederick Lyman, June 14, 1913.

28. Blackman to Pratt, October, October 3, 1914.

29. Blackman, "Whom God Has Joined"; Trustee Minutes, February 1915.

30. Blackman to Lyman, October 17, 1913.

31 .[Trustee] Edward Bower to Ward, April 17, 1916; Ward to Board of Trustees, April 12, 1916; Trustee Minutes, February 16, 1916.

32. Ward to Board of Trustees, January 25, 1916; Trustee Minutes, February 1918.

33. Trustee Minutes, February 1919.

34. *Ibid.*, November, 1919; *Tampa Tribune*, February 18, 1921.

35. Treasurer Annual Reports, 1920,1921; Trustee Minutes, November 1921.

36. President's Annual Report, 1923.

37. *Ibid.*,1924; Trustee Minutes, February 1924.

38. Memorandum to Sprague, March 7, 1924. Sprague Papers.

39. Trustee Minutes, May 1924.

40. *Ibid.*, 1925.

41. *Ibid.* Evidence suggests that Wier was involved in an affair with his secretary.

Chapter 5

THE EARLY HOLT YEARS;
ERA OF REFORM, 1925–1932

IN 1890, AN aspiring young writer named Irving Bacheller sent a poem to the prestigious *Independent Magazine.* To Bacheller's great delight, the editor, Hamilton Holt, agreed to print his poem. The young poet never forgot the incident and the editor who made his first professional publication possible. Afterward he and Holt formed a close association. In 1918, Bacheller built a palatial home in Winter Park and a few years later accepted a position on Rollins' Board of Trustees. In the midst of the search for a Rollins leader, Bacheller, now chairman of the board, suddenly remembered his friend Hamilton Holt and wrote a letter asking him if he would be interested in the position. Holt's positive reply led to a two-month long negotiation. Finally, on October 25, 1925, the trustees announced that Hamilton Holt had been appointed the 8th president of Rollins College. Thus, in a twist of fate, a poem printed by a magazine would serve thirty years later as a catalyst for a decision that changed forever the future of Rollins College.[1]

Given the past decade of problems with presidential succession and considering the recent refusals by qualified candidates, why did the trustees take so long to hire a man of Holt's stature? Ironically, Holt's very prominence made him suspect. Some thought him "too big a man for the job."[2] Born to an illustrious New York family and a graduate of Eastern preparatory schools and Yale University, Holt had risen after college to the editorship and subsequently ownership of *The Independent,* a family owned influential turn-of-the-century magazine. He had established himself as a national leader in the pre-World War I international peace movement, helping to found the prestigious League to Enforce Peace. Immediately after the war, he worked closely with the Woodrow Wilson administration on the League of Nations. Holt's name was linked with Presidents Woodrow Wilson and William Howard Taft and with Republican presidential candidate Charles Evans Hughes. He counted as personal friends luminaries such as Franklin Roosevelt, Bernard Baruch and Colonel Edward House, Woodrow Wilson's chief adviser.

Holt's background revealed a man whose views seemed wholly at odds with traditions of Rollins College and also with the conservative outlook of most trustees. After assuming the editorship of *The Independent*, Holt had turned the magazine into a liberal journal of opinion, which espoused most of the political and social causes of the progressive movement during the first two decades of the 20th century.

He wrote many articles supporting liberal reforms and, at one time, he even flirted on the edges of socialism. During the late 19th century, when southern states were passing Jim Crow laws, the magazine under Holt's leadership vigorously championed the civil rights of African Americans. In 1920 Holt ran as a democrat for the United States Senate seat in Connecticut, losing in part because his opponent successfully depicted him as a radical. If Holt's background reflected his true views, some trustees felt he would not be a good fit in conservative Winter Park, not to mention in a racially prejudiced Central Florida.[3]

Moreover, many trustees doubted that the college could financially afford Holt. In his original letter inquiring about Holt's interest in the college, Bacheller mentioned a salary of $5,000 plus a presidential residence.[4] Holt's reply could not have been encouraging. He was committed until December to promotional work on behalf of internationalism, he wrote, but he would accept a "preliminary" call to the presidency on the terms mentioned by Bacheller. In the meantime, he would study the "present and future policies" of the college. Holt then stated his jaw-dropping terms: "If after, the Board wants me to continue on a permanent basis, I will do so for not less than $10,000 a year and a home, although my income for the past decade has varied from $21,000 to $28,000 a year. I could not accept the terms you offer as I am unwilling to have any permanent connection with an educational institution that is compelled to underpay its Presidents and Professors." Holt admitted that he was short on educational experience, but, he argued, he had proven fund raising qualifications. "The real question," he bluntly told the trustees, "is whether your Board is such as can be depended upon to get enthusiastically behind a sane, liberal expanding program."[4]

The salary demand by Holt was wildly out of line with past presidential salaries. As Bacheller noted, "certain small businessmen were frightened at that amount." The board had paid Sprague only $4,000. With great reluctance they had been forced to offer Weir $6,000. Moreover, in 1925 the highest faculty salary was $2,000 and that went to the director of the music conservatory. The average faculty salary was just over $1,000. Former President William Blackman wrote a letter gently warning Holt that too wide gap between the President's "income and the salary paid Professors could create serious morale problems.[5]

For all these reasons, when the trustees met on August 7, 1925, to discuss presidential candidates, Holt's candidacy was laid aside in favor of another prospect named S. Walter McGill, who was an executive member of a southern Presbyterian association. Several trustees were attracted to McGill because he had a proven record of successful fundraising for southern Presbyterian colleges. As president he could perhaps revive the effort to unite the college with the Presbyterian Association. Trustee Raymond Greene wrote Holt (with a syntax that must have caused raised eyebrows from the former editor) that he had learned the trustees wanted "a man that can get money rather than a big personality." After unsuccessful negotiations for two weeks, McGill withdrew his name. Rejected by McGill, the trustees turned reluctantly to Hamilton Holt. In October, they appointed him on Holt's original terms.[6]

The trustees need not have been anxious about Holt's perceived "radicalism." Typical of early 20th century progressives, Holt remained loyal to the Republican party. In 1912, he chose conservative William Howard Taft over two self-proclaimed progressive candidates, Woodrow Wilson and Theodore Roosevelt. A Connecticut editor perhaps best understood Holt's essential moderateness. Although depicted as a radical, the editor wrote, Holt "was in fact quite sane and a fine type of educated man of today who takes an active part in everything that leads to the better education in the modern world."[7]

The final question concerning Holt's candidacy is why did such a prominent public figure accept the leadership of what appeared to be a tottering educational institution? The uncertainty of Holt's immediate financial and career prospects suggests one answer. The call from Rollins came at a critical period in Holt's career. He had turned *The Independent* from a religious magazine into a respected and influential secular journal. Although he increased annual circulation from 20,000 to more than 150,000, the magazine was never a financial success. It lost money almost every year, and when he left it in 1922, Holt had incurred a $33,000 personal debt. Before the war, he held a lucrative leadership position in an international organization, but in the era of post-war disillusionment, peace organizations began to atrophy. By 1923, Holt was without a steady income. In debt, plagued by a mild diabetic condition and concerned that in the past decade he had been neglecting his family, Holt was searching for more remunerative work and a more stable life style.

Additionally, Holt had his eye on Florida prior to the Rollins call. Along with many northeasterners, he was attracted to the Florida land boom of the early 1920s and its possibility of quick wealth. Not surprisingly then, Holt found Bacheller's proposal of July quite appealing. Though the salary in his counter-proposal was smaller than he anticipated, it would be steady and dependable and could perhaps be supplemented with lucrative land investments. Thus, like so many others who came to Rollins, it was the college's location that attracted him. Holt admitted later that he would not have accepted the presidency of such an institution in any other state, because Florida, he thought, was synonymous with achievement and creativity. The Rollins presidency would allow him to meet his family obligations while offering him the challenge of turning a failing college into a respectable institution of higher learning. With typical New England shrewdness, Holt drove a hard bargain but he also experienced considerable relief when the trustees accepted his terms.[8]

The public reception of Holt's appointment undoubtedly dissipated any lingering trustee concern, as congratulations from high places came pouring into the college. Political notables such as Florida's Senator Duncan Fletcher and former President William Howard Taft, now Chief Justice of the Supreme Court, sent their felicitations. Congratulations from the academic world came from the presidents of America's leading colleges: J. K. Kirkland of Vanderbilt, James Angell of Yale, John Greer Hibben of Princeton, Henry King of Oberlin and Glenn Frank of Wisconsin.[15] In its 40-year history, no other Rollins appointment had given

TOP Early Winter Park, 1884

MIDDLE, LEFT TO RIGHT
Loring Chase, Alonzo
Rollins, Francis Knowles

BOTTOM, LEFT TO RIGHT
Frederick Lyman, Lucy
Cross

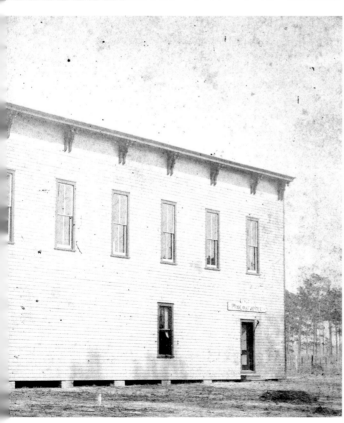

TOP, LEFT TO RIGHT
Original Rollins
Campus, First
Congregational Church

BOTTOM, LEFT TO RIGHT
President Hooker,
Ergood Store

Collegiate Department. 10

TERM.	CLASSICAL COURSE.	SCIENTIFIC COURSE.
	Livy. Rhetoric. Geometry.	Livy. Rhetoric. Geometry.
2.	Tacitus. Memorabilia. Trigonometry.	Tacitus. English History. Trigonometry.
3.	Horace. Demosthenes. Trigonometry.	Horace. History of the English Language. Trigonometry.
	Sophocles. Chemistry. Analytical Geometry.	History of Civilization. Chemistry. Analytical Geometry.
2.	Juvenal or Plautus. Chemistry. Mechanics.	Juvenal or Plautus. Chemistry. Mechanics.
	Zoology. Logic. Mechanics.	Zoology. Logic. Mechanics.

(FRESHMAN YEAR / SOPHOMORE YEAR) ROLLINS COLLEGE, WINTER PARK.

	German. Physics. Astronomy.	German. Physics. Astronomy.
2.	German. Physics. Botany.	German. Physics. Botany.
	German. Botany. Whately's Rhetoric.	German. Botany. Whately's Rhetoric.
	Mental Science. English Literature. Constitutional and International Law.	Mental Science. English Literature. Constitutional and International Law.
	Moral Science. English Literature. Geology.	Moral Science. English Literature. Geology.
	Political Economy. Geology. Evidences of Christianity.	Political Economy. Geology. Evidences of Christianity.

(JUNIOR YEAR / SENIOR YEAR) ROLLINS COLLEGE, WINTER PARK. 11

COURSE OF STUDY LEADING TO THE DEGREE OF BACHELOR OF ARTS.

I.

GENERAL COURSES
- English IV.
- Moral and Political Sciences.
- Modern Languages.
- Natural Sciences.
- Mathematics III.
- History.

NOTE.—At least one course throughout three terms in each of the above six subjects is required of every candidate for the degree.

II.

SPECIAL GROUPS
- I. Moral and Political Sciences, History and English.
- II. Latin and Greek.
- III. Latin and Moral and Political Sciences.
- IV. Latin, History and English.
- V. Latin and Modern Languages.
- VI. Latin and Natural Sciences.
- VII. Modern Languages.
- VIII. Natural Sciences.

NOTE.—The candidate for the degree must select one of the above eight special groups and devote the entire work of one year, i. e. forty-five (45) points, to the group selected. The work need not, however, be taken in any one year, but may be divided among the entire four years; and, furthermore, any one of the preceding General Courses that falls within the province of a group may be counted towards the completion of the group.

III.

THESIS.

NOTE.—A written or printed Thesis on some subject connected with the special group and embodying the results of

TOP Faculty and Students, c. 1890

MIDDLE, LEFT TO RIGHT Classical and Elective Curricula

BOTTOM John Ford

TOP Charter Faculty, Pinehurst Hall

MIDDLE, LEFT TO RIGHT President Fairchild, President Ward, Williams O'Neal

BOTTOM President Blackman and Family at Home

rise to such national interest. The mere announcement of Holt's appointment engendered the kind of public recognition that had only been a dream to other presidents during four decades of tireless efforts.[9]

Holt assumed the presidency of an institution in disarray. It was several thousand dollars in debt, and its most profitable program, the Preparatory Department, had been dropped, leaving the liberal arts college to its own resources. The previous administration had virtually lost control of the institution. The dean of women submitted a special report to the board in August 1925 protesting the "lax methods of discipline." Academic standards, long the pride of the college, had declined dangerously. Students cut classes at will without much repercussion. One parent, on paying a late bill, complained he was throwing money away anyway since his daughter did little in the past term but "hang around with football players." A local pharmacy in Winter Park, which served as the college's bookstore, reported in July 1926 that the store was left with over half the textbooks. An investigation revealed that many professors did not require students to purchase them. Both Holt and the trustees understood only drastic reorganization could save the college. At the appointment meeting in October 1925, the board gave Holt carte blanche authority to devise a reorganization program "as to curriculum, professors, grounds and buildings for a student body not to exceed 700."[10]

Holt's first goal was to strengthen the college sufficiently to receive accreditation from the Southern Association of Colleges and Schools, the region's principal accrediting agency. No one would take the college seriously until it was accredited. Unfortunately, the association had turned down the college's application two years earlier. To gain accreditation, Holt decided to hire a reputable dean of the college with experience in this area. After extensive search, he found such a person in George Carrothers. The new dean had earned a PhD from Columbia University in education, was teaching at Ohio University and at the same time was serving as a consultant for a midwestern college association. After looking at the condition of the college, the new dean predicted it would take three years to gain accreditation. Actually, it would take only two, but not without an academic transformation.

Little in his background had prepared Holt for this new work. He later called his reforms an "adventure in education," but the term more aptly applied to his own decision at the age of fifty to enter the field of education. Holt did possess personal qualities that counter-balanced his lack of educational experience. Above all, he was a supremely self-assured person. After overcoming a period of insecurity at Yale, his experiences in journalism and in the peace movement had given him supreme confidence in his ability to lead and to administer an organization. Most importantly, in the past few years, Holt had given some thought to the state of American higher education. He thought he understood what was wrong with it and believed he knew how to improve it.

Holt's unhappy experiences at Yale left him with negative view of the prevailing system of higher education, particularly the pedagogical practices of lecture and recitation. In his early years at Rollins he told anyone who would listen that the lecture system was the "worst pedagogical method ever devised for imparting knowledge because though a lecturer may serve to inspire a student who has some familiarity with the subject, it invariably mostly discloses the personality--good or bad--of the lecturer." "The assumption," Holt argued, "that knowledge may be poured into another and assimilated without the other going through something of the same process of preparational [sic] study is perhaps the greatest fallacy of modern pedagogical psychology." During his two decades of visits to scores of campuses, Holt became convinced that another fault of American education was its "insatiable impulse to expand materially." He came to the conclusion that the passion for expansion was harming the university systems. For colleges, he argued, expansion seemed to be the end, not the means, of education. They were forced to devote "their chief energies to drumming up students and multiplying buildings [while] the students and professors are ground between the millstones of materialism."[11]

Holt's unfavorable impressions of American higher education were further strengthed when he edited a series of articles written for *The Independent* by its literary editor Edwin Slosson. After visiting several American universities including Yale, Harvard and the University of Chicago, Slosson found a monotonous similarity of pedagogical methods—the lecture, the recitation—which had changed little since the Colonial period. He found students "sitting like automatons in lecture classes oblivious to the efforts of the professors to engage them in the learning process." Slosson's sweeping indictment of higher education received withering criticism, but, because his conclusions reinforced

Holt's own predisposition, the new president accepted them without questioning their validity.[12]

Holt first revealed his own thinking on higher education in an article published by *The Independent* in 1920 entitled, with unintended prescience, "The Ideal College President." Holt's ideas were far from original. His ideal college president should decide on the size of student body, get it approved by the trustees, build a proper physical plant and raise enough money to pay the faculty more than any other institution. He should then discharge or pension deadwood professors and attract quality students. No evidence exists that Rollins trustees read Holt's article, but if they had, they could not have been reassured by such platitudes.[13]

Although Holt brought no educational experience to the Rollins presidency, he did possess an active, eclectic mind sharpened by his editorial work in prior years and by his ideas of the need for educational change in higher education. Perhaps more importantly, growing out of his participation in progressivism, he brought a powerful belief in the transforming possibilities of reform. He was convinced that there were new educationally beneficial ways to create more human contact between teacher and student.

He often compared his apprentice experience in the editorial offices at *The Independent*, where he seemed to have learned so much, to his classes at Yale, where he claimed to have learned so little. He blamed this unfavorable learning experience on the methods of teaching. The lecture system created a barrier between student and professor allowing little opportunity for the instructor to help shape young people's character or personality. On the other hand, at *The*

Independent, Holt worked in close contact with associates who not only taught him the complexities of the editorial room but also helped him mature. Holt thought he detected a serious irony: "My colleagues in the editorial room who never had thought of teaching me anything taught me everything while my professors at Yale and Columbia that were paid to teach me taught me virtually nothing." The difference, he felt, was in the sense of association, the idea that learning was a cooperative effort. Thus the solution to the problems of American education, it seemed clear to Holt, could be achieved by somehow transferring the associational experience of the editorial room to the classroom.[14]

In essence, Holt envisioned an interactive educational process that brought the professor and the student into a closer relationship, thus making that relationship as important as the subject matter. In this sense both teacher and student would actively participate in the educational process. Apparently on his own, Holt had arrived at an insight that formed the foundation for a new American educational movement termed "progressive education." Led by educational philosopher John Dewey, who would later guide Rollins in a curriculum revision, progressive educators stressed a humanized system that placed the student at the center of the educational process. Within a short time after assuming the presidency of Rollins, Holt became a full convert to this progressive education movement, a decision made easier because he had earlier worked out its basic principles himself.

As many educators discovered (and continue to discover), it is no simple matter to turn theoretical ideas into a concrete academic program. Holt was full of educational ideas but he possessed no practical experience in a college educational setting. Dean George Carrothers did possess that experience and thus was a key player in the creation of what they would call a "new Rollins." Shortly after Carrothers accepted the position, Holt began bombarding him with his ideas for pedagogical reform, many of which Carrothers later admitted shocked him. To implement his idea on teaching reform, Holt wanted professors to develop courses that lasted for half a day at a time, and in classrooms that would contain all the required books, sources, references and equipment. Students would then select courses that interested them, moving from one professor to another as their interests guided them. Carrothers had difficulty taking seriously such an unorthodox system, which, if nothing else, would be a logistical nightmare. However, on a trip to Rollins in April 1926, he found Holt determined to carry it through. Disturbed by Holt's insistence, Carrothers made a second trip and, after hours of discussion, persuaded Holt that the Southern Association would never accept such an informal arrangement and would certainly reject the requirement that professors remain so long in a classroom. The normal requirement for students, Carrothers reminded Holt, was one hour in the classroom and one hour of study outside the classroom. Well then, Holt suggested, why not have the students spend both hours in the classroom--one hour for classroom work and one hour for study under the professor's supervision. Carrothers agreed that such a plan was possible. Thus was born the Two-Hour Conference Plan. Even though much more orthodox than Holt had originally envisioned, it still contained his essential principle of close association for an extended period between professors and students. The plan satisfied Holt's dream of allowing for constant interaction as the professor advised and supervised the student during the two-hour class.[15]

Throughout the summer of 1926, Holt and Carrothers worked out the details of the plan. The end product established a four-period day, with two-hour classes meeting three times a week. An additional supervised fourth period would be devoted to varied activities, such as field trips, laboratory work or physical education classes. Professors were required to teach three courses each term with all required work to be accomplished in the classroom. Teachers would assign no homework although students were encouraged to undertake additional study outside the class. Moreover, in the two-hour periods students would proceed at their own paces. More mature, intelligently capable students would be given the freedom and opportunity to explore more complex material, while the slower students might require more supervision from the professor. As stated in the first catalog, ideally the plan promised "the free exchange of thought between pupil and teacher in personal conference during which the student is helped over difficulties, shown how to study, and given an illustration of a scholarly attitude for knowledge."[16]

A few professors worked with Holt and Carrothers during the summer months, but the majority of the faculty had not seen the plan until they returned for classes in September. The calendar for 1926-1927 called for the first faculty meeting on September 17 and for student class registration on

September 27. It seemed unlikely that the Conference Plan could be voted on and implemented before student registration for the 1926-1927 calendar year. Yet, at a special faculty meeting called on September 24, three days before registration, the faculty began debating the new plan. Despite Carrothers' assurance the plan could be successfully put into effect during the coming academic year, many faculty members remained skeptical. Professor Lyle Harris of the English Department proposed introducing the new plan gradually during the morning periods. But instead of considering that proposal, the faculty voted on a motion by chemistry professor Frederick Georgia proposing that the college go over entirely to the two-hour period. With apparent blind faith, the faculty voted in favor of the motion.[17]

With classes already scheduled and only two days remaining before students were required to register for them, the new program created a registrar's nightmare. That evening and during the next two days, Dean Carrothers and his staff worked furiously to revise class schedules. Incredibly, by the time the students arrived on September 27, the administration was ready to register student for the new classes.

Holt and Carrothers believed that the new plan would represent more than a simple change in the number of hours students spent in the classroom. They intended that the reform would provide a more meaningful structure within which new and innovative teaching would take place. They hoped the expanded time would give professors the framework to design a variety of activities for the students, ranging from research to reading, from written to oral reports, from general discussion to individual conferences. Without doubt

Hamilton Holt's ingenious plan opened countless ways for professors to engage students in the learning process. The possibilities would be limited only by the professors' imagination. But would professors accustomed to generations of the well-established lecture method of teaching, be willing and, more importantly, be creative enough, to make the new approach work? The success of the plan depended on the a favorable answer to this critical, yet uncertain, factor.[18]

During the first term, both the president and the dean advertised the rationale and possibilities of the plan. Holt tended to articulate the purposes of the plan in practical terms. The purpose of the plan, he stated *ad infinitum*, "was to put academic life on a more practical basis by placing class attendance on par with the hours and duties of a business office or editorial room." To Holt the most significant aspect of the new two-hour plan was the opportunity to maximize the interactions between professors and students, where immature and untrained students would receive systematic supervision from master teachers. Holt saw "the chief departments of the college domiciled in large, lighted study rooms, attractively furnished, eventually with open-air connecting piazzas." As Holt envisioned it:

The students would have their desks and easy chairs in this room where they would study under his supervision and in [the professor's] presence. For the brighter students it would be enough to assign them reading and writing projects. The slower students would have to be coached when necessary, but there would be little of the old style of recitation or lecturing in the common workroom. The professor would know what the students were doing or not doing, and in the course of their studies if they came to difficult problems, he would be at their elbow to help them. Under this system there would certainly be sufficient work, both intellectually and physically, but under conditions where the impact of the teacher's mind is at its maximum than under the system where the professor sits on the throne in a repugnantly furnished classroom for a few hours a week and lectures the students before him, a large portion of whom are trying to get by with the least possible effort.[19]

As the plan developed, Dean Carrothers began to have new insights into its possibilities. If the faculty approached the plan with a spirit of open-mindedness, Carrothers noted, significant, perhaps even profound, innovations could be developed. The two-hour classroom period, he thought, allowed professors to recognize student individual talents and differences. Students could be allowed to move at their own paces and to work in various directions. A sense of freedom could pervade the classroom, with students involved in a variety of activities, some studying individually and others studying in groups. They could leave and return to the classroom as if it were a workshop. Rather than being enclosed within a recitation room and restricted by a lecture and a textbook, learning then would be limited only by the imaginations of students and the professor.

To guide the professors toward these possibilities, Carrothers wrote a long letter to the *Sandspur* in January 1927, suggesting a host of creative approaches. The conference plan, Carrothers explained, "may mean individual or group discussion, it may mean some students working in the library while others are working in the classroom; it may mean a complete break in the continuity of all group and individual activity and the sending of the entire class to the open air for a relaxation; it may mean leaving breaks and study time to the discretion of the individual students." These ideas, Carrothers hastened to add, were merely suggestive; "no administrator could or should state in detail just what [would take place] in the classroom. Critical decisions should be made by the instructor but with the cooperation of the students."[20]

Earlier reforms had unshackled the students from the prescribed classical curriculum and replaced it with the elective system. Few academic institutions were prepared to offer the kind of freedom to professors and students suggested in the conference plan. Although neither Holt nor Carrothers used the phrase "progressive education" clearly they were attempting to implement one of the basic principles of this new educational theory—the recognition of individual differences in students and of the need to provide students with the freedom to express those differences. Later, when Holt began to perceive the similarities between the conference plan and progressive education theory, he would move swiftly to place the college firmly in the progressive reform tradition. For the time being, he and his staff found themselves on the cutting edge of excitingly new innovative educational reforms.

The hasty inauguration of the plan gave professors little opportunity to readjust their teaching methods, resulting in a mixed bag of teaching efforts. Some dropped the lecture method altogether and began experimenting with discussion and conferences; others made a partial attempt by lecturing one hour and trying other methods in the second hour. Some professors, unable or unwilling to break old habits, simply lectured for two hours. The administration expected this mixed outcome. Holt had predicted that they were likely to encounter unforeseen difficulties and, working from this assumption, the administration arranged "experience meetings" where professors could share accomplishments and problems. In addition, less than a month into the term, the administration called for an evaluation of each class. Students were asked to state what changes had been made, how they were responding and what improvements could be made. A majority of the students expressed enthusiasm for the new plan. Comments from those taking classes where professors had attempted to revise teaching methods indicated that the students were having new and stimulating educational experiences. Many students criticized professors for assigning additional homework despite the claim that they could complete all the necessary work in the classroom.[21]

In his history class, professor Jenks abandoned lecturing altogether and began to conduct brief discussions and to allow most of the time for supervised study. Professor Frederick Georgia's chemistry classes was built around a kind of self-paced study with one student on page 170 of the textbook while another had reached only page 75. Professor Grover's class on the history of books was held in an "ideal environment" with students seated at a round table and before a wall lined with books. Following the student evaluation reports, the administration held an all-college meeting to discuss the two-hour system. Although student representatives voted enthusiastically for the plan, when Carrothers urged them to criticize the plan if they desired, he opened the door for a barrage of complaints, primarily centered on the fact that some professors were not changing their methods and that many were requiring work outside the classroom. Still, the meeting ended with a sense that although improvements were necessary, the new system was working. Even more importantly, the meeting began a discourse on the curriculum that would continue for months afterward. By the end of the first school term, the conference plan was firmly entrenched and most faculty members were adjusting their teaching methods to the new system.[22]

Commencement exercises in May 1926 concluded one of the most stimulating and fruitful academic experiences since the college had opened 40 years earlier. In one short year, the college had embarked on a direction that within a decade would bring national attention to its innovative approaches. The conference plan had furnished a catalyst for a reawakening. Faculty and students who had fallen into a kind of academic stupor suddenly came alive to the excitement and possibilities of a new way of learning. Holt and Carrothers, with the help of a few faculty members, had devised the plan, but the entire college became involved in its implementation. Faculty meetings, traditionally a time for discussing such day-to-day institutional minutiae as course and examination schedules, student discipline and grade problems, were transformed into three-and-four-hour forums for debating pedagogical methods. Students, who had passively accepted an academic structure as something handed down from on high, found themselves not only expressing their own views on the new changes, but also encouraged to participate in its revision. In the prior systems, student discontent usually manifested itself in some rules violations; in the new system they were encouraged to voice that dissatisfaction with their education with some assurance that their voices would be heard. For generations students had accepted an enforced silence about their own education. Now they were encouraged to expressively participate in the development of a new system. The community involvement not only gave Rollins singularity in the 1920s and 1930s, but this democratic approach to community would also form the foundation upon which the college would grow and develop in the decades ahead.[23]

Despite the excitement created by the conference plan, it contained a potential problem. The most innovative aspect of the two-hour conference plan was its effort to place the student closer to the center of the educational process. Early brochures proclaimed that Rollins had "shifted its emphasis and its focus of responsibility from faculty to the students." But the fixed two-hour class requirement seemed to conflict with the intended openness of the conference plan. The division of the day into two-hour blocks potentially restricted the goals of self-directed individual education. Leland Jenks, who enthusiastically supported Holt's innovation and immediately grasped the student-centered nature of the changes, maintained that Holt had the right idea but had placed that idea in too rigid a framework. Why not, he argued, schedule class times and then allow the student and professor to arrange the conference times. "My suggestion," he wrote the administration, "is that the student work out his own schedule for individual self-directed activity subject to the special limitations of announced conference hours and of the instructor's giving part-time instruction." Holt never seemed to grasp the contradiction between the rigid structure of two-hour blocks within which all learning would take place and the goals of self-directed education. He remained steadfast in his belief that all teaching-learning should function within two-hour periods. Holt's two-hour class idea began as an experiment and ultimately drifted into certainty and finally into rigid orthodoxy. By the mid 1930s it had become Holt's signature achievement and no one was allowed to touch it.[24]

In the meantime, Holt used his publicist talents to advertise to the world that a small provincial college in Central Florida had undertaken "an adventure in common sense education," the title of a speech extolling the successes of the conference plan. He managed to get the speech published in several educational magazines, such as *World's Work, School and Society* and *High School Quarterly*, to name a few. In addition, between 1926 and 1929, he wrote over a score of articles for important national journals including *Review of Reviews, Forum* and *The Nation*. Carrothers wrote four articles himself. Stories about the plan appeared in newspapers throughout Florida as well as in the *Boston Globe*, the *New York Times* and the *New Republic*.[25]

Holt was particularly adept at coining catchy phrases such as, "adventure in common sense education," Rollins has abolished "lock-step education," at Rollins the professor is not a "lecturer but a guide, a philosopher, and friend" and his most oft-quoted, though problematic, slogan: "Rollins has put Socrates on an eight-hour day." In 1930, Holt contributed an article to *The Nation's* popular series on educational experiments in higher education.[26] Holt's article, "The Rollins Idea," indicated how thoroughly the college community had embraced progressive educational ideas. At Rollins, Holt declared, "we hold the belief that the individual student's growth and development are the all-important things, and that to justify itself, every course, by its subject matter and manner of being taught, must deepen and broaden the student's understanding of life and enable him to adjust himself more quickly and more effectively to the world in which he lives. This theory assumes an approximation of college life to normal living as well as a correlation of subjects to be studied. On this premise, we have shifted our emphasis and our forms of responsibility from the faculty and administration to the students. We find that because young people really accept responsibility willingly and carry it well, because they like being treated as adult, reasonable beings, they seem to lose, if they have it on entrance, the average student's resistance to things academic. They learn to recognize education for the thing we believe it should be: a joint adventure and a joint quest." This was one of Hamilton Holt's most profound observations on the purposes of a liberal education and its insights will guide the college for decades to come.

Holt closed his article suggesting that the college was prepared to explore additional progressive educational reforms. In the past five years, he explained, the faculty at Rollins had been experimenting with new progressive teaching methods. Now that those methods had become firmly established, the college was embarking on a study of the courses themselves with a view to making a major curriculum revision. For that purpose, he said, he had called a curriculum conference composed of leading national educators to advise the college on its revision. Holt proudly announced that he had persuaded John Dewey, progressive education's leading theoretician, to head the conference. It was scheduled for the middle of January 1931.[26]

By the time Holt's article appeared, the college community was in another academic ferment. A curriculum committee, chaired by chemistry Professor Frederick Georgia, had been studying a number of suggestions for a "comprehensive reconstruction of the curriculum." Before the summer break of 1930, the committee presented the faculty with a report that proposed dividing the college into lower and upper divisions. At Holt's suggestion the faculty took the unprecedented step of approving student participation. Several students were given a course credit to study and to present their ideas for curriculum reform. Another group calling itself the independent student-faculty committee, "stimulated by an interest in the subject of education, and by the prospect of the conference in January," began meeting in November 1930. This group presented its curriculum report in January 1931.[27] The student committee, chaired by the president's son, George Holt, presented a proposal at the end of Fall break. It reflected student excitement over a recent speech given at the college by Goodwin Watson, a young progressive professor at Teachers College, Columbia University. Watson, an early proponent of a branch of progressive education called "life adjustment," called on the college to abandon the old academic departments and create new "functional" ones based on areas such as health, home participation, vocation, leisure and citizenship. All student activity, he proclaimed, should be "worthwhile and important to life." The student report then suggested a parallel course of study designed to prepare students for life--to prepare them to "become diligent and efficient workers, intelligent and socially minded citizens, tolerant husbands and wives, fathers and mothers." They specified such courses as "Health -- Mental and Physical; Value of Money and Time; The Individual and the Family; The World We Live In."[28]

Yet another report came from independent faculty/ student committee headed by Professors Malcolm Forbes and Edwin Clarke. This group argued the other reports had fallen short of a truly progressive educational program.[29] The independent group wanted John Dewey's theory of student interest to shape curriculum reform. "We believe," the group argued, "that interest is a very basic and important factor in the progress of education and of getting an education. We therefore wish to have the interests of the students discovered, in order that they may study those things which interests them and thereby have their learning properly motivated."

The independent report then stressed four Deweyian principles: "1) Specific Learning, meaning that all courses should be worthwhile in themselves; 2) Individual Differences, meaning that a curriculum ought to take into consideration that no two people are alike in mental capacities, interests, attitudes or needs; 3) Interests, meaning that a curriculum ought to provide for the fact that there is more learning, retention and continuation of interest in a subject chosen voluntarily than one that is prescribed; and 4) Use, meaning that a curriculum ought to provide a structure for the implementation of these principles."[29]

Thus, by the time Holt convened the curriculum conference in January 1931, the Rollins College community had already embarked on an exciting and substantive debate on the nature of a progressive liberal education and on the degree to which Rollns should adopt its principles.[30] Holt had achieved a major coup when he secured John Dewey to chair the conference, for this guru of progressive education quickly attracted several disciples. The final list included a stellar constellation of progressive stars. John Dewey, of course, headed the list. In 1931 he was professor of philosophy at Columbia University with duties that included counseling graduate students and consulting with his colleagues. One of the most prominent public intellectuals of this period and the era's leading philosopher, Dewey had written extensively on the nature and meaning of progressive education. In *School and Society* (1896), already a classic in educational literature, he had expounded the basic principle for what later became known as progressive education— namely, that human experience should provide the motivating force for all educational programs. In *Democracy and Education* (1916) he asserted that the development of individual freedom ought to be the goal of all education. Between 1896 and 1904, Dewey successfully tested these theories at the University of Chicago Experimental School (which he organized), where he directed his thoughts and efforts toward elementary and secondary schooling. The call from Holt gave the aging philosopher his first opportunity to put his fertile mind to work on higher education. So far as the record shows, Dewey's only specific ideas on undergraduate education came at the Rollins Conference.[31] Other leading figures in higher education include historian John Harvey Robinson, Dewey's colleague at Columbia and author of two influential books on education: *Making of the Mind (1921)* and *Humanizing of Knowledge (1923),* where he called for the abandonment of the old conservative ways of teaching and for the construction educational systems that freed individuals for a "life of creative thinking." Another leading educationist participating in the conference was Joseph K. Hart, professor of education at Vanderbilt University, who had recently published a study entitled *Discovery of Intelligence (1924),* where he argued that education was a community endeavor. Education, he wrote, was more than training children; it was "the problem of making a community within which children cannot help growing up to be democratic, intelligent, disciplined to freedom, reverent to the good life, and eager to share in the tasks of the age."

In addition to Dewey, Robinson and Hart, the conference membership included Henry Turner Bailey, a nationally recognized innovator of creative arts in schools, A. Caswell Ellis, author of books on educational psychology and an authority on adult education, John Palmer Gavit, associate editor of *The Survey,* who had recently studied over thirty colleges in preparation for a widely read article on education, and Goodwin Watson, whose recent talk had stimulated the Rollins community's interest in curriculum reform. Also present were three college presidents: Arthur Morgan of Antioch, an institution involved in cooperative educational experiment, Constance Warren of Sarah Lawrence, a new two-year women's college constructed on progressive principles and Rollins' Hamilton Holt.

The report from the three-day conference ringingly endorsed the overarching principles of progressive education: the significance of individual differences, the primacy of individual interests and the relationship between education and life. Most of the conferees had presented these ideas in reference to primary and secondary education. The Rollins conference gave them their first opportunity to apply these principles to liberal education. Dewey expressed this special value of the conference in his closing remarks: "It is significant that while many conferences have discussed problems of secondary and primary education, and some groups have taken up social problems of college teaching and curricula, this conference is, so far as I know, unique in devoting itself to the fundamental principles of college education as distinguished from those both of lower schools and of the university. While differences of opinion marked some phases of the conference we have precipitated the essentials necessary to further development of the college of liberal arts."

Armed with a set of guidelines for constructing a progressive curriculum, in May 1931, the faculty passed a final version of the new curriculum. In harmony with the curriculum conference, individual interest became the centerpiece of a new curriculum now called "Individualization in

Education." The catalogue, published the following year, proclaimed that the revised course of study would "substitute learning for instruction," "encourage intellectual curiosity and enthusiasm" and, most importantly, would allow students to develop "in the manner best suited to them." For admission requirements, the college now emphasized an individual's character and over all achievement rather than some fixed number of units studied in secondary school. Admitted students would be assigned to advisers who would guide and nurture them as they pursued their individual goals. Even though the lower division required nine specific courses, students would be allowed considerable flexibility in devising a plan to meet requirements for entrance into the upper division. In further recognition of individual differences, the curriculum placed no time limit for completion of work within either division. Finally, the college determined a student's qualifications for graduation not by the number of course credits accrued, but by the student's "accomplishments, intellectual ability and degree of application."[31]

Starting with the freshman class of 1931, the college community placed itself at the cutting edge of small colleges that had embarked on innovative progressive experiments in higher education. With its individualized curriculum, the college could (and most loudly did) proclaim that it was in the forefront of progressive higher education, basking proudly in its national reputation of an institution eager to experiment with fresh educational ideas. The most immediate benefit of the new curriculum, however, was the intellectual ferment that engulfed the campus during the early thirties. The faculty, the students, the independent curriculum reports and the curriculum conference kept the entire college community involved for over a year in an intensive debate over educational ideas. This discourse itself was a significant learning experience at Rollins, and it precipitated an ongoing dialogue within the community for over two decades.

In this sense, the spirit of the educational reforms meant more than the structure of the curriculum changes. The debate and the new curriculum, coupled with Holt's original conference plan, left a permanent legacy of experiment and innovation. The educational transformation in the first two decades of the Holt era came not only from the introduction of innovative pedagogical devices and the launching of a new curriculum, though these two would occur with increasing frequency. The real and more permanent legacy of this period came from the emergence of a spirit of reform and the sense that true education came from a mutual cooperation between administration, faculty and students. Above all, the creation of a democratic educational community, where innovation and change were encouraged and became everyone's responsibility, proved to be the greatest achievement of the Holt era. Generations afterward, the Rollins community's openness to educational innovation and its belief in democratic governance became the college's principal source of identity.

1. Trustee Minutes, October 15, 1925.

2. Raymond Green to Holt, August 7, 1925. All the following Holt correspondence found in the Holt Presidential Papers, Rollins Archives.

Ray Greene served the college from 1913 through the 1950s. He came to Rollins as "special student" because he enrolled at the age of 25. While studying for his degree, earned in 1921, he served as physical education director. In a short period after World War I he was secretary to the president and at one time was co-president along with William O'Neal. While director of the Alumni Association, he ran a successful real estate business. He was elected to the Winter Park City Commission and later served a term as mayor of the city. He and his close friend Rex Beach founded the Florida Parks Association and identified Highland Hammock as Florida's first state park. In 1967, President McKean established the Raymond Green Chair of Health and Physical Education. Greene died in 1979 at the age of 90.

3. Holt's background is covered thoroughly in Warren Kuehl, *Hamilton Holt* (1950).

4. It is not clear who authorized Bacheller to write Holt or whether he simply made the approach on his own impulse. His promise that he could get Holt "an unanimous call from the Board," proved to be unfounded. Bacheller to Holt, July 3, 1925; Holt to Board of Trustees August 2, 1925.

5. Bacheller to Holt, August 10, 1925; Trustee Minutes, March, 1925; Blackman to Holt August 12, 1925.

6. Trustee Minutes, August, 1925; October, 1925; Green to Holt, August 7, 1925.

7. Quoted in Kuehl, *Holt*, 62.

8. *Ibid.*; Holt to Morgan Gress, June 29, 1925; to William Blackman, June 30, 1925 and Bacheller, June 30, 1925.

9. Trustee Minutes, April, 1926; Holt to Father, April 27, 1926.

10. Trustee Minutes, October, 1925; William Short to George Carrothers, July 17, 1926; August 16, 1926.

11. Kuehl, *Holt*: Hamilton Holt, "Rollins in the Making, "*Rollins College Bulletin*, 19 (March, 1926); Holt, "Ideals For the Development of Rollins," *RC Bulletin* 19 (June, 1926).

12. Edwin Slosson, "The Great American Universities" *Independent*, January 1909-March 1910. Slosson published these essays in book form in 1910 and dedicated the book to Hamilton Holt. Included in the book was a statement that Holt repeated many times: "The lecture method of teaching was largely informational and the attitude of the student was passive receptivity." A scientist by profession, Slosson published books and articles interpreting complicated science theories to the layman.

13. Holt, "The Ideal College President," *Independent* 102 (May, 29, 1920), 285-287.

14. Holt, "Adventure in Commonsense Education," *World's Work,* 55 February, 1928), 423-24.

15. Carrothers to Friend "Jack," August, 1958. Copy in Holt Presidential Papers.

16. Memorandum to the Faculty, "The Two Hour Study Plan," November, 1926.

17. Faculty Minutes, September 24, 1926.

18. *Ibid.*, October 25, 1926.

19. Holt, "Ideals For Rollins."

20. Carrothers, "Freedom in the Two Hour Plan," *Sandspur,* June 27, 1927.

21. Faculty minutes, September and October, 1926; *Sandspur,* October 1, 1926.

22. *Sandspur*, October 15, 1926; Memorandum, Dean's Office, "Report of the Students on the Two Hour Plan."

23. *Ibid.*.

24. Holt, "The Open-Air College of America," *RC Bulletin,* 25 (March, 1930); Leland Jenks to Dean Short, January 21, 1927.In 1917 Jenks had started his academic career as instructor in History at the University of Minnesota. From 1919 to 1920 he was Assistant Professor of History and Political and Social Science set Clark College. Later he was appointed Associate Professor of History and Social and Economic Institutions Amherst College He came to Rollins in 1926 and left in 1930 to teach at Wellesley College. He was awarded a Guggenheim Fellowship in 1936.

25. See Kuehl, "Holt Bibliography," copy in Holt Presidential Papers, for a complete listing.

Holt's editorship of *The Independent* provided him with a talent for publicity. In addition to his speeches and articles about Rollins, he and Osgood Grover conceived other another publicity scheme to advertise Rollins: the Animated Magazine. Another publicity schemed to emerge from Holt's fertile mind was the Walk of Fame See Appendix for fuller descriptions.

26. Holt, "On the College Frontier: The Rollins Idea," *Nation,* 131 (October 8, 1930.), 322-373.

27. All three reports were printed in "The Curriculum for the College of Liberal Arts," *RC Bulletin* 26 (February, 1931).

28. Student Curriculum Committee Report in IBID., 24-3l. Watson's speech was published in *Sandspur*, November 10, l5, 1930 and republished in *Progressive Education* (December, 1930.)

29. Independent Student-Faculty Report in "Curriculum for the College of Liberal Arts," 31-39.

30. The following discussion of the conference is based on the verbatim type-

script compiled in three volumes located in the Rollins Archives. For a fuller discussion and analysis of the conference see Jack C.Lane, "Rollins Conference and the Search for a Progressive Liberal Education," *Liberal Education.* (Winter, 1984).

31. Catalogue, 1931-1932.

Chapter 6

THE COLLEGE IN CRISIS: THE RICE AFFAIR, 1933

WHEN HAMILTON HOLT assumed the presidency of Rollins he found a better qualified faculty than he anticipated. Historian Leland Jenks and chemistry Professor Frederick Georgia were outstanding. They enthusiastically embraced Holt's conference plan idea and helped other faculty members adjust to the new changes. Jenks, a Ph.D. from Columbia University in economic history, was an established young scholar who had arrived at Rollins just before Holt. Georgia, a stalwart in implementing the conference plan, would later be instrumental in creating the progressive curriculum. From the beginning, Holt assumed sole responsibility of hiring administrators and professors he believed would be committed to his educational ideas. When vacancies occurred, Holt himself searched for replacements. A department head would learn about the appointment *after*

Holt had hired the new member. Whatever the faculty thought of his methods (many grumbled), within a few years Holt had assembled a stellar group of what he called "golden personalities.". These included Thomas Bailey, a Phi Beta Kappa and a Ph.D. in Philosophy and Psychology from the University of South Carolina who had written controversial works on race orthodoxy in the South; Charles A. Campbell, dean of the chapel, sympathetic student counselor and outstanding preacher; Edwin Clarke, a Phi Beta Kappa from Clark University with a Ph.D. in Sociology from Columbia University; Royal W. France, a professor of economics who served as the college's socialist in residence; Fred Pattee, a Phi Beta Kappa from Dartmouth and author of several books on American literature; Willard Wattles, professor of English, Phi Beta Kappa from University of Kansas, author of several books of poetry and the college's poet-in-residence; and Theodore Dreier, a Harvard Phi Beta Kappa and professor of physics. From a professional point of view, some of the appointments seemed idiosyncratic. One was Ralph Lounsbury, a lawyer whose only qualification was his friendship with Holt. He was the president's classmate at Yale. Another unusual appointment was Edwin O. Grover, a former book publisher and Holt's personal friend. Holt could find no academic department for Grover so he named him the world's only professor of books. Despite their meager academic experience, both men made valuable contributions to the college. The gem in this collection of "golden personalities" was a professor of classics named John A. Rice.

Rice came to Rollins through the usual route: Holt was

looking for a Rhodes scholar who could enhance the college's academic reputation. While on an English holiday in the summer of 1930, he dropped by Oxford University to interview John Rice, whose name had been earlier mentioned to him. Characteristically, Holt hired Rice on the spot. A graduate of Tulane University, Rice had taught Greek at the University of Nebraska and Rutgers before accepting a Rhodes scholarship at Oxford University. His father-in-law, Frank Aydelotte, president of Swarthmore College, had recommended Rice to Holt. Typically, Holt made the appointment without thorough investigation and without consulting Rollins professors. Had he done a more thorough evaluation, he might have hesitated before hiring the classicist because the brilliant scholar and engaging teacher possessed some unfortunate traits. This superficial assessment of John Rice meant that President Holt knew nothing of these characteristics. In time he would rue that oversight.[1]

Holt attracted these substantial talents to the campus with adequate salary offers, and most often by promoting the college's innovative educational schemes. After they were hired, they enthusiastically joined Holt's headlong drive to build a new and innovative college. They took seriously the college's commitment to the principles of progressive education, not just in the course of study, but throughout the college community. Such principles included recognition of student freedom to develop personally and academically according to their own interests and of faculty participation in flexible governance structure. These principles also implied the democratic community tolerated, even celebrated, individual faculty and student differences and beliefs.

In terms of college community relations, the principles proved transformative. There was probably no college or university in the South more liberal and open-minded than Rollins, even though Holt readily found he had to walk a fine line between the college's progressive culture, Central Florida's conservative values and southern racial prejudices. He eagerly befriended an unknown African American novelist/playwright named Zora Neal Hurston, former resident of Eatonville. At the suggestion of Theater director Robert Wunsch, Holt allowed Hurston to present on campus her folklore play performed by African American actors and dancers. To Hurston's dismay, his only caveat was that no African Americans be allowed in the audience. The play was a huge success, but as expected, Holt received serious criticism from the Winter Park community. Rollins was the first predominantly white institution of higher education to confer an honorary degree upon Mary Bethume Cookman, the nationally recognized president of Cookman College in Daytona. In the 1920s Holt, with faculty and students, chartered a bus to Tallahassee to protest a Florida legislative decision to pass a law preventing the teaching of evolution in public schools. Holt unflinchingly supported the socialist, activist Royal France, despite being frequently bombarded by local criticism complaining the college harbored communists.

Thus, in terms of community social relations, Holt presented the face of a steadfast progressive who would willingly take a stand for his progressive principles. However, in the realm of college governance where Holt's authority or judgement was involved, his liberalism and openness was sorely tested. The ferment generated by the curriculum revision, led faculty to push for more reforms and, in doing so, ran head into some of President Holt's sacred cows. In the minds of these young reformers, some parts of college life seemed at variance with the progressive "spirit" of the new Rollins reforms. In the aftermath of the curriculum changes, a group of faculty boldly moved to alter aspects of college life yet untouched by the reform efforts. In their attempts, they consistently came in conflict with the president. Thus, for all its significance as a revitalizing force on campus, the reform movement also served as a catalyst for conflict, one that would rob the college of its best talents and tarnish its national reputation as a progressive institution.

The first trouble erupted in the spring of 1932, when several faculty members criticized the Greek system as unrepresentative of the new Rollins democratic spirit. In response to these complaints, Holt appointed a special committee of faculty to investigate, naming John Rice as chairman and authorizing the committee to state its objections to the fraternity system. What Holt expected to come from such an effort remains unclear, but what he received was a thorough indictment of college fraternities in general and the Rollins system in particular. The committee report declared fraternities did not accord with Rollins' new progressive changes. They "fostered elitism, exclusiveness, snobbishness, superiority, and promoted an unnatural and unhealthy relationship and even social discrimination." The Greek system was "undemocratic and therefore out of harmony with Rollins College life." In contradiction to Rollins' educational ideals, the report continued, the fraternities subordinated individuality to the group. "We preach here," the Committee noted, "the gospel of individual development. We then proceed to nullify it by tolerating a fraternity system, which of necessity submerges the individual in the group, which at most produces types not personalities. If it be our serious purpose to produce a fraternity type, let us frankly admit the fact and advertise it accordingly." Additional charges were directed at the disrupting tendencies of "rush," the immaturity of oaths of secrecy and pledges, the division of loyalty between fraternity and college, the distortion of campus politics by the fraternities' clannish interests and the emphasis on social over academic aspects of college life.[2] Holt then asked the fraternities for responses to the report. The committee's criticism hit the organizations like an explosion and spawned an all-out effort at rebuttal. Indignant reactions came pouring into the president's office.[3]

Holt seemed eager to stand above this controversy, serving as a kind of broker between the various factions. Yet there was no doubt he strongly supported the fraternity system because he encouraged its growth in the years since he came to Rollins. Between 1925 and 1932, the college had authorized the establishment of fifteen fraternities and sororities. True, Holt had earlier voiced concerned with some of the fraternity excesses, in particular the wild parties during the rush period. Still, he was uncomfortable with such a virulent attack on the entire system. In an attempt to appear neutral, Holt named Edwin Grover and Ralph Lounsbury as a committee of two to digest and summarize the two positions. To his surprise, controversy arose even here. Grover and Lounsbury could not agree and, therefore, wrote separate reports. Grover claimed the student reply satisfactorily answered the committee charges while Lounsbury maintained, even in their replies, the fraternities attested to their undemocratic nature.[3] At this point, Holt simply filed the reports away and within a few weeks the fraternity brouhaha died quietly. However, the incident revealed a growing rift between the reformist faculty and the president. The fraternity incident would prove to be a prelude of things to come.[4]

A more serious crisis followed closely on the heels of the fraternity controversy. In the January 1933 faculty meeting, the Curriculum Committee proposed abolishing the two-hour class system because it was "incompatible with the new Rollins plans." If the new curriculum was based on achievement rather than time, the committee argued, and if it was designed to "enable the individual to develop in his own way and along the lines of his own interests as fast as his ability will admit," then, the college needed class periods elastic enough to "permit more hours in class, less hours in class or no hours in class." The Curriculum Committee's proposal caught Holt by complete surprise even though the details of it had been clearly outlined in the minutes submitted to him several days earlier. He later admitted he had not read the minutes carefully. He told the faculty he was stunned they would view the new curriculum as a basis for abolishing his cherished two-hour plan. He failed to see a conflict in the two innovations. The president immediately suggested, and the faculty voted for, a motion to table the resolution until a special faculty meeting could be called to more carefully discuss the entire matter.[5]

A few days before the special faculty meeting, the president met with the Curriculum Committee members at his home to inform them that this effort to make basic changes in the curriculum usurped his authority. He warned the committee if the resolution passed either he would resign, or a certain group of faculty would have to go. Later, at the special faculty meeting, Holt delivered a long and emotional argument for the conference plan. He still insisted that the two-hour classroom period did not conflict with the new Rollins plan. Following Holt's speech, the faculty voted to table indefinitely the Curriculum Committee's resolution.[6] Holt prevailed but the larger and far more serious issue remained unresolved. Who controlled the academic program, the faculty or the president?

A few weeks later, the Curriculum Committee challenged the President's authority in two other areas. On January 18, the committee, "as a committee and as individuals," protested the administration's practice of holding Tuesday and Wednesday convocations that extend beyond the 10:30 a.m. class period. A "convocation of doubtful value," the Committee charged, "disrupted and in fact led some faculty to disband classes." Additionally, the committee chided the administration for permitting students to miss classes to listen to tennis pro Bill Tilden, whose sole purpose was "to advertise an exhibition of tennis professionals." Holt, stung by the sharp and condemning tone of the protest, admitted the administration's mistake in infringing on class time but added a poignant retort: "The slur of your phrase concerning tennis professionals implies a motive on the part of the administration that I am sure on reflection you will wish to withdraw."[7]

Clearly the campus was on the brink of turmoil. Many of Holt's golden personalities, caught up in the excitement of this reformist fermentation, were pressuring the administration to make changes they assumed coincided with the high standards and spirit of the new curriculum reforms. They argued the new Rollins plan implicitly foretold a more democratic community and particularly a more democratic governance of the college. The fraternity controversy, the curriculum proposals and the complaints of over-extended convocations revealed a faculty asserting itself forcefully into the college governance system.

These were uncharted waters. When Holt assumed the Rollins leadership position he inherited a long small college tradition of unchallenged presidential authority. Particularly when their jobs were on the line, faculty members rarely disputed presidential decisions. Holt clung to this tradition but unfortunately he had given mixed messages. During the early academic reforms, he involved the faculty in the conference plan *after* he presented them a fait accompli. With the new curriculum, he allowed the faculty to take the lead, assuming the role of facilitator. Were these new faculty undertakings simply logical extensions of the academic reform and, thus, a way of making a transition from a traditional to a progressive democratic governance system? Or was this faculty assertiveness a kind of insurgency against authority and, therefore, a challenge to presidential leadership? Holt's answer came on February 23, 1933. He fired Professor John Rice, leader of what Holt saw as the "rebel" faction.

It is impossible to separate the personalities of Hamilton Holt and John Rice from the sequence of events that led to Rice's dismissal, Rice's subsequent appeal and the crisis that ensued. Holt held an expansive view of the college presidency not only because this was a time-honored, traditional way of seeing the office. Also his attitude was derived from the fact that he was perceived as the one person responsible for turning around a failing provincial institution. His successes were seen as Holt creations to such an extent that the phrase "Holt is Rollins and Rollins is Holt" became commonplace. Trustees, administrators and faculty happily bowed to his dynamic leadership, and Holt responded by treating individuals with generosity and civility. Holt presented himself as a kind of an enlightened patriarch who desired sweet harmony among the members of the family community he was so painstakingly nurturing. So long as an issue was undecided, Holt encouraged the widest possible debate. But once the president had decided the appropriate course, Holt deemed further discussion not only unnecessary but also counter-productive.

Two souls resided in the personality of Hamilton Holt. One soul celebrated openness and was receptive to new and innovative ideas, and the other treasured loyalty above all other virtues. The former reflected the 20th century liberal Holt: honest, broad-minded, forthcoming, openhearted, humorous, generous and kind—a delightful and lovable person. The latter revealed a 19th century presidential Holt: possessive, assertive, paternalistic, autocratic and, like most Victorian fathers (and college presidents), demanding complete authority within his realm. Holt vaguely sensed these two souls. He once told a friend he could not understand how the reformers had made a lifelong liberal appear conventionally conservative. In the first decade of his presidency Holt was guided by his progressive soul. John Rice brought to surface Holt's heretofore hidden patriarchal illiberal persona. Better had it remained concealed because when it emerged, the creature was instrumental in transforming a single faculty dismissal into a raging crisis.

Rice's own personality contributed to and shaped the affair that shook the campus in the spring of 1933. No one doubted Rice was one of Holt's brightest golden personalities. Many of his colleagues at Rollins and a sizable number of students, realizing they were in the presence of a profound mind, sought and enjoyed Rice's company. He frequently displayed a sharp biting wit. For example, when the dean of academic affairs of Nebraska asked him why he came to that university, he replied, "Dean, I've been trying to figure that out ever since I came here." During formal and informal faculty discussions, Rice consistently raised challenging and interesting questions and more than often offered plausible answers. Within a year of his appointment, Rice had become a major campus figure, serving on several important committees (chairing some of them), and acting as a kind of catalyst for progressive reform that swept the college shortly after he arrived.

When he wished, Rice could teach a class in a manner many students had never before experienced and would never forget. One day he walked into his classroom and pinned on the wall a calendar pinup of two scantily clad females. After two days, when one student asked about the purpose of the drawings, Rice turned the question on him. "Why, don't you like them?" The student's negative answer launched the class into a two-day profound discussion of the meaning of art. With such Socratic methods, Rice prodded students into deeper thought than many believed themselves capable.[8]

He was probably one of Rollins' most effective teachers, but he was not a prudent man. The college hired him to teach classical languages but his interests were much too eclectic to remain locked in the mechanics of an ancient language. In fact, he rarely taught Greek or Latin languages, preferring instead to roam in the larger fields of Greek art, literature and philosophy. Many students who needed and wanted to learn Latin and Greek left his classes virtually as ignorant of the two languages as when they entered. Rice casually ignored their needs thereby breaking his contract with both the college and the students. He rationalized this questionable behavior by criticizing other professors who did teach their assigned subjects as dull pedagogues wedded to textbooks. Some were probably guilty of these charges, but that hardly justified Rice's teaching methods.

The persona that John Rice most reveled in was that of an iconoclast. His greatest enjoyment came from attacking sacred cows and shattering beliefs of pious, self-righteous people. His favorite target was the Christian religion. Shortly after he arrived, the college held a religious conference on the topic of "The Place of the Church in the Modern World." Leading religious scholars from throughout the country attended. Rice's performance at one of the meetings set town-gown relations back several years. Rice refused Holt's invitation to participate but did agree to attend and ask "thought-provoking" questions. At a session in the Winter Park Congregational Church filled with the town's citizens, Rice dutifully rose to speak: "I live in Winter Park," he declared, "and I should like to ask a question that has to do with the churches in Winter Park and those of us who live here. The question is: If I should come along Interlachen Avenue tomorrow, Sunday morning, and instead of churches I should find green grass growing, what difference would it make and to whom?" When one indignant preacher jumped to his feet and retorted that the Congregational Church had founded Rollins, Rice noted sarcastically that now he understood to whom it would make a difference, and asked if someone would answer the first part of his question. No one ever did to his satisfaction. The pious never forgot John Rice's performance that day and Holt grew weary of explaining why he continued to retain such a blatant atheist on the Rollins faculty.[9]

A similar Rice incident later shocked both the college and the Winter Park community. As the college's sole place of worship nothing could have been more sacred than Knowles Memorial Chapel. Built in 1932, the chapel was Holt's pride and joy. Designed by the nationally famous architect Ralph Adams Cram, modeled after a Spanish chapel and consistent with the college's Spanish Mediterranean style, it was Holt's signature achievement. To show off his crowning triumph, Holt invited dignitaries from across the country and Central Florida for the opening service. John Rice would barely control his wrath as he watched what he described as a contrived Protestant service conducted in a chapel more appropriate to a Catholic mass. Harmony, he believed, required a balance between liturgy and the physical form of the building. He later sat in aesthetic agony through the chapel's first Christmas service that ended with an artificially lighted star glowing in a darkened chapel. As the audience filed out of the vestibule, Rice, in a loud voice, called the service "obscene." It was the one Rice indiscretion Hamilton Holt never forgot or forgave.[10]

Often Rice's withering criticisms led to outright meanness. He disrupted faculty gatherings and committee meetings with long, rambling, monotonous harangues. His vicious attacks against faculty members often went beyond the bounds of human respect. The Dean of the College regularly received complaints from faculty members charging Rice with unwarranted attacks on their character. Rice pursued these attacks on individual faculty members in his classrooms. He frequently disparaged individual faculty as "incompetent" and "old-fashioned pedagogues who were wedded to a book." He verbally attacked one member of the faculty with such vehemence many expected the incident to erupt into violence.[11]

More seriously, Rice treated some of his students in much the same manner. He attracted a small group of disciples who viewed him as generous with his time and caring with his advice. But many other students feared and disliked him intensely. Less capable students or those who found his teaching methods and spicy language objectionable became a victim of his venom and rancor. He spoke disparagingly of them in class and often badgered them unmercifully. Rice could be incredibly arbitrary. *His* students appearing before the Board of Admissions to the Upper Division received the most solicitous treatment, but those he disliked could expect a rigorous examination and were, at times, subjected to malicious personal criticism. In his personal relations, Rice seemed lacking in that sense of moderation and proportion the civilization of his own field of study valued so highly. He wrapped those he liked in kindness, but those he disliked were treated with disdain and disrespect.[12]

If all this was not sufficient for concern, Rice's personal habits grated against a village and college community still guided by cramped Victorian mores. He paid little attention to his personal appearance and, as he once admitted, sometimes looked like a tramp. Many complained of his immodest dress. At a time when men still wore swimsuits covering most of their bodies, Rice often appeared at the college's New Smyrna beach house dressed in very brief swim trunks, so skimpy by any standard of the day that he was later accused of parading around in nothing more than a jockstrap. Rice often greeted unexpected visitors at his home in dress considered inadequate by any standards. One professor often repeated a story of escorting a prim female potential donor around the campus. They came upon Rice in his own backyard (Rice lived in college housing) dressed in extremely revealing underwear. Unconcerned, Rice stood for fifteen minutes conversing with them as if fully dressed. To the chagrin and disapproval of the administration and of not a few parents, Rice frankly discussed sex in his class and openly criticized what he called the "prude Victorian" views on the subject. It was rather commonly believed he was "having an affair" with one or more students.[13]

Thus, academically, socially and professionally Rice was an extremely unsettling presence on the Rollins campus. The college community had been moving toward a more liberated educational system but far from one that would tolerate such unorthodox behavior from one of its faculty members. Rice seemed unwilling to moderate that behavior to conform within a socially conventional institution located in a conservative village. In this sense, Rice's dismissal was probably inevitable. The ensuing turmoil came not because Holt had insufficient reasons for the firing, but because in a professed democratic environment his methods appeared arbitrary to a large number of the faculty and students.

In a meeting on February 23, 1933, where Holt fired Rice, the president told him that faculty and students had been coming to him for the past year complaining of Rice's intolerance, his insulting and unethical conduct, his intemperate language and his immodest dress and behavior. Holt concluded this damning review by suggesting that Rice undertake "an old-fashioned religious conversion; that is, get love in your heart and banish hate." Rice protested saying he did not hate people, he would be willing to see the school psychologist and change his ways if Holt would reconsider his decision to fire him. Holt agreed to postpone his decision for a few days, even though he later admitted he had no intention of changing his mind. The postponement proved a fateful one.[14]

News that the president intended to, but had not finally decided to fire Rice hit the campus like a bombshell, splintering the college into factions. Those who had been deeply hurt by Rice formed the largest group. They pledged their loyalty to the President and strongly encouraged him to remain firm in his determination to fire Rice. Another large group, probably fearful of losing their jobs, faded into the background and quietly watched the whole affair from a safe distance. A smaller but highly vocal faction supported Rice but for a variety of reasons. A number of students (including campus leaders such as George Barber, editor of the *Sandspur*, and Nathaniel French, president of the student body) reacted strongly against Rice's dismissal. Many had come to the college because of its progressive reputation and believed Rice was the leader in progressive experimentation. They aligned themselves with a group of progressive faculty who viewed the Rice dismissal as a serious blow to progressive education. Still, another group, of which Ralph Lounsbury and Frederick Georgia were the most important members, worried about the methods employed by Holt. Influenced by the recent democratic developments at Rollins and the national effort of all faculties in higher education to assume more authority in college governance, they saw the Rice dismissal as arbitrary and unjust in its procedures and potentially threatening to every faculty member who disagreed with administrative policy. Except for the students, no one in these groups was particularly friendly with Rice, although few seemed to hold animosities toward him.[15] For different reasons, every faction elevated the Rice dismissal to a *cause celebre.*

After hearing all sides of the case and after talking with Rice on two separate occasions (one a long meeting at Holt's home that lasted from eight in the evening until midnight), Holt remained convinced that Rice would never conform.

The president sent him a formal letter of non-reappointment on March 21. "I have listened to all who care to see me in regard to my decision," Holt explained, "keeping my mind completely open and free from all rancor or personal ties, but I have now come to the final and definite conclusion that I cannot reconsider my decision, and I write to inform you of this fact." He offered Rice the dignity of resignation provided he tendered it by March 23. In the meantime, Holt had sent out letters advertising a teaching vacancy in Greek and Latin.[16]

One such letter was directed to a professional organization of college professors called the American Association of University Professors (AAUP). The AAUP was created in 1915 to "enhance the security and dignity of the scholar's calling throughout the country." In its first two decades, it concentrated on promoting the principles of academic freedom, faculty involvement in promotion and reappointment decisions and the establishment of a tenure policy. By 1933, having established criteria for these principles, the AAUP had begun the process of persuading universities and college administrations to accept them. Even though the organization had reached a membership of over 5,000 in more than 200 institutions, it still had persuaded only one-half of the institutions to accept its criteria. During that period, it had conducted institutional investigations and had published in its bulletin the results of these inquiries, placing violators on its list of unacceptable institutions. Few institutions paid heed to such censure, but most felt uncomfortable with being held up to public scrutiny as an institution with serious internal problems.[17]

In late March 1933, almost simultaneously with Holt's advertisement for Rice's vacant position, the AAUP head-quarters received information Rollins College was expe-riencing tenure problems. The General Secretary, H. W. Tyler informed the Rollins president that the Association had learned "that the particular vacancy in the Department of Classics may be due to dismissal not in accordance with our principles." Holt immediately answered Tyler. Rollins professors, he informed Tyler, were all on one-year appoint-ments. Associate and full professors who served in those ranks for three full years were given "automatic reappoint-ments. In the case of the professor in question, he had not served those three full years."[18]

Holt then turned his attention to another concern. How did he AAUP learn of Rice's dismissal? Concluding that one of Rice's supporters was responsible, Holt began a search for the culprit. At one point, he even interrupted Rice's class to ask him if he had written to the association. All denied writ-ing the AAUP, but Holt remained convinced one or more of them had perpetrated what he considered "an act of great disloyalty." In fact, they were telling the truth. Knowledge of the dismissal came to the association from a source outside the college family. Rice's father-in-law, President Frank Aydelotte of Swarthmore College, had written Tyler. By this time, a condition of mutual suspicion and distrust hovered like a dark cloud over the campus.[19]

Rice's supporters may not have written the AAUP but they were determined to keep alive the issue of Rice's dismissal. Students and faculty debated the topic in the classrooms and held community forums where they openly criticized the president. They held almost nightly meetings in Rice's home. No one missed the meaning in the weekly chapel speech by Professor Allan Tory, a Rice supporter, entitled "The Faith that Rebels," where he spoke of the need to struggle against authoritarian decisions. Repeatedly, Holt and other administrators cited this "agitation" as additional justification for Rice's dismissal.[20]

Rice himself brought the situation to a head on April 24 when he informed Holt that he had submitted his case to the AAUP. The news only served to harden the president's resolve. The following day Holt persuaded the Executive Committee of the Board of Trustees to issue a statement that laid to rest any lingering doubt as to who governed Rollins College: "Resolved: That the Board of Trustees of Rollins College has sole authority to make all rules and regulations for the conduct of college and to delegate and to revoke such authority; that the President of Rollins College is the executive representative of the Board of Trustees with full authority to oversee and conduct the affairs of the corporation in the intervals between meetings of the Board of Trustees and the Executive Committee."

In a separate statement, the president then decreed: "In view of the above authoritative ruling, I now formally dismiss John Rice for the remainder of the academic year 1932-33 effective this date." Rice, he continued, must remove his personal effects from the campus by noon April 28, 1933. Then he added an ominous caveat: "It is of course obvious that any further agitation for the reinstatement of Professor Rice on the part of any employee of the college, among each other or with students or outsiders, either individually or in groups, will be an act of disloyalty to Rollins College and must be dealt with summarily." Privately Holt told a friend that if Rice insisted on "appealing to those outside, he must fight the College from the outside."[21]

On the afternoon of the 26th, Holt called to his office 13 faculty members considered opponents of Rice's dismissal. They included Frederick Georgia, Ralph Lounsbury, Allan Tory, Edward Clark, Royal France, Richard Fuerstein, Cecil Oldum and Theodore Dreier. Holt explained the "constitutional legitimacy of his authority over tenure" and told them that the Rice case was now closed. The faculty members suggested Rice deserved an impartial hearing. They requested Holt invite the AAUP to come down and, to their surprise, Holt agreed. Before he terminated the interview, the president handed each of them a loyalty form to sign. They were dumbfounded. After a long period of silence, Lounsbury spoke: "Look, Hammy," he said in a soft voice, "you don't want to do anything like this. If you take my advice, you'll collect these forms and not let anyone else see them." Holt hesitated, and then quietly went from one member to another collecting the forms. When Dreier and Clarke later requested copies, he refused. Holt also left no copies of the loyalty form in his papers.[22]

A few days later Holt sent a letter to Secretary General Tyler of the AAUP, inviting "representatives to visit Rollins for the purpose of permitting me to place before your Association all the material at my disposal on which we based our decision."[23] Two weeks later, on May 16, an investigative team comprised of Arthur Lovejoy of Johns Hopkins University and Arthur Edwards of the University of Georgia arrived in Winter Park to investigate the Rice dismissal. Lovejoy, a nationally recognized scholar in philosophy and a founder of the AAUP, took charge of the investigation, interpreted the findings and wrote the final report while Edwards remained unobtrusively in the background.[23]

Rice's appeal to the AAUP charged the administration with violating the association's tenure principles, which stated that before dismissal, every professor of associate rank or above should be entitled to have the charges against him stated in writing. Afterward, the faculty member would be given a fair trial on those charges before a faculty-elected judicial committee where he would have the opportunity to face his accusers. Lovejoy wanted to deal with the issue of the absence of a professional tenure policy at the college but Holt demurred. Lovejoy agreed to leave the issue until after the committee investigated the Rice dismissal.[24]

The investigative hearings took place in the sacristy of the Chapel where Holt (along with Treasurer E. B. Brown and Dean Winslow Anderson) presented evidence against the dismissed professor. Rice was supported by Georgia and Lounsbury. Day after day, Holt read letters and signed statements from students and from faculty, staff and townspeople critical of Rice for one reason or another.[25] Altogether, Holt listed a dozen charges against Rice, including claims he failed to teach Latin and Greek languages, he had spent class periods on irrelevant topics of religion and of sex, he punished students who did not hold his ideas, he influenced students to leave fraternities and sororities, he bullied students who came before the Board of Admissions of Upper Division, he "scoffed" at services in the chapel, he criticized the churches of the town and he was at times "immodest in dress." A final charge contained a blanket accusation: Rice "destroyed youthful ideals without inculcating anything equally constructive and commendable in their place." Professors who were supposed to encourage students to keep open minds in order to seek their own way, to come to their own conclusions now were expected to "inculcate" young people with "constructive and commendable ideas." Thus, the Rice affair had seemingly caused Holt to violate his own basic beliefs.

Rice was initially shocked at the accumulation of condemning evidence Holt presented but then relaxed considerably when he realized in their particulars they were often distorted, trivial or entirely false. In Rice's mind, Holt's efforts to articulate Rice's pernicious influence on the campus seemed nothing more than disagreements over policy or petty differences over lifestyles. Did Holt personally look into Rice's teaching of Greek and Latin, asked Lovejoy? Well, no, said Holt, but he had considerable information from students. Did Rice characterize a chapel service as obscene? Rice admitted he had, but for good reason. Form should follow form, Rice argued. "You can't put on a vaudeville show, pink spotlight and start singing with a choirmaster standing with his back to the altar in a Catholic style chapel without incurring the charge of obscenity." Didn't Rice encourage student disloyalty to the college? "My students," Rice replied, "are loyal to Rollins as they want it to be but not necessarily as it is, that is an unwise loyalty." Rice also denied he "dressed immodestly." Did you parade around the beach house in a jockstrap? Holt asked. "No,"

Rice replied, "I don't own a jockstrap." And so it went for several days: Holt reading charges from signed affidavits, Rice either disputing them or trying to explain them away.

Finally, although Holt wanted to avoid the issue, Lovejoy brought the hearings around to the heart of the matter. Did Rollins have a tenure policy, and if so, were Rice's rights violated under that policy?[40] Holt answered that, at the request of the faculty several months earlier, the trustees had issued policy guidelines: "Until Rollins College achieves a greater measure of financial stability, Trustees find it impossible to establish permanent standards for tenure of office. Therefore, while it is necessary to continue assistant professors and instructors on the one-year appointment basis, the Trustees are glad to assure professors and associate professors who have served in this rank for three or more years that the policy of the Trustees will be to continue their services without annual notification unless reasonable notice be given to the contrary." Lovejoy reminded Holt that Rice was asked to leave the campus two days after he received his non-reappointment letter. Did Holt consider that "reasonable notice"? Holt replied "yes."[26]

Lovejoy and Edwards left on May 24. Several months would elapse before they completed their report, but Holt knew by the manner of Lovejoy's handling of the hearing and by the tenor of his questions and comments he would find fault with Rice's dismissal. Even before the hearings ended, Holt determined that Lovejoy had placed not just Rice, but the president and the college on trial. He thought Edwards "a fair investigator," but was convinced that Lovejoy was devious and prejudiced.[44] Holt felt betrayed when

Lovejoy handed a "preliminary report" to local newspapers before he left town. It criticized the college's "rules for tenure" as "ill-defined" and found in Rice's behavior "nothing seriously reflecting upon either the private character or scholarship of Mr. Rice or on his ability as a teacher."[27]

With the investigation completed, Holt now prepared to play out what he called "the fourth act in the great college drama, Rollins versus Rice." He intended to deal with Rice's friends. One by one he called the Rice supporters into his office and asked them all the same question: "Will you give your loyalty and support to reducing the cleavage on the campus and in carrying out policies of the Trustees, the faculty or acts by myself or any others in authority even though you may intellectually differ with them?" Those who replied affirmatively found their positions secure. Those who resisted were dismissed. Allan Tory, an English historian and Oxford graduate, told Holt he would work to repair campus rifts, but would refuse to be a "yes man." Despite a previous verbal contract, a promotion to associate professor and appointment as a faculty representative to a prestigious international organization, Holt fired Tory the following day. The president wanted to fire physics Professor Theodore Dreier, but hesitated. He was the nephew of Margaret Robbins Dreier, an influential trustee. Holt informed Ted Dreier he "could come back next year" but would not be asked to return the following year. Dreier resigned. Professor of history and crew coach Cecil Oldham had resigned earlier for reasons stemming from the Rice affair. Despite Holt's pleading, Robert Wunsch, a brilliant associate professor of theater, quit in July. Total casualties, including resignations and dismissals, stood at eight faculty members, all Rice defenders in one form or another. The college had lost one-fourth of its faculty.[28]

Frederick Georgia and Ralph Lounsbury presented Holt with special problems. An important force in Holt's rebuilding program, chairman of several major committees and organizer of the 1932 curriculum conference, Georgia had held his professorship for over seven years and seemed protected from dismissal. Lounsbury had completed three years as professor and had only recently (March 11) received a letter from Holt stating "though professors who have held a professional rank three or more years need not be notified of their reappointment I am writing you this personal note for I hope you will continue at Rollins where you have made an enviable reputation for yourself."[29] In a letter to his dean, Holt frankly admitted that, because the college had no case against the two professors on "specific grounds," their dismissal had to rely on the fact that they "were disturbing elements and we must have harmony." On June 6, the day after commencement, the executive committee permitted Georgia and Lounsbury to resign with one-half salary. Both men refused, arguing that the settlement was inconsistent with the policy of due notice. Their contract for 1933-34 must be honored, they said. The executive committee voted not to re-employ Georgia and Lounsbury for the following year, and one month later, the Board of Trustees upheld that vote.[30]

Lounsbury's case was perhaps the saddest. The president's closest personal friend since their college days at Yale and a political and economic conservative, Lounsbury seemed curiously out of place among the liberal and progressive supporters of John Rice. Yet, he sympathized with their professional educational goals, saw much inflexibility in the two-hour classes and most of all believed principles should guide a person's life. More than any others, he supported Rice not out of sympathy with the eccentric iconoclast, but because he thought Rice's dismissal struck a devastating blow against the integrity of the teaching profession. Lounsbury never doubted the administration's authority to fire Rice, but he very strongly questioned Holt's dismissal methods. Try as he might, Lounsbury could not make Holt understand the consistency of his loyalty to Holt and his support of Rice. In mid-March he had written of his concern that Holt saw his efforts to improve policies or methods as evidence of his disloyalty. "I have gone and shall doubtless continue to go upon the supposition that loyalty does not call for mere subserviency or for clothing an honest expression of opinion. College professors who are willing to surrender lightly the thing which is very fundamental to their profession—namely their mental integrity—are not apt to be of any value to Rollins." Two months later when the Rice dismissal became a crisis, Lounsbury vainly tried to clarify his (and "also his colleagues") position in a letter to the president: "I should be sorry if you thought that our opposition to some things and our efforts to help another had any personal aspect towards you. We have been fighting not Hamilton Holt as an individual and friend but for what we believe to be the integrity of our profession; and may I say that no man who will not fight for that has any business to be in [a profession]." He then added a poignantly moving plea:

"So Hammy please try to overlook my failings and believe that whatever I have of head and heart is devoted to even a bigger and better Rollins. If the roads by which we seek that result seem now and then divergent, I know that we are both trying to attain that goal and I beg you to believe it too."[31] However reasonable and moving his plea, Lounsbury entirely misread the situation. Hamilton Holt was incapable of separating his personal mission from that of the college. He seemed to have completely internalized what others had been saying: "Holt is Rollins and Rollins is Holt."

With hindsight, one can see the Rice dismissal need not have degenerated into a crisis. Only the president could have prevented it. Even more to the point, as chief officer of the college, it was his responsibility and his alone to make sure Rice's dismissal did not turn into an explosive situation.[32] He had only to turn the Rice problem over to an appropriate faculty committee, to charge it with conducting hearings and to use its findings simply as recommendations. Given Rice's behavior, the committee undoubtedly would have recommended dismissal. But even if it had not, the president could still have acted independently, with no more unfavorable consequences. Many faculty members and at least one trustee had suggested this solution. Professors Tory and Edwin Clark thought such a committee would create "a new morale and hope for the future."[32] The most perceptive advice along these lines came from Board of Trustees member Margaret Drier Robbins. A childhood friend of the president, a liberal reformer and a militant leader of the women's labor movement in the 1920s, Margaret Robbins tried in several letters and with a personal visit to divert Holt from a collision course with his faculty. She begged Holt to elect a faculty committee to consider the discipline and even dismissal of Rice. In that way, she sagaciously contended, rather than Holt's shouldering the entire burden, the faculty would bear with him responsibility for that decision. Wasn't such an effort simply an extension of "your own liberal policies? My dear Hamilton Holt," she pleaded, "why not add this jewel to your immortal crown?" Holt never answered her questions.[33]

As a college president, Holt was much more conventional than Mrs. Robbins supposed. With prodding from the AAUP, a few institutions had established systems giving the faculty a greater role in college governance, but in the overwhelming majority of colleges, employer-employee concepts still characterized president-faculty relationships. Few presidents held more strongly to this attitude than Hamilton Holt, who consistently described his efforts at Rollins in business terms. Like businesses, his two-hour class system would place education on an eight-hour day; students must be responsible in attending classes in the same way as workers were responsible for showing up at work. Holt regarded *The Independent* reporters and Rollins professors in much the same way. He respected their professionalism, and even though many were close friends, in the final analysis he was their boss. As president he held the authority of a conventional employer who could personally hire and fire employees. When, in the midst of the Rice affair, some faculty questioned that authority, he promptly persuaded the trustees to issue an interpretation that provided him with unlimited authority in matters of faculty discipline and dismissal:

"Subject to the approval of the Trustees it is the duty of the President to appoint or dismiss all employees of the college including the faculty," read the trustee minutes.

Holt bluntly stated his personal management style in a letter to the Southern Association of Colleges explaining why he had dismissed the Rice supporters: "It is fundamental of [the] employee's duty that he should yield obedience to all reasonable rules, orders or instructions of the employer." More to the point when asked why he would not allow a faculty review committee, Holt replied, "When you fire a cook you don't go out and get a committee of neighbors to tell you what to do."[34] In Holt's mind, cooks and professors were on the same level when it came to the presidential authority.

Holt found others than Margaret Robbins on the Board of Trustees with more supportive advice. Successful businessmen John Goss and Milton Warner, Holt's classmates at Yale, and William O'Neal, a local Trustee, all interpreted the Rice affair as a power struggle between a group of liberal dissident faculty and the president. They advised Holt to stand firm in his authority, or else he would lose complete control of the college governance. Throughout the crisis, Goss, who was especially influential, wrote long pages of advice Holt followed almost to the letter. At one time or another, Goss advised Holt to "go at this Rice matter firmly, decisively, and without hesitation;" "to get the Rice supporters together and make them pledge themselves to be loyal." After the AAUP hearings, Goss counseled Holt "to clean the decks just as quickly as possible of all disloyalty and of all disintegrating influences personal or otherwise that have surrounded this Rice problem." Holt was so receptive to Goss's advice that more than once he repeated word for word an odd aphorism that the trustee said guided him in his business affairs: "When principle and right conflict, throw away your principles and do what is right."[35]

By the beginning of the new school year in September 1933, the Rice affair had receded beneath the surface of Rollins' community life. An uneasy peace had returned to the campus. The Rice affair resurfaced, however, in November, when the AAUP published Lovejoy's report in its bulletin. The report conceded Rice "had unquestionably much disturbed the harmony of the local community," had "fallen into some serious errors of judgment and some of taste." Still, it concluded, Rice's dismissal "eliminated from the faculty a teacher who appears on the one hand to have done more than any other to provoke questioning, discussion and the spirit of critical inquiry and on the other to have aimed with exceptional success at constructive results both in thought and character."[36]

The Lovejoy report accused Holt of exceeding his authority, of autocratically interpreting the college bylaws, of demanding excessive personal fealty and of expecting more harmony and like-mindedness than should be found in the college. It further accused him of hypocritically proclaiming liberal ideals but of practicing the opposite. The report specifically noted the mass dismissals subsequent to the Lovejoy hearings, citing them as evidence of the President's "autocratic powers contrary to academic customs and principles of this profession and not sanctioned by the college charter or bylaws." The association placed Rollins on its ineligible list indicating to its members that the college had violated AAUP principles of academic freedom and tenure.[37]

Maddened by Lovejoy's report, Holt refused to let the matter drop. In December, he and the Executive Committee published a response entitled, "Rollins College versus The American Association of University Professors," charging the Committee of Inquiry with "attempted coercion if not bribery; [with] misrepresentation if not defamation of character of bias; and [with] prejudice if not malice and suppression of evidence." The report further lashed out at "the small body of willful men who controlled the Association in the year 1932-33." It also belittled the organization which approved "the attack of a prejudiced and hostile investigator." The college then distributed several thousand copies of the report to college and university administrations throughout the country. Afterward, the administration finally allowed the Rice affair to rest. In February 1934, Holt wrote a friend with some relief that "the storm through which our academic ship of state passed is now over and we are now in calm waters."[38]

The Rice affair produced another and more positive outcome. When Rice, Georgia, Lounsbury and Dreier gathered during the summer to consider the future, they were drawn to the idea of putting in practice what they had been preaching. Why not start their own college, one of them suggested. With the nation in the midst of a deep economic depression the idea at first had seemed absurdly naive, but they agreed to explore the possibilities. By August, they had found a ready-made campus, the Baptist summer retreat in Black Mountain, North Carolina, and enough funds to make a beginning. In September 1932, four of the dismissed

Rollins faculty members opened Black Mountain College, destined to become in the next decade one the nation's most exciting, significant and progressive experiments in American higher education. Rather than resentment, Black Mountain College evoked considerable pride from the Rollins community. Many sensed an affinity with its efforts, believing correctly Rollins had provided the educational spawning grounds for the experiment. The Rice affair thus seemed to be ending on a much more pleasant note than the President's strident reply to the AAUP report.

The struggle left behind two unfortunate casualties. The first was Ralph Lounsbury who died unexpectedly in 1933 of heart failure. Previous attacks had led him into what he thought were the peaceful confines of academe. More than a few of his colleagues at Black Mountain believed his row with Holt and his subsequent dismissal had contributed to Lounsbury's untimely death. The second casualty was the incipient progressive educational reforms begun with such high optimism in 1930. The college did not abandon its progressive posture, but the Rice affair had diverted the community's energy into an unproductive struggle that substantially smothered a fledgling spirit of reform. Moreover, John Rice took with him to North Carolina imaginative progressive ideas that within limits could have been developed at Rollins. It is true the radical communal educational experiments attempted at Black Mountain could never have happened at Rollins (and perhaps no other place than Black Mountain's rural isolated location). It is true as well the city of Winter Park would have been uncomfortable with the bohemian behavior of the many students and faculty who populated Black Mountain. The loss of Rice and seven other leading faculty members, however, robbed the college of individuals who could have taken the institution to even greater progressive heights. As Holt indicated in the aftermath of the Rice affair, by 1934 the academic ship of state had receded from the stormy seas of conflict, into the more calming waters of academic conventionalism. Unfortunately, the secure haven into which Holt had anchored his vessel shielded it as well from the excitement, the adventure and the promise of the turbulent seas of innovative education.

The final and ironic chapter of the Rice episode was written several years later in 1938. In that year Black Mountain College refused to reappoint John Rice on grounds similar to those that had led to his dismissal at Rollins. That same year the Rollins Board of Trustees adopted the AAUP statement of principles on academic freedom and tenure. In December 1938 the Association removed Rollins from the unapproved list.[39]

1. Jenks left Rollins in 1930 for Wellesley College and later achieved scholarly recognition for his book, *Our Cuban Colony: A Study in Sugar (1972)*

For Rice's background and his own description of how he was hired see John Rice, *I Came Out Of the Eighteenth Century* (1942). Holt's version, not significantly different from Rice's, may be found Holt Memorandum on the Rice Affair, May 1933.

2. Holt to Rice, March 16, 1932; Rice to Holt, March 18, 1932; "Report of the Committee on the Fraternity System," March 1932.

3. Memorandum from the President to the Fraternities, March 26, 1932.

4. Grover to Holt, April 10, 1932; Lounsbury to Holt, April 10, 1932.

5. Curriculum Committee Report, January, 1933; Faculty Minutes, January 1933.

6. Holt to Howard Bailey, January 22, 1933; Faculty Minutes, January 1933; Curriculum Committee Report.

7. Curriculum Committee to President Holt, January 18, 1933; Holt to Curriculum Committee, January 19, 1933.

8. Rice, *Eighteenth Century*, 306-08; Martin Duberman, *Black Mountain College* (1972), 3.

9. Rice, *Eighteenth Century*, 301.

10. Duberman, 4.

11. Willard Wattles to Holt, March 10, 1933; Dean Anderson's Memorandum on John Rice to President Holt, March 1933.

12. *Ibid*, where Anderson cites student and faculty complaints against Rice.

13. Interview by author with Rhea Smith; Carol Hemingway Gardner to author, February 10, 1979; Dean Anderson's Memo.

14. Holt's Memorandum on Rice Affair.

15. For example see Wattles to Holt, March 10, 1933.

16. Holt to Rice, March 21, 1933.

17. Holt to the American Association of University Professors (AAUP) March 1933.

18. Tyler to Holt, April 8, 1933; Holt to Tyler, April 18, 1933.

19. Interview by author with Theodore Dreier; Statement by Arthur Lovejoy, "Rollins College Report," *Bulletin of the AAUP* 19, No. 7 (November 1933). Rice, "Eighteenth Century, 306.

20. Tory's speech printed in *Sandspur*, April 8, 1933. Wattles warned Holt of the agitation in a letter on April 10, 1933. See also Winslow Anderson's Report on the Rice Affair.

21. Rice to Holt, April 21, 1933; Executive Committee, Trustee Minutes, April.

22. 1933; Holt to Rice, April 22, 1933; Holt to Asa Jennings April 27, 1933.

22. Rice, *Eighteenth Century*, 307. Interview by author with Theodore Dreier.

23. Holt to AAUP, May 6, 1933; Holt Memo on the Rice Affair, May 1933. In Lovejoy Holt had a formidable adversary. To say that Arthur Lovejoy was an "established scholar" is something of an understatement. At the time he was America's foremost intellect who had written the seminal study in the history of ideas entitled *The Great Chain of Being (1936)*. The book has since become a major classic. Lovejoy was also a passionate defender of faculty free speech. In 1901 he resigned from Sanford University when the administration fired a professor over a disagreement with a trustee. The faculty at Harvard wanted to hire Lovejoy but the president vetoed his appointment on the grounds that he was a troublemaker. He was later hired at Columbia University.

24. Printed in AAUP, "Report on Rollins College," Appendix A, 439.

25. I have reconstructed the following discussion of the hearings from hand written notes kept by E. B. Brown, Holt Papers; from Rice, *Eighteenth Century*; from Holt Memo on the Rice Affair and from the AAUP, "Report on Rollins College."

26. AAUP, "Report on Rollins College," 423; Trustee Minutes, February,1932; Notes kept by E.B. Brown on the Rice Hearings.

27. Holt to Beard, May 24, 1933; *Orlando Sentinel*, May 25, 1933; AAUP, "Report on Rollins College," 439.

28. Memorandum on Conference with Rice Followers, June 2-5, 1933.

29. *Ibid*.

30. Holt to Lounsbury, March 11, 1933; Trustee Minutes, June 1933; Holt to Anderson, June 21, 1933.

31. Lounsbury to Holt, March 16, 1933; May 7, 1933.

32. Holt to Beard, May 24, 1933.

33. Margaret Dreier Robbins to Holt, May 24, 1933. Margaret Drier was one of the college's most intriguing members of the Board of Trustees. As a former president of the Women's Trade Union League, she was its most unconventional as well. It must have been a bit awkward for a Board consisting of mostly conservative businessmen to sit at the table with someone who had organized strikes, perhaps against one of their own corporations. She was also married to Raymond Robbins who was on speaking terms with Lenin and Trotsky of the Soviet Union. Margaret and Raymond owned a home in Brooksville, Florida called Chensegut which they offered to donate to Rollins in their wills, but Holt turned it down. It is now a historic home run by the University of South Florida.

Robbins resigned from the Board in September, 1933. In the resignation letter she reiterated her long "abiding friendship with Holt. "For your progressive ideas in education," she continued, "and the spirit of freedom and comradeship in teaching for both students and professors that you pioneered, I have keen sympathy and admiration. But with the policy of faculty dismissal I find myself in settled opposition. Under these circumstances, I send you my resignation." Robbins to Holt, September, 1933.

34. Trustee Minutes, April 1933; Report of the Southern Association of Colleges [no date], copy in Holt Papers; Holt's testimony Before the AAUP Hearings, copy in Holt Papers.

Holt's use of the term "drama" reinforces the perception that he saw the Rice affair as pure theater and envisioned himself as collegiate King Lear defending his kingdom from a family assault. Reading all the documents and letters left me with the impression that Holt enjoyed every minute of his stage performance.

35. John Goss to Holt, May 15, 1933; Holt to Goss, May 26, 1933.

36. AAUP, "Report on Rollins College, 427.

37. *Ibid*. 429.

38. Printed in *Bulletin* 29 (December 1933).

39. Duberman, *Black Mountain, 152; Trustee Minutes, April 1938.*

After his dismissal, Rice wrote a memoir that included a chapter on his experiences at Rollins. Holt purchased a copy and carefully annotated virtually every page indicating where he thought Rice lied about many incidents. Holt's copy is located in the Rollins Archives.

Today, over sixty years after its founding, interest in Black Mountain College as a quintessential experiment in progressive education has reached the level of a kind of cottage industry, generating scholarly articles, conferences and workshops almost every year. In all this assiduous attention, the place of Rollins College in the origins of Black Mountain College has been relegated to one of derision: a conservative college dismissed four brilliant progressive professors who took their theories to North Carolina and started a new innovative institution.

Still, a strong case can be made that the open, receptive venue at Rollins College was one of the few places where progressive ideas were given the freedom to germinate. The first Black Mountain curriculum of Junior and Senior Divisions with entrance into the Senior Division dependent not on number of courses but on passing oral and comprehensive exams was lifted directly from the Rollins progressive curriculum of 1933. Rollins faculty and students were fully prepared to accept many of the far reaching programs introduced in the first years of Black Mountain. Even though he initiated the progressive educational reform movement at Rollins, ironically it was President Hamilton Holt, not the faculty members, who brought sweeping progressive reforms to a halt. Nevertheless, it may be said, without Rollins there would have been no Black Mountain College. Ironically, Holt's imperious resistance to radical progressive reforms was responsible for the conditions that led to the creation of those reforms elsewhere. Holt seemed to take pride in Rollins' role in Black Mountain's success, as long as such experiments occurred some other place.

Chapter 7

THE LATER HOLT YEARS:
DEPRESSION AND WAR,
1932–1949

HOWEVER REGRETTABLE THE Rice affair, it could neither obscure nor diminish the substantial accomplishments of the Holt administration. Even more amazing, they occurred in the midst of an unprecedented devastating depression. During this period, the college undertook major curriculum reform, doubled the size of its faculty and continued to attract large numbers of students with high academic qualifications. Holt also virtually built a new campus, adding 32 new buildings all constructed in the Spanish-Mediterranean architectural style. These changes evidenced the transformation and drama of a small, provincial college undergoing a profound and often wrenching metamorphosis into a nationally celebrated institution.

In the early years of his presidency, convinced the faculty was the keystone of the academic structure, Holt much of his time and the college's resources to finding qualified professors. He first cleared the community of what he perceived to be "academic deadwood"—that collection of poor teachers and aged professors which he had inherited. He replaced them with "golden personalities." As defined by Holt, these luminaries would be teachers with a fund of knowledge, combined with the creative and engaging styles that made learning interesting, exciting and worthwhile. "It is professors who make a college great," Holt proclaimed repeatedly, "and yet how rare a great teacher." GPs, as students and faculty irreverently dubbed them, were those "rare souls whose personality appeals to young men and women, who possess the gift of teaching and the nobility of character to inspire youth." Most institutions of higher learning were looking for more tangible evidence of skills, such as advanced graduate degrees, particularly PhD's. Holt did not disregard these concrete factors, but he more often relied on his own intuition in hiring his "golden personalities." For several years, Holt alone interviewed and hired most of the faculty.[1]

For the most part, Holt's personal judgment served him well. Within five years he had assembled a well qualified and interesting collection of "golden personalities," who were certainly the most impressive faculty the college had ever seen. It was also a group that compared favorably to those of quality colleges in the Northeast and Midwest. Eleven of his faculty appointments possessed earned doctorates from universities such as Cornell, Columbia, California and Pennsylvania, and foreign universities such as Dublin and Heidelburg. Holt made these appointments in an era when

PhD's were scarce. The group also included seven Phi Beta Kappas. Several of the professors had published or would make important scholarly contributions later in their careers. Willard Wattles, professor of literature, had already published several volumes of poetry when he arrived in 1927 and continued publishing after coming to Rollins. Leland Jenks, professor of economic history, published several scholarly articles on Cuba while at Rollins and, after leaving in 1931, completed an important study on Cuban-American policy. Holt also managed to hire three graduates from Oxford University: Cecil Oldam, Allan Tory and the Rhodes scholar, John Rice.

Even so, the president remained adamant that a collection of graduate degrees and a list of publications did not necessarily add up to good teaching. He valued the "universal gift of teaching" as more important than research and student testimony about professors more than the praise of their colleagues. Having himself entered academia without a graduate degree, Holt downplayed its significance in effective teaching. "While no one cares less for a degree than I," he wrote John Rice in 1930, "I rather hope you can arrange to get your M.A. from Oxford. It looks good in the catalogue and is supposed to be an academic plus." Holt's patronizing—if not unfriendly—attitude toward the academic professional led him to seek "golden personalities" outside the educational sphere. One of his first appointments was Edwin Osgood Grover, former editor-in-chief of Rand-McNally and Holt's colleague in the publishing world.[2]

Grover's academic qualifications included an honorary degree from Dartmouth, a few publications of his own private press and a knowledge of publishing, qualifications not much different from Holt's. Since Grover possessed no traditional academic area of expertise, he could not be assigned to an existing academic department. Holt created a new one, the Department of Books and gave Grover the unique title of professor of books. College literature proclaimed it to be the one and only such professorship in the world. So far as we know, the claim went unchallenged. The idea of starting heretofore unknown positions excited Holt. Only the failure to uncover supporting funds kept Holt from appointing a professor of hunting and fishing. In 1930, he appointed the famous writer, Corra Harris, as professor of evil. Holt never bothered to explain how a southern novelist who revealed deep racial prejudices in national magazine articles—Holt published many of those articles in *The Independent*—had managed to acquire expertise in the subject of evil. Students often complained that her sole source for the meaning of evil came from the Bible. When she became ill after teaching three classes, someone quipped that this might have been an example of life imitating art.[3]

These quixotic notions aside, Holt's faculty appointments from outside academe generally worked well. Edwin Osgood Grover proved be a credible teacher, made significant contributions in several areas of college life and became a valued citizen in the Winter Park community. He became close friends with a little known writer named Zora Neal Hurston and was instrumental in getting Hurston's first book published. In addition to his many contributions to the college, he was active in Winter Park's African American community. He and his wife Mertie established the Welbourne Day Nursery for the children of working African-American mothers. He was the chief contributor to the Hannibal Square Library, helped form the Hannibal Square Associates and raised most of the money for the DePugh Nursing Home. His final gift to the community was putting together the land for Mead Gardens, forty-five acres of a natural environment that became Winter Park's crown jewel.

Royal France may have been one of Holt's most interesting and also one of his most challenging appointments. France came to Rollins after a successful career as a New York attorney and as president of two large corporations. One was Triangle Film, a company that distributed the films of Thomas Ince, D. W. Griffith and Mack Sennett. Paramount Pictures later absorbed the company. Through Joseph Irving France, his brother and a U. S. Senator from Maryland, Royal moved among the highest levels of Washington and New York societies. He knew personally both Woodrow Wilson and Theodore Roosevelt. Over the years France had developed an increasingly liberal outlook on life, which made him more and more uncomfortable in the corporate world. An earlier experience with a progressive preparatory school had interested him in education, and in 1928 he wrote Holt: "I think that one who has majored in Economics and Law in college and has practiced both, ought to be able to teach those subjects better than someone who has just read about them in books."[4] Naturally, this appeal struck a responsive chord with Holt. He met France in New York and characteristically hired him on the spot to teach economics. France became not only an outstanding teacher, but his presence also added immeasurably to the college community because, like Ralph Lounsbury, he was a highly principled man. For example, France publicly criticized Holt's methods in firing John Rice while at the same time pledging his loyalty to the president. Holt's acceptance of France's claim of a fractured loyalty, while rejecting a similar one from Lounsbury, is proof of the president's high respect for the economist.

In the national election of 1932, France worked for the socialist candidate Norman Thomas, and afterwards became chairman of the Socialist Party of Florida. If this were not enough to disturb the sensibilities of conservative Central Florida, he became an active public critic of the southern segregation system. France and his wife established a close friendship with Zora Neal Hurston, who often stayed overnight in the France home when she was in Winter Park. Such incidents brought notoriety to the campus, but Holt continued to support the professor's right to speak out on controversial issues. In 1951, at the age of 70, France left the "comforts of his home" in Winter Park, and the comparative calm of Rollins College, for the civil liberties struggles of the McCarthy era. He gained national prominence for his defense of communists hauled before the House Un-American Activities Committee. In 1952, he presented an amicus brief in an effort to reduce the death sentence of Julius and Ethel Rosenberg. At the time of his death in that year, he was organizing a rally to protest the McCarran Internal Security Act.[4]

The early Holt era also brought an increase in the quantity and quality of students. When he arrived in 1926, the college reported a total of 368 students. Holt envisioned increasing that number to 700, but the Depression, cause of many college woes, created a nationwide decline in student enrollment. Thus, ten years after Holt arrived, enrollment stood at 470. This number remained relatively steady until the outbreak of World War II when it dropped precipitously.

If the college failed to reach the optimum number Holt wanted, its educational reforms did attract higher quality students and particularly students intensely interested in the kind of education they received at Rollins. Many came to the college specifically because of progressive reforms. The statement of Carol Hemingway, sister of Ernest, was commonly subscribed to: "My first impression of Hamilton Holt came from an article I read of his describing the Conference Plan. I determined to go to Rollins because of that article."[5] Because the students arrived at the campus with an interest in education, they sought to take an active part in the entire educational process. The college encouraged this participation by periodically asking students to evaluate the conference plan, and involving them in the curriculum revision. As a result, students at Rollins directly participated in the educational process and responded to their new opportunities with a zeal surprising to all campus visitors. One of such visitors was Dr. Charles H. Judd of the University of Chicago. Judd, who visited the campus on behalf of the Rockefeller Foundation, exhibited less than ardent support for college progressive programs, but he could not deny the positive attitude of Rollins students: "There is evidently a spirit of the greatest enthusiasm for the college among the students. The Rollins conference plan is discussed even in class exercise and is thought of by the students as a unique and very inspiring undertaking. Some of the students characterized American college education elsewhere as a failure, and declared that in their judgment the Rollins plan is destined to replace all types of organization. The whole community seems to be alive in a kind of enthusiastic ecstasy."[6]

Holt, who had always shown a special interest in literature, took advantage of the large colony of reputable artists and writers who wintered in the "Park." Holt often invited them to take part in campus life and their presence helped attract imaginative, creative students whose talents and enthusiasm soon became evident. They transformed *The Sandspur* into a regular-sized newspaper organized in the format of *The New York Times* with sections that included editorials, reviews of books and movies and various essays. In 1930 and 1931 the newspaper played an important role in encouraging a college dialogue on the curriculum revision. In the 1927 winter term, the college authorized a fiction and poetry seminar with writing taught by nationally known poets and novelists including Irving Bacheller, poets Cale Young Rice and his wife Alice Hegan Rice, as a well as Clinton Scollard and his wife, Jesse Rittenhouse.[7]

Perhaps the most significant student creative endeavor of this period was *The Flamingo*. This monthly "literary magazine of the young generation," first published in March 1927, contained original poems and short stories. Students edited the magazine and contributed most of the material. The magazine attracted wide attention, reinforced the reputation of the college as a progressive, creative institution and popularized Rollins as a home of fine literary talent. Writers such as Marjorie Kinnan Rawlings and editors such as Maria Leipes of Simon and Schuster praised the stories and poems from the magazine as of "immensely high caliber." In the 1935 edition, a short story entitled "The Key" received critical acclaim and won for its student-author, Frances Perpente, first prize in a national short story contest. Carol Hemingway caused a sensation on campus when *The Flamingo* published her short story about a lesbian love affair. A winter visitor from the Rockefeller Foundation noted "anyone wishing to gain an estimate of the kind of work done by the better students at Rollins should examine *The Flamingo.*" Holt once remarked the magazine had become a "veritable sport on the campus," the kind that encouraged community-wide creativity.[8]

The Flamingo set the tone for a burst of creative energy that permeated the entire campus. Holt hosted poetry readings and discussions every Sunday in his home on Interlachen Avenue, and similar activities often spilled over into evenings at professors' homes or on campus. Students gathered at John Rice's house almost nightly; Theodore Dreier, a physics teacher, often escorted students on excursions to explore nature's aesthetic delights around the campus; and Richard Fuerstein, who taught German, directed impromptu drama in the evenings. The completion of the theater in 1932 brought quality drama to the campus for the first time. At the helm was a star of legitimate theater, Annie Russell, for whom the theater was named. Productions that year, which included Russell's own *Major Barbara*, were simply one of the many indicators that Rollins College had suddenly blossomed as a cultural center of the Southeast. The spirit of progressive experimentation had clearly unleashed latent talent within the community, transforming the college into a creative workshop.

Perhaps Holt's most innovative and popular contribution to the college's national reputation was the *Animated Magazine.* The concept came from the fertile publicist minds of Holt and Osgood Grover. Holt was searching for a way to take advantage of his experience as an editor and to use the acquaintances he had developed over the years to create an event that would bring national attention to the college. According to tradition, Holt and Grover were discussing ways to bring national attention to Rollins. Holt suggested publishing a magazine, taking advantage of his contacts in the fields of art, literature and public affairs. Grover suggested a one-day event where artists and politicians would "speak" their articles. He proposed calling it the Animated Magazine. That's it, replied Holt. He organized the first "issue" for February 1927 using mostly artists and writers from the little Winter Park art colony. The "publication" of this annual magazine caught on immediately and became the major cultural event each year for Central Florida. As one writer has described it:

"The *Animated Magazine* grew steadily in size and fame over the years, keeping pace with (and, to some degree, inspiring) Florida's booming tourist trade. *Time magazine* touted the event in 1932; for years, CBS Radio in New York broadcast selections and the *New York Herald Tribune* published the program event in its magazine section. Speakers included journalist Edward R. Murrow '49H; actors Mary Pickford '52H, Greer Garson '46H, and James Cagney '55H; FBI director J. Edgar Hoover; civil rights leader Mary

McLeod Bethune '49H; U.S. Army Generals Omar Bradley and Jonathan Wainwright '48H; and authors Carl Sandburg '40H, Willa Cather and Marjorie Kinnan Rawlings '39H. Each paid his or her own traveling expenses and did not receive a speaking fee—remarkable proof of Holt's powers of persuasion. Many received honorary degrees from the College."[9]

Academically and artistically, these were exciting times for the college, but Holt was not able to turn around the deplorable financial situation he had inherited in 1925. He had raised over one and a half million dollars for various peace organizations in the pre-and post-World War I period. Surely, if he could raise that much for something as abstract as peace, he could attract sufficient funds to endow a small college. Failing that, he was certain he could rely on his eminent acquaintances among the wealthy and powerful men of the Northeast. The perennial and burdensome college deficit that had leveled several former presidents appeared to Holt as a bully good challenge, and his first effort at fund-raising simply reinforced his confidence in his ability to meet that challenge.

In 1926, Holt persuaded an old peace movement friend, William Short, to join the college as treasurer. That summer and fall Short reorganized the institution's financial structure and, in April 1926, he launched a campaign in Orange County to raise $300,000 to pay operating expenses. The administration, relieved of the chore of raising funds for operating expenses, devoted its full efforts to increasing the endowment. If the college expected those outside Florida to donate funds, Holt argued, it must first garner local support. The administration began solicitations on April

1926, and one week later it announced cash pledges totaling $304,000, an over subscription of $4,000. Subsequently, Holt's first attempt to raise funds outside the state brought $25,000 for student loans from President Elbert Gary of the United States Steel Corporation. Thus, the college seemed financially well secured for the future even before the trustees had held formal inauguration for the new president. This early rush of success swept the Holt administration with a wave of optimism.[10]

But just as quickly as they had appeared, the early successes were followed by a sudden economic disaster. In the summer of 1926 a destructive hurricane swept away millions of dollars in property and precipitated the land boom collapse which had brought Floridians unprecedented (though, as it turned out, false) prosperity. Within a fortnight of the land crash, the real estate given to the college during the campaign could not be sold at any price. Countless pledges simply could not be collected. Subscription pledges for the 1926-27 academic year totaled only $20,000 by January, one-third of the anticipated $60,000. In January 1927, Treasurer William Short presented Holt with a dismal "analysis of Rollins College's finances." Not only would the college not retire the debt Holt had inherited but it would also accrue even more deficit by the summer. Even more frightening were the current bills that had to be urgently paid within a matter of days. Short's long range predictions proved equally discouraging. Local banks were reluctant to make loans to the college until they had collected the February tuitions, he explained, "because they know we have no further income." Besides, he said, local banks also had fallen on hard times. This critical financial situation was additionally complicated by the fact that in the halcyon days of the previous summer, Holt had ordered a deferred maintenance program. The true total of the deficit would likely stand at almost $150,000.[11]

In the midst of this financial crisis, dissension developed within the administration. Short's concerted efforts to collect tuition angered students and his methods jarred the conservative sensibilities of the crusty former treasurer, William O'Neal, the college's oldest and most powerful trustee. He was appalled by Short's insistence on continuing repairs during the financial crisis. Unwilling to endure the bitter crossfire of criticism, Short resigned in June 1927. Holt, who had persuaded Short to come to Rollins in the first place, deeply regretted his old friend's resignation. "If I had my own feelings to consider," he wrote later, "I would never have let him leave Rollins. He suited me there absolutely. His going was one of the griefs of my life."[12]

At O'Neal's suggestion, Holt replaced Short with Erwin T. Brown, an experienced and competent treasurer. Even so the old trustee was not placated. He proposed shocking Draconian measures: "cut expenses at every corner, reduce salaries, make no repairs not absolutely necessary." The college had completely drained its Florida resources, O'Neal claimed, because every president had conducted a local campaign promising that "if a given amount was subscribed it would be ample for present needs." In his judgment, he told Holt, "it would be impossible to raise anymore money in Orlando and vicinity" for sometime to come. Do not rely on the trustees, he warned. He had seen them "shut up like clams..." saying "it is heartbreaking [that this is happening to the college] but that's the way of the world." His final advice: "close the college until endorsement interest revives." Holt's answer was he had accepted the call to Rollins to build not to destroy.[13]

On the premise the best defense was an all-out offense, in June 1928, Holt and Treasurer Brown presented the Board of Trustees with plans for a two and one-half million dollar endowment fund raising campaign. The trustees authorized the campaign but in face of the college's inability to meet day-to-day operational problems, the endowment campaign was a bold, aggressive—and some thought foolish—move. Despite this need for daily operational funds, Brown supported the new endowment campaign because, he told Holt, "there is only one direction we can go: forward," and because "I have faith in you and that faith has caused me to stay at Rollins for another year." In August 1928, Brown wrote Holt, who was summering at Woodstock, he could not meet even necessary maintenance costs and had no idea how he would pay faculty salaries for September. To add to these problems, Brown discovered over one-third of the enrolled students had failed to pay fees and tuition. Trustees John Goss and Milton Warner kicked off the guarantee fund by contributing $25,000 each, but contributions came in a slow trickle thereafter. It was not until February 1929, that a last minute gift from William Bingham enabled the administration to complete the guarantee fund.[14]

While the administration strained every effort in the fund campaign, college deficits from operating costs continued to mount at an alarming rate. To use Holt's metaphor: a "financial sword of Damocles," suspended tenuously by the "gossamer thread," swung menacingly over their heads. The new campaign was an enormous gamble, for failure would drag the entire institution down with it. Nevertheless, in February 1929, the Board of Trustees authorized the firm of Tamblyn and Brown to open the two and one half million-dollar campaign. Unfortunately, in another bit of pure bad luck, the campaign announcement coincided with the stock market crash of October 1929. Even a $125,000 gift from H. H. Westinghouse (the college's largest gift yet) failed to brighten the dark cloud spread over the campaign after the crash.

Then, at that darkest hour, and while Holt was canvassing furiously in Pittsburgh, there came a sudden burst of hopeful, financial light. On January 31, 1930, Holt received a stunning telegram from his old and close acquaintance, Dr. John Gering, a physician and financial advisor to philanthropist William Bingham II: "On this last day of the first month of the year the word of the Lord came to a certain Samaritan saying write my servant Hamilton Holt offering the sum of $500,000 and send it now but with no publicity save to the Trustees." Kenneth Wilson, a Tamblyn and Brown agent working with Holt in Pittsburgh, later recalled Holt's stunned reaction to the news. "As he stared at the message his cheeks flushed and his body became rigid. He seemed almost paralyzed by the news." Wilson suggested Holt prepare a reply to the incredible message, but when Holt tried to put his appreciation into words, the potential implication of the gift came flooding in on him, and according to Wilson, the President "broke down and

wept."[26] Only later did Holt learn how the momentous decision had been made. Gering, with little success, had been
bringing the college to Bingham's attention for several
months, but then, Gering reported, on the morning of the
31st, Bingham "came to me to inquire as to the welfare of
Rollins College followed by a declaration that he would like
to give a half a million dollars toward it."[27] As the first of the
college's major gifts (it almost doubled the endowment),
Bingham's donation was valued more highly than any other,
since Holt believed it proved that his new educational plan
could attract financial support. In a letter of appreciation
to Bingham, the president spelled out its meaning to the
college: "Rollins was reaching a turning point in its career.
I had about exhausted every available liquid asset short of
mortgaging the campus and I feel that this great and most
timely aid will bring me safely past the first big milestone
and give every friend renewed courage and strength for the
tasks ahead in upbuilding the little college I have learned
to love." Holt saw the gift so critical to the college's survival
that he celebrated its anniversary every year.[15]

The increase in endowment income satisfied the
college's immediate financial needs (even though those
needs had increased enormously by Holt's determination
to maintain small conference classes, hire more teachers at
higher salaries and make major improvements in the physical plant). Holt understood the new funds, however, offered
no long-term panacea for the college's financial condition.
As the Depression deepened, depleting the college's normal
resources, the campaign lagged and finally atrophied.
On February 18, 1931, the trustees canceled the Tamblyn

contract. The campaign had netted just over $900,000, a sizable amount but still far short of the two and one-half million-dollar goal. Holt wrote a friend that he, Brown and his assistant Fred Hanna would "go it alone."[16]

When Holt decided to go on the offense rather than retrench during the national economic depression, few would have imagined he would embark on a building program that would completely transform the physical appearance of the campus. From the beginning, Holt envisioned an architectural design consistent with the Florida landscape and at the same time congruent with the college's progressive academic changes. Thus, when he received funds for a new dormitory, he was determined to find an architectural style which would reflect the new educational programs and in turn take advantage of Rollins' semi-tropical location. He chose a Spanish-Mediterranean style because, he thought, that design blended best with "palms, bamboos and brilliant sunshine." He once told a group he was looking "for the most beautiful buildings of Mediterranean type in Florida, then find who designed them, then get that man to design every building on our campus..., all in harmony and all parts a unified whole." The college's unified curriculum purpose, Holt argued, ought to be reflected in its architectural style. Holt also maintained that, since the college was located in the land of sunshine, its buildings should be designed with spacious and open breezeways. Holt hoped that one day Rollins would have a logo that would proclaim it was the "Open Air College of America."

Holt found the architect he wanted in Richard Kiehnel of Miami. During the 1920s Kiehnel established a national reputation in South Florida for adapting the Spanish-Mediterranean style to the Florida landscape. Kiehnel was a perfect match for Holt's new architectural vision. When the cousin of Alonzo Rollins gave the college a generous donation in 1929, Holt immediately hired Kiehnel to design Rollins Hall, the college's first Spanish-Mediterranean building. The following decade, Kiehnel was responsible for designing 15 buildings, beginning with Rollins, Pugsley and Mayflower Halls (1930) followed by Annie Russell Theater (1932). Through his connection with the Roosevelt administration, Holt was able to wrangle funds from the Public Works Administration to pay for three more Kiehnel dormitories—Gale, Lyman and Fox (1936-- placed along Holt Avenue. In the next five years Kiehnel designed Cross and Hooker Halls (1937), Woolson House (1938) Strong and Dwyer Memorial(1939), and Alumni House, Student Center, and French House (1941).

The *piece de resistance* of Hamilton Holt's contribution to the built landscape came with the construction of a theatre-chapel complex. When Francis Knowles' daughter, Frances Knowles Warren, agreed to donate sufficient funds for the construction of a chapel, Holt immediately set out to acquire the services of the world renowned college and church architect, Ralph Adams Cram. Cram agreed provided he could design a chapel similar to one he had seen in Toledo, Spain. The result became the college's signature building and the spiritual center of the community. In Cram's owns words: Knowles Chapel was "designed in a modified version of the style common in Spain in the 17th century, when earlier versions of Renaissance fashion had given way to somewhat more classical forms, but before Spanish builders had gone to the lengths of elaboration found in churches in Mexico." Craftsmen were imported from New England and marble came from as far away as Italy. Through the subsequent years, in addition to Sunday services, the chapel served as a community venue for weekly all-college forums.

While the chapel was under construction, the college received a gift from Mary Curtis Bok for a theatre to honor her friend Annie Russell, a highly successful and nationally known actress. The Kiehnel-designed Annie Russell Theatre was placed along side the Knowles Chapel and separated by a formal garden. Physically, spiritually and academically, the theatre-chapel complex now stood at the center of the campus representing the college's commitment to intellectual, artistic and spiritual values.[17]

Holt's other major addition to the college campus came with the construction of the Student Center and the Alumni House in 1942. The center's beautiful Florida style large interior, with its stylized Spanish design, whirling ceiling fans, snack bar and post office boxes, became the true social center of the campus for the next fifty years, serving as a place where the faculty and students gathered daily for coffee and conversation. Other buildings included four dormitories on the east side of the campus, which were connected by covered walkways, and five on the west side, also connected by covered walkways. A classroom building, Orlando Hall (1949), designed to accommodate the conference plan curriculum, the Mills Memorial Library (1951), the Warren Administration Building (1947), Casa Iberia (1944), the French House (1941) and finally two one-room buildings for social/academic meetings, Woolson(1938) and Sullivan Houses (1947), comprised the rest of the constructions. Thus, in addition to creating a quality progressive academic institution, Hamilton Holt had also left the college with a historic architecturally unified campus. The two accomplishments were deeply intertwined: the educational program was based on the progressive principle of individual student interest and perennial innovative change, while the unified Spanish-Mediterranean style reminded the college of the significance of community and unity of purpose.[18]

All of this construction came at a cost, and unless large sums of money suddenly began pouring into the college coffers for operating expenses, something had to be given in exchange. That "something," which came at the end of the college year in 1932, was faculty salaries. The payment of salaries in June 1932 had completely emptied the college treasury, and with a debt destined to soar over $300,000, banks declined to lend until the next academic year. With salaries for the summer months soon to be paid, Holt gave faculty the cheerless news: the college would withhold fifty percent of all salaries through the summer months. The trustees added an even more ominous note to the announcement: "If adverse financial conditions continue, faculty members may be requested a) to donate to Rollins College on or before October 15 a given percentage of the payments withheld as defined above, or b) to accept a percentage reduction in salaries for the year 1933; or c) to face a possible reduction in personnel." During the summer months, Holt and Fred Hanna, the president's new assistant, made valiant efforts to forestall any of these alternatives. "We have been wearing out automobile tires and shoe leather," Holt wrote a friend in August, "chasing around the country seeking whom we can financially devour. I confess it is gall and wormwood to beg in this strenuous way. I have gone to some of my real personal friends which I swore I would never do."[19]

By a combination of hard work and good luck, the administration managed to meet the July, August and September payrolls, but, with no further prospects, it decided to make additional economies. Following a meeting of the trustee finance committee in Connecticut on August 11, Holt wrote the faculty informing them their salaries would be reduced by 30 percent in the coming year.[36] The trustees hoped to repay this reduction, but Holt warned the faculty not to count on it. He deeply regretted the action and assured the faculty no one would blame them if they decided to leave Rollins to improve their personal situations. The "retain" caused serious hardship among the faculty who were receiving an average of only $1,800 per year, a sum well below that of southern sister colleges and, by Holt's own admission, less than half the average salary of northern institutions.

The faculty, without exception, chose to remain at Rollins but not without some grumbling. In autumn 1932, the faculty of the local AAUP delivered a pointed letter to the president complaining that extensive capital outlays, not large faculty salaries, had created the college's precarious financial predicament. The committee letter bluntly set forth the position: "an underpaid faculty now faced the prospect of paying for capital improvements made in the past by accepting a salary scale below their present living cost. The obligations of the college are thus being converted into private obligations of faculty members." Holt bristled at the tone of the letter and the barely hidden accusation his extravagant spending policy had caused the college's financial problems, but he made no reply. It is possible that Holt's spending policies and the corresponding loss of faculty income created a lingering resentment among the faculty that contributed to the Rice uprising. After Holt fired Rice and several of his colleagues, the administration announced that a 20 percent salary "retain" would now be entered in the books as a "donation" from the faculty to the college. Not a single voice of protest arose from the faculty ranks.[20]

Certain that he had exhausted every outside resource available to the college, particularly after the Rice affair, and determined that the faculty would not further shoulder the burden of college finances, Holt decided that the students would pay a larger share of the cost of their education. In the fall of 1933, the administration announced its innovative tuition program called the "unit cost plan."[21] Starkly uncomplicated, the plan divided the annual operating budget by the estimated enrollment producing a unit cost per student. In the year 1933–1934, with a budget of $675,000 and an estimated 500 students, the new unit cost came to $1,350, an increase of $400 per student over the previous year. Endowment income was used to assist students unable to pay the higher fees. With the nation at the nadir of economic depression, it was a bold (some would argue potentially disastrous) move to increase tuition so drastically, but the college had prepared a compelling, equalitarian explanation for its "simple scientific and concrete" new plan. In the past, Holt argued, society had justified meager student contributions (half of the actual cost) because graduates entered some form of public service such as the fields of ministry or teaching. In the 20th century, students attended college for personal or professional considerations. "It would seem therefore that under these changed conditions, the well-to-do students should be expected to pay for the benefits received, and the endowment income in gifts heretofore distributed equally throughout the student body should go to those unable to pay the full cost of education."[21] In another rationalization, the administration depicted the unit cost plan as "the third noteworthy step in Rollins' progressive educational development" and "our third academic departure from existing college practices." The college, Holt implied, had completed the progressive circle: the conference plan humanized teaching; the new curriculum individualized learning, the unit cost plan democratized college financing where the burden of cost was shared by those able to pay.[22] This was Holt at the philosophical heights of his progressive thought. It was precisely where many of the progressive faculty wanted to take the college before the Rice debacle.

Theoretically, the additional monies accruing from increased tuition would balance the budget, but, in fact, the plan never lived up to its expectations. Probably because of the higher fees, student enrollment dropped by 100 in 1933-34, with a corresponding loss in anticipated funds. Moreover, the college had promised exemption for currently enrolled students from the rate increase to if those students could show that they would have to "leave the college if required to meet the increase." That number proved much higher than expected (most likely because many students whose families could afford $1,350 tuition too easily convinced the administration they could not pay), further diminishing anticipated income. In addition, two-thirds of the student body received some kind of aid. Altogether, the total income from students actually fell in 1933-34, and in the first year of the unit cost plan the college still ran a deficit of over $46,000.[22]

In 1936, the Treasurer Brown was forced to announce that the unit cost plan was less than a success. "We adopted it too soon," he told Holt. "Our clientele was not firmly enough established; we did not have uniform housing conditions, and in general we had no physical attraction to justify such a move." Enrollment had dropped by 25 percent, meaning another deficit at the end of the academic year.[24] A memorandum to faculty in 1939 indicated how much of a toll the depression was taking on the college's finances: "Due to the fall of Rollins securities and the interests on our endowments the last few years of the depression, we are about at the end of our borrowing capacity and if Rollins is to get "over the hill" in 1939–1940 we must have an increase in the number of full paying students. It seems to me the faculty, whose future employment and salaries depend upon the success of the college, could devote sufficient time this summer to securing one such student." In the fall of 1941, increased enrollment raised hopes the college may be "over the hill." The Japanese attack on Pearl Harbor in December dashed all optimism overnight.

The war years, coming on the heels of the Great Depression, meant even more travails for Rollins. Male students left campus in large numbers for military service or defense jobs. The slow enrollment decline of 1941–1942 became an avalanche in 1943, and in 1945 only 250 students registered for the fall term. In that year, fewer than 30 female and no male graduates received Bachelor of Arts degrees from Rollins. The college enrollment remained constant at about 200 throughout the last years of the war.[23]

The administration began its own war on the declining enrollment and decreasing funds. Retrenchment was the keyword. Through retirement, leaves of absence and non-reappointments, the faculty was cut from 80 to 40, and course offerings were trimmed to bare essentials. The list of courses in the 1940 catalogue covered nearly forty pages. In 1945, it occupied only 17. In November 1942, Holt asked the faculty for a $20,000 "retain," assigning to a faculty committee the determination of apportionment. These reductions, plus a cut in maintenance funds, permitted Holt to reduce the budget by 23 per cent. The college then embarked upon a campaign dubbed by Holt the "war adjustment financial program," a title suspiciously similar to the familiar President Roosevelt's national war agencies.[24]

The administration also attracted Army and Navy training units to the campus, a move that not only generated desperately needed funds, but also brought a male constituency during the war years. The training personnel occupied several dormitories and used Pinehurst as military headquarters. Service men marching to and from classes and holding retreat on the horseshoe in the evening brought the community face to face with the reality of war. Despite these valiant efforts, the ubiquitous debt continued to accumulate, but doors remained open during ehich even Holt admitted were the college's darkest hours. Several times Holt stood against the pressure of the O'Neal group to close the college for the duration. The commencement of 1945, just after the surrender of Germany and two months before Japan's capitulation, graduated only 32 females and 2 males. Nonetheless the college was still alive, poised to take advantage of four years of suppressed educational demands.[25]

With war's end in August 1945, students inundated the college with applications. The fall term began with the largest freshman class in the history of the institution, and, by January 1946, total enrollment reached a record high of 534. One year later it stood at 640. For a decade the administration had been laboring toward such a favorable situation. However, the growth in enrollment proved to be a mixed blessing because the sudden increase caught the college woefully unprepared. Even before the war, one half of Rollins' students had lived in substandard housing, and little money went for repairs in the years thereafter. The college faced skyrocketing enrollment with not only a housing shortage, but also with the pressing needs of deferred maintenance. Expanding facilities and providing the necessary repairs, all at inflated prices, placed expenses far beyond anticipation, even with the increased income from the surge of new students. Moreover, to align its tuition and costs in accordance with similar institutions, Rollins discontinued the unit cost plan, lowering tuition and room and board charges. An embattled Holt prepared another (and final) financial offensive: the "victory expansion program." By

1948, he had raised several thousands in new money and had received pledges from Frances Knowles Warren for a new administration building, from philanthropist Henry Strong for a new dormitory, from the citizens of Orlando for a new classroom building and from the Davella Mills Foundation for a new library.[26]

In the midst of this optimistic turn in the college's financial fortunes, Holt had to deal with a serious personnel problem. When he authorized an increase in faculty salaries to meet inflation costs, Treasurer Brown flatly rejected the proposal. As in the Rice affair, Holt found himself in a power struggle, this time with his own treasurer. Now, however, he had the support of the students and the faculty.

At a special meeting in June 1948, Holt told the Board of Trustees that no one questioned Brown's loyalty or dedication but his behavior had alienated a large portion of the college community. He asked the trustees to discharge Brown and then to amend the bylaws making the treasurer report directly to the president. Because a large majority of the trustees were Holt's nominees, and because he had the support of virtually the entire college community, the president undoubtedly felt assured of a favorable vote.

Apparently, Holt was unaware of Brown's strong standing in the Winter Park community, or the strength of the treasurer's support from the board. In a close vote, the trustees not only rejected Holt's bylaw amendment, but also answered his demand for Brown's dismissal with a resounding resolution proclaiming "complete confidence in the Treasurer's professional ability and competence." Stunned, Holt delivered an impassioned extemporaneous speech accusing the trustees of ignoring "unanimous opinion of the students and of the faculty and now of myself. I respect your right to vote for or against me but, honestly, I do not think I can come back to the campus and do much good. When students and faculty comes to me next fall asking about his meeting today, I do not want to be put in a position of feeling I have to defend you. I cannot defend you. I take my stand right here and now with the faculty and students and as I have lost confidence in you and you have lost confidence in me, I think it's better that I ask you to release me from coming back to Rollins next year. This is the hardest thing I have had to do in my life but I do not believe you would respect me if I did not do it."

Faced with the unwelcome possibility of starting a school year with a vacant presidential office and a disgruntled college community, Brown's supporters made a hasty retreat and the board moved promptly to salvage a suddenly deteriorating situation. One of Holt's supporters moved and the board adopted a resolution stating the trustees interpreted the bylaws to give the president "final authority over all activities and personnel of the college." Holt agreed to return in September. Brown resigned in December 1948.[29]

Holt replaced Brown with Assistant Professor of economics John M. Tiedtke, a graduate of Dartmouth College's Tuck Business School and a businessman with land holdings in Florida. Tiedtke and Holt immediately "went north," and, after a few weeks, they negotiated a loan with Connecticut Mutual Life Insurance Company. The college paid its debts for the year, surmounting what Holt called "the gravest crisis that has ever confronted Rollins College." Holt always believed that John Tiedtke's "leadership and devotion saved Rollins" in his hour of desperation. In complete agreement, the trustees named Tiedtke treasurer of the college.[30]

However unsettling the Brown crisis, Holt always thought the outcome of that struggle was his most satisfying victory for no other reason than he had the college community solidly behind him. Coming on the heels of the Rice incident, where he seemed to be battling former friends and students, the Brown affair had provided Holt with a stage to dramatically display his best qualities. He often told others that his spontaneous speech before the Board of Trustees on June 28, when he courageously placed his career on the line, was his finest hour. He sent the speech to Dean Wendell Stone suggesting he circulate copies to students and faculty as well. "I would like them to know some way," he mused, "that it was largely because I have tried to fight their battle that I have taken the stand that I have." When he returned in September, he found the college community more affectionate and loyal than at any time during his presidency. However, Holt had fought his last battle. The board had already formed a committee to search for the aging president's successor. Holt's call to service almost 30 years earlier was coming to an end. The academic year of 1948-1949 would be his last at Rollins.

Hamilton Holt had a profoundly deep impact on Rollins College. His influence on the life of the college community and on the college's future is almost incalculable. He came to the institution when it was teetering on the edge of extinction, pulled the college from that abyss, provided it with stability and then guided it into the world of academic respectability. But most importantly, he gave the college a new identity. By the end of the Holt era, the Rollins community saw itself as a progressive institution, as a place where academic experiment and innovation were not just tolerated, but also encouraged and even expected. This progressive democratic spirit permeated the entire college life, giving faculty, students and staff a sense of ownership in the community. Despite his sometimes arbitrary paternalism and at other times his sense of entitlement, Holt left the entire community with a feeling of empowerment, giving all the belief they could play a role in shaping the future of the college. This became another source for Rollins' identification. Future leaders who ignored or remained ignorant of this democratic tradition found themselves in serious conflict with the college community.

Holt's ability to lead the college through these fundamental changes was his greatest strength, but also a grave weakness. As we have seen, the expression "Holt is Rollins, Rollins is Holt" was more than a catchy expression. Holt actually internalized this view of his presidency. Within a decade after he assumed the leadership of the college, he was unable to separate the institution and its policies from his personal ambitions. Holt saw any attempt to question or change certain aspects of the college community as a personal attack on him. Particularly at those times when his authority was challenged, Holt never left any doubt that Rollins was **his** college. This attitude was a fateful flaw. Holt began to see differences over policy as personally threatening. At such times, he behaved uncharacteristically imperious.

This possessiveness had an even more lasting effect. The

latter half of his life was so intertwined with the life of the college Holt simply could not let go of Rollins. So much of him would be lost if he stepped down. Thus, at a time when most college presidents rarely served more than a decade, making way for fresh leadership, Holt held on three times that long, almost half the institution's history. Only ill health led him to retire. A poignant photograph was taken at his last commencement. He is sitting alone in a chair on the commencement stage seemingly lost in contemplation, perhaps recalling the memories of the glorious time he had building a great institution.

Hamilton Holt's unusually lengthy tenure meant that he cast a long, imposing shadow which was not altogether healthy for the college. Prolonged incumbencies provided much needed continuity and stability, but they left an institution with a potentially serious problem. Such was the case with Holt's drawn-out presidency. Only a very special person would be able to respect the Holt legacy and at the same time move beyond Holt's shadow to give the college the benefit of new progressive leadership. Holt's successor would inherit the very delicate and difficult task of navigating between an institution molded by a beloved president and the necessity of responding to the dramatic educational changes taking place in the post-war era. Clearly, one of the chief challenges facing the new president would be negotiating the Holt legacy.

1. Holt to Gehring, October 29, 1928; Holt, "Ideals For the Development of Rollins College."

2. Holt to Dewitt Keech, May 10, 1926; Holt to John Rice, June 13, 1930; Holt to George Kirchway, June 15, 1931.

3. The Holt and Harris friendship lasted for over two decades. For an analysis of the curious relationship between a Northeastern liberal and Southern racist see my article "Race and the Hamilton Holt/Corra Harris Friendship," at scholarship.rollins.edu/cgi/view content.

4. France to Holt, January 10, 1928; I have reconstructed France's career from his autobiography, *My Native Grounds* (1957). For a fuller discussion of France's life and career see Jack C. Lane, "Introduction" to a reprint of the autobiography. scholarship.rollins.edu.

5. Carol Hemingway Gardner to Author, October 3, 1979.

6. Report of Charles Judd, January 27, 1930. Rockefeller Foundation

7. Catalogue, 1927; Comment by the authors in *Flamingo*, 1927; H.E. Hawkes Report on Rollins, January 27, 1930. Rockefeller Foundation Archives; Holt to Gehring <no date>. Dee Brown from George Washington University and later the author of the best selling book *Bury My Heart At Wounded Knee*, won Third Prize that year.

8. Carol H. Gardner to author.

9. This paragraph comes from a delightfully written essay by Mary Seymour (daughter of President Thaddeus Seymour) published in the *Rollins Magazine,* Fall, 2014.

Not every artist accepted President Holt request. Holt had published Robert Frost's first poems in the *Independent* and assumed the poet would repay the favor. Frost refused, writing: "I can never be drawn into a show like your living magazine. People have learned that my modest kind of entertainment is better when it has the occasion all to myself." Frost to Holt, December, 1936.in the Holt Papers.

10. Trustee Minutes, April, 1926; Treasurer's Report, 1927; Holt to Milton Warner, November 8, 1927.

11. O'Neal to Holt, July 16, 1927; Holt to O'Neal, July 25, 1927.

12. Trustee Minutes, June 6, 1928.

13. Brown to Holt, August 2, 14, 1928; December 15, 1928; O'Neal to Holt, November 22, 1928; August 2, 1928.

14. President's Annual Report, 1929; Trustee Minutes, December 1919.

15. Gehring to Holt, January 31, 1929; Kenneth Wilson, "Recollections" Manuscript, Holt Papers; Holt to Bingham, February 8, 1930; Holt to Gehring, January 31, 1930.

16. Holt to Harold Strong, April 29, 1931.

17. Trustee Minutes, February 19, 1930.

18. *Ibid.*, May 1931.

19. *Ibid.*, October 1932. October 1932; President's Annual Report, 1933

20. Rollins AAUP Committee to Holt, January 21, 1933; Holt's Statement on Rice Affair, April, i933.

21. Holt seems to have first conceived the idea of the unit cost plan after hearing from the Rockefeller Foundation. College literature claimed that the plan was a "program entirely new in college finance." President Robert Leigh of Bennington College quickly informed Holt that his college had used the method since 1928. Leigh to Holt, March 13, 1934; Holt to Leigh, April 19, 1934.

22. *Rollins Record*, November, 1933.

23. Carlton South to Dean Anderson, June 18, 1934; Brown to Holt, August 7, 1934.

24. Treasurer's Report, 1934; Trustee Minutes, April, May 1934; Bingham to Holt, May 14, 1934; Brown to Holt, May 23, 1935.

25. Catalogue, 1940-45.

26. *Ibid.*; Professor George Waddington to Holt, November 10, 1942; "Brochure" WAP, March, 1942; *Sandspur*, March 18, 1943; Brown to O'Neal July 31, 1942; Holt to Anderson, October 13, 1943; O'Neal to holt, July 22, August 8, 1943.

27. Catalogue, 1946.

28. Trustee Minutes, March 1948.

29. Treasurer's Report, 1948; Holt to Trustees, December 12, 1948; Mrs. Stanley Cleveland to Mrs. Warren, May 30, 1948; Brown Memo to Trustees. June 19, 1948.Report from the Faculty Administration Board, February 1948.

30. Trustee Minutes, February 1948. Holt to Wendell Stone, July 2, 1948; Holt to Trustees, July 2, 1948; Trustee Minutes, September 1948. Holt to Stone, July 2, 1948.

Chapter 8

A LEGACY OF THE HOLT ERA: THE WAGNER AFFAIR, 1949–1952

AT THE BOARD of Trustees' request, Holt agreed to inter-view the candidates for his replacement and make recom-mendations before he left for his home in Connecticut. One morning, while Holt was meeting with a prospective candi-date, a man walked into the president's outer room and declared, within earshot of the candidate in Holt's office, he would like to interview for the Rollins presidency. It was an awkward, embarrassing moment for Holt. The visitor was told to come back later. Holt did not see the man until well into the evening, and even then he did so with great reluctance. It was late in the day and Holt was tired. He was prepared to dismiss this impulsive creature who had rudely marched into his office seemingly off the street. As the man launched into a speech about how well qualified he was for the Rollins presidency, Holt thought him brash and egotistical, the kind of super-salesman personality that warred against Holt's New England sensibilities. But, as the evening wore on, Holt began to change his mind. He found him more and more appealing and by the time the man left, Holt had decided to recommend him to the search committee. On May 31, 1949, the Board of Trustees unanimously elected Paul Wagner, Rollins' ninth president.

The unorthodox way in which Wagner came to be appointed president of Rollins College was perfectly consistent with his past performances—and it was a performance because Paul Wagner was nothing if not theatrical. Like a professional actor upon a stage of his own choosing, he overwhelmed Holt, the search committee, the faculty and students and finally the Board of Trustees with a series of stunning interview performances. He often captivated his audience with novel audio-visual presentations, a new technology, he argued convincingly, that would transform American education. He was attracted to Rollins, he told admiring college audiences, because of its tradition of educational innovation and experimentation, as a place receptive to new educational ideas.[1]

To those who knew him well, Wagner's extraordinary interview performance would have come as no surprise. A mere account of this 33-year-old phenomenon's meteoric career left most people breathless. With eyesight severely weakened at an early age by a measles attack, he struggled through elementary and secondary school by listening to his mother read to him and by taking all of his examinations orally. Despite this handicap, he graduated with high grades from high school at the age of 16. His sight weakness outgrown, he completed four years of work at the University of Chicago in three years, acquiring his B.A. degree at the age of 19. While teaching English in a Chicago secondary school during his senior year, Wagner drew wide attention with his innovative use of audio-visual material. Impressed by the young teacher's effort, the head of Chicago's Department of Education offered Wagner a teaching position at the University's Experimental High School, originally headed by John Dewey and based on his progressive educational theory. Wagner remained in Chicago for three years, left for a year to earn a master's degree at Yale and then returned to the university as an instructor.

Throughout these years, he had been experimenting with the use of film and other visual aids in teaching. At the outbreak of war in 1941, Wagner offered his services to the Great Lakes Naval Training School where he perfected the use of graphics in training recruits. Impressed by his innovations, the Navy Department offered him an officer's commission to introduce audio-visuals at the Naval War College. Wagner created the Navy's first audio-visual laboratory where he developed training aids and made hundreds of indoctrinatory motion pictures. After the war, he accepted a position at Bell & Howell, a leading photography company. He was eager, however, to return to education. In the summer of 1949, when he learned that Rollins was looking for a new president, Wagner hurried to Rollins College on an impulse.

The public announcement of Wagner's appointment caused a national sensation rivaling that of Holt's. The tall, handsome new president, with a winning smile and a Hollywood persona, was greeted as if he were an academic celebrity. At 33, he was the nation's youngest college president. Only Robert Hutchins, Wagner's mentor, had been younger (age 30) when he assumed the presidency of the University of Chicago. In fact, most news reports of Wagner's appointment drew implicit comparisons between the two men. *Newsweek* made Wagner's appointment its major educational story of the week. In a three-page article, *Collier's* magazine called him "Education's New Boy Wonder." It depicted him in very flattering terms as a dynamic, even brilliant, young man full of novel ideas on how to make Rollins a better college. Wagner's inauguration attracted over fifty college presidents including, appropriately, Robert Hutchins, who served as the keynote speaker. Wagner seemed a worthy successor to the beloved Hamilton Holt and a perfect fit for a college known for its academic experimentation.[2]

During the first months of his administration, Wagner appeared to exceed these large expectations. In his inaugural address and in his formal and informal conversations with the faculty and students, he talked of continuing the principles of Hamilton Holt, particularly Rollins' progressive tradition. A January 1950 editorial in the *Sandspur* proclaimed he was governing with these convictions: "Dr. Wagner has already achieved his goal of establishing a friendly sort of basis between himself, the faculty and the students." Most faculty members, in retrospect, invariably commented on the favorable impression Wagner made in these early months.[3]

Only a couple of early incidents clouded the bright beginning for the young president. In the fall of 1949, in the midst of football season, Wagner decreed the demise of that program. The announcement sent a small tremor through the campus. Hadn't he traveled with the team, even diagramming a few plays at half time, and hadn't he told some students Rollins would have a football team as long as he was president? He had, but he found it impossible to reconcile that commitment with the sport's $50,000 annual deficit. The trustees persuaded him to drop the football program after the 1949-1950 season. He told the community the administration might have to discontinue other inter-collegiate sports after January 1951 if they too reported deficits.

Wagner cleverly diffused a potentially explosive student reaction by holding a two-hour meeting with the entire student body. He not only convinced them the football team was not worth the deficit, but he also sold them on the idea of a substitute program of useful life-long sports such as golf, tennis, swimming, sailing and perhaps even chess. Students, who had entered the Annie Russell Theatre meeting initially hostile, burst into applause after Wagner's performance. It was model exhibition of salesmanship.[4]

A second ripple of concern came during Wagner's first year, as he began to shape his own administrative staff. Almost immediately friction developed between former President Holt's dean of men, Arthur Enyart, and the new president. The 68-year-old dean had served Rollins since 1911 and he had become almost as beloved as Hamilton Holt. He rivaled Holt's title as "Mr. Rollins." From the beginning the aging dean had trouble adjusting to Wagner's youthful style. After a stormy meeting where Wagner exclaimed that he was tired of Enyart's constant "infantile" behavior (he was particularly speaking of Enyart's opposition to dropping football), the old dean announced his resignation. Wagner may have had sufficient reasons for losing his patience with someone who perhaps should have retired earlier, but his behavior toward Enyart alienated many of the dean's friends, some of whom were influential alumni who held deep affection for Enyart. It was not a propitious beginning for the young president.

With the Enyart problem behind him, Wagner turned his attention to other issues. Typical of all new presidents, he wanted to know the overall condition of the college. He gave the Dean of the College Wendell Stone the task of conducting what Stone referred to as a "lengthy and exceedingly complicated" survey of the college's economic and academic condition. He then appointed Horace (Tolly) Tollefson, the current director of the library, as his executive assistant and "coordinator." Former presidents had involved the entire Rollins community in such institutional assessments, which allowed all constituencies to claim ownership of and take responsibility for the outcome. The arbitrary decision to name only two individuals to conduct such a study was not only unprecedented; it also raised serious questions concerning the new president's governing style. Was this decision simply the result of his inexperience in college administration or, even more seriously, did this arise from an imperious personality? Or was it both?[5] The college community needed answers to the questions because a combination of inexperience and imperiousness could prove pernicious.

The arbitrary appointments came as a complete surprise to the college community since it flatly contradicted Wagner's statements about the way he would govern. He was attracted to Rollins, he often repeated, because of its progressive democratic traditions. In his inaugural address, he spoke at length of the need to take seriously the idea of a democratic institution where everyone would be encouraged to participate. Whatever changes made at Rollins, he told the inauguration audience, would be the result of the participation of the entire college community. Future plans for the college, he promised, would be "fashioned by the faculty, staff and student body. Only by experiencing life in a truly democratic community can we hope to develop a true and abiding faith in democracy."[6]

Although those early appointments of Stone and Tollefsen caused only a ripple of grumbling among the faculty, those concerns deepened when Wagner began to rely on his own staff rather the college governance structure (faculty committees and faculty meetings) for the development and implementation of policies. He frequently presented the college with *fait accomplis*. The community never debated, for example, about the termination of the football program. Wagner simply informed faculty and students of the necessity for abolishing the sport. As a result, many remained unconvinced that the team could not have been saved, although few objected its abolishment.

A more serious uneasiness arose later when Wagner announced he intended to launch an "educational aim study" designed to revise the curriculum. By his own admission, this approach was unconventional. Rather than following the traditional method of appointing a special faculty/staff committee to organize such a study, he asked each individual faculty member to submit a report based on an outline of "what every educated adult should know about factual information, general knowledge, attitude, appreciation, techniques." Many faculty members resented this extra burden heaped upon them during the summer vacation and became irritably impatient as they tried to grapple with what one called "a rigid, inelastic, superficial approach that left out vast areas of learning." Stone himself thought it showed a lack of understanding of the liberal arts. More important, the faculty sensed that in the areas of traditional prerogatives and responsibilities, their only contribution would be merely to provide information to the administration, while the president would determine significant educational policy decisions. This was not their view of democratic governance.[7]

Subsequently, nothing came of the "educational aim study" because, in the fall of 1950, rumblings of serious financial problems surfaced. Despite knowledge of the college's perennial deficit during the Holt era, the faculty was surprised by the news. The new administration had consistently issued cheery financial reports in the past few years. As late as the September 1950 meeting, Treasurer John Tiedtke had announced "that the position of the college was financially sound and that it had been for two years." But underneath the optimistic facade, the administration was deeply worried about the college's future. Two external pressures on enrollment caused concern. First, as with most institutions of higher learning, rampant post-war inflation threatened to deplete the college's already meager treasury. Between the end of World War II and 1950 the cost of operating a college had soared nearly 70 percent, causing even prestigious institutions to run deficits. Second, World War II veterans, who had been responsible for a swell in the number of college enrollments, suddenly were no longer enrolling in large numbers. Many colleges were left with dangerously over-expanded programs, buildings, staff and faculty. These difficult problems were exacerbated by the outbreak of the Korean War. A call for military manpower mobilization threatened to deprive the college of an additional portion of its male population.[8]

When the college opened the 1950–1951 academic year, all these forces began to weigh heavily on the mind of the youthful president. Congress had authorized only a partial manpower mobilization with exemptions for qualified college-bound young men. But what this meant for college enrollment, no one knew. In December, Wagner attended a Washington conference for 400 college presidents and returned with a pessimistic report. The Defense Department predicted that, after the election in November, Congress would authorize the drafting of all 18-year olds. Still, Wagner reported to the faculty that many politicians disagreed with the Defense Department's predictions. All this, he noted, made "crystal gazing very difficult." The report left Rollins' future very much in the air, and Wagner inserted yet another uncomfortable observation: "In the event that we should lose 200 of the 356 men to the draft, there are several possible but undesirable answers including a reduction of faculty and staff." At the end of his report to the faculty he added the United States Commissioner of Education had told him nothing in the past fifty years would affect higher education as greatly as a national mobilization.[9]

During the fall of 1950, Wagner tried to meet this impending crisis in two ways. As a way of combatting communist propaganda, the United States State Department created a Meet America Program (MAP) aimed at educating foreign students in this country. Wagner presented a proposal to bring 400 to 600 Latin American citizens to Rollins, for a period of six months, where they would be taught American traditions and values. The State Department showed interest, encouraging the college to submit a detailed proposal. The president involved almost all faculty members at a cost of hundreds of man-hours of labor. In the end it came to naught. Somewhere in the labyrinth of the State Department bureaucracy, it simply disappeared.

At this point, Wagner's style of governance led to ruinous consequences. Instead of involving the community in solving what he perceived to be a looming enrollment problem, he took sole responsibility himself. Without consulting the faculty, Wagner appointed Wendell Stone to collect and analyze information on the college's probable economic condition for the 1951-1952 academic year. Specifically, he wanted Stone to determine probable enrollment for the following year by investigating the validity of draft deferments and by estimating the dropout possibilities for winter. While working with Dean of Admissions John Rich, Stone was expected to "plot the probable number of men and women we can reasonably expect to be admitted next fall."

The president told Stone, using these estimates, to determine the probable income for 1951-1952. The college, he said, must "play it safe by assuming that the total amount of student fees will be the operating budget for the coming year." It would not depend on endowments to cover debt payments, nor would it rely on "gifts of free money" because such funds constituted an exceedingly doubtful factor. Wagner also instructed Stone not to count on State Department MAP contracts or on the possibility of obtaining a ROTC unit. Finally, he instructed Stone to estimate next year's operating costs and to specify what cuts would be required in order to balance the budget. Wagner left no doubt that on the basis of this proposal some faculty and staff would be dismissed. The actual number would depend on the size of the gap between the operating budget and the income from student fees. The president then gave Stone the most painful charge: on the assumption cuts were necessary, Stone was to construct "a system of related values for determining who would be dropped."

Wagner admitted to Stone much guesswork would be involved in this survey but "if we err," he told the dean, "I hope it would be on the side of being too pessimistic rather than too optimistic." The college could always hire or rehire additional faculty and staff, but "the opposite surprise would leave us in an embarrassing position of having contractual obligations we would not be able to fulfill." Such a study ordinarily would take a group of people an entire year to complete. Wagner asked Stone to finish the survey by February 1, so he could "digest, discuss and articulate it to the Board of Trustees at the February 1951 meeting."

Through a herculean effort of working night and day, on February 1, Stone was able to present Wagner the results of his efforts. They were precisely what the new President suspected—a very pessimistic evaluation of the present and future conditions of the college. Treasurer John Tiedtke's equally gloomy financial predictions gave Wagner the final information he needed to present the trustees with a comprehensive plan to deal with a coming budget crisis.[10]

At the February meeting of the Board of Trustees, Wagner found himself again in the familiar role of the super-salesman. True to his reputation, he gave the board a performance of a virtuoso. Armed with a plethora of visual material (graphs, charts, scales) and spontaneously constructing his own charts and messages on large sheets of paper, ripping and casting them aside as he talked, Wagner completely awed and overwhelmed the trustees with his apparent grasp of the present and future prospects of the institution. Not in war nor in peace nor in depression had the college ever faced such a crisis, Wagner informed the trustees. With a message businessmen would understand, he warned them that the college would have to face decisions in a "tough minded way." Businessmen, he said, lived not in a "romantic" but in a "realistic" world, and a college "is in effect a business." We are, he said, "in a corporation selling a highly competitive commodity, college education." Seen from this perspective, he argued, the college must balance its budget in the following academic year. It must reject the financial philosophy of "embrace deficits and pray for gifts" or "pay now and pray later" and make once and for all the tough-minded decision to spend no more than its income.

Regretfully, he said, 88 percent of that income came from student fees, and the recent national draft policy had made student enrollment highly volatile. Thus, in determining the budget, he concluded, the college must start with admissions. With his graphs and charts he presented the board the dismal enrollment numbers he had predicted after his Washington trip and with the aid of the admissions office. All colleges, including Rollins, expected a 30 percent drop in enrollment. The admissions office reported an already-serious decrease of 25 percent per week in applications from the previous year. Thus, Wagner continued, he was planning for a total of 449 students, a decline of 29 percent or 200 students. He thought these were not "hysterical figures"; if anything, they were too optimistic. "If you ask me to swear that we will get more than this number, I just wouldn't; if you ask me to swear that we will not get more than this number I will swear it." Finally, Wagner told them these were not short-term conditions. He predicted the situation would last at least seven years.

All these figures and data led Wagner to his major point. If the 1951–1952 budget depended entirely on income from student fees, then given the precipitous drop in student enrollment, the college faced a sizable decrease in income. In fact, Wagner estimated a decrease of over $150,000. To balance the budget would require a $150,000 cut in expenditures. John Tiedtke, he said, after decreasing costs by $39,000 last year, had figured out a $77,000 cut for 1951-1952. The only area of expenditures that had not felt the cutting knife was the educational program budget. Now, Wagner proclaimed, the time had come to make one of those tough-minded decisions. He recommended decreasing the educational budget by $87,000, a move requiring the release of 15 to 20 faculty members.[11]

The trustees were overwhelmed by Wagner's performance. The president's argument seemed logical, but most of them found it impossible to absorb all those figures and statistics in one gulp. Several times Wagner had scribbled figures on large newsprint, had ripped them from the board, crumbled them, and thrown them on the floor. He presented, however, no information in the form of a written report, and neither did he offer alternatives. He explored other plans, he explained, but, with the exception of the one he presented, all others were found wanting.

Tiedtke and Stone followed Wagner's performance, but neither had any advance knowledge of the details of the president's presentation. Wagner had turned their research to his own purposes. Tiedtke conceded that, because of the perennial deficit, the college had lost or would soon lose its borrowing power. "I understand," he explained, "the terror of trying to raise money when you have gone the limit to your ability to borrow." He believed if "the college ran into that situation again," it would surely go under. But Tiedtke was also concerned with the potentially serious consequences of retrenchment. Rollins, he said, offered premium education. "We have a Cadillac assembly line and we cannot turn out Cadillacs without fenders or radiators or wheels; nor can we turn out Fords for we are not built that way." He was worried that dismissing professors and reducing courses would damage the college's reputation for quality education. None of this, he pointed out with some compassion, consid-

ers the human suffering that would ensue from a retrenchment policy. The treasurer had no solutions to offer, but he
asked the trustees to consider all of the ramifications of a
deep faculty cut, again offering a stark analogy: "I look at
this very much like a cancer. To save your life you may have
to amputate your hand, but it's a serious matter to amputate
your hand." He could not predict faculty reaction to a cut,
but he did warn of a possible "kickback from the students."
In general, Tiedtke presented a less-than-cheery report
whose tone and even substance supported Wagner's basic
premises.[12]

Stone, who had not known how Wagner would use his
months of research, presented a picture of faculty hardship
already brought on by low salaries. Many, he said, moon-
lighted simply to make ends meet. Here again, as in Tiedtke's
report, Stone's dismal presentation reinforced Wagner's
report since the president had argued his plan would allow
the college to raise the salaries of those who remained.[12]

After these discouraging reports and gloomy forecasts,
the trustees voted unanimously in favor of Wagner's recommendations. They then issued an ominous public statement:
"Because of present conditions which seriously impair the
financial security of Rollins as well as other colleges, it has
become necessary to curtail expenses. The Board of Trustees reluctantly instructs the President to reduce the faculty
in the various divisions to conform to the budget voted by
the Board according to the following plan: Faculty members
aside from the following exceptions shall be retained in
accordance with seniority in their area of study. Exceptions to the seniority factor: 1) Part-time instructors may

be retained if it appears financially advisable to do so. 2) All regular faculty members with Social Security benefits at the end of the academic year 1951-1952 would retire. 3) Retention would include a professor who is the only one in a division qualified to teach a particular subject that is considered essential."[13]

Having dispensed with the matter of the budget and faculty cuts, the board's executive committee members, who had prior knowledge of Wagner's proposal and unanimously supported it, moved abruptly to solidify Wagner's position at the college in preparation for a predictably unfavorable reaction against this plan. The trustees unanimously voted the president a $2,000 raise beginning in March, 1951, and promised him a $500 annual increase until his salary reached $15,000. They concluded with a declaration of unconditional support for the president: "The Board of Trustees recognizes and appreciates the intelligent and thorough manner in which Dr. Wagner has carried on the work of his office, has analyzed the problems of Rollins and has presented constructive plans for the future of the institution."

The following day, February 28, the executive committee handed the Board of Trustees additional motions. The first recommended that Wagner be given a 10-year contract in order to protect the president from possible opposition to the retrenchment policy. Several board members vigorously opposed this unprecedented step, but eventually agreed to compromise on a five-year agreement. As a final bulwark, the board cemented the authority of the president in a by-law amendment, stating that "the president shall have the sole power to hire and discharge employees and to fix administrative and educational policies of the college subject to the veto of the Board of Trustees." Although several trustees were dismayed by the effort to cover the president with monetary awards and verbal accolades and to increase his power and authority, they did not oppose the motions. A few, however, expressed their opposition by recording their abstentions. Most must have left that February meeting with an uneasy feeling about the propriety, and perhaps even the ethics, of raising a president's salary and handing him a five-year contract while simultaneously voting to deprive 25 faculty members of their sole means of support.[14]

Although they had discussed the methods of faculty dismissal, the board chose to leave the selection of individual choices to the president. Wagner thought to involve the faculty in the decision process, but he reconsidered when it became obvious that the number would exceed earlier expectations. Asking the faculty to dismiss one-third of its membership, he concluded, would "have created an impossible psychological situation." He now began to study the report on the faculty provided by Wendell Stone. Stone's survey of the personal financial conditions of most faculty members indicated that from 15 to 20 were financially secure or able to survive a year's leave of absence. He also provided the president with an analysis of departmental conditions, in which he identified those areas where dismissals would most harm the college academically. In addition, Wagner requested from Tiedtke a list of faculty he expected to be financially secure following dismissal. The treasurer found himself in unfamiliar territory. He finally submitted a list but not without considerable prodding from the president.

With this information and with the criteria stipulated by the Board of Trustees, Wagner began constructing a list of faculty who would be required to leave at the end of the academic year.[15]

In the midst of this effort, the president appeared before a regularly scheduled faculty meeting on March 5. In an abbreviated repetition of his trustee presentation, Wagner informed the faculty of the new retrenchment policies. The board, he told them, had voted to reduce the present budget and it would be necessary to cut student scholarships, to reduce faculty salaries and later to make additional operational reductions. Even so, the college would still carry a deficit that would allow for no contingencies. Some faculty would have to be let go. He presented the board's "mathematical formula" for faculty dismissals. These objective criteria, he explained, were designed to obviate the need to make judgments on a personal basis. He added a chilling warning: for obvious reasons there would be "no appeal and no discussion" following the announcement of dismissals. The faculty left the meeting reeling from the news they had just heard.[16]

The president had staged another dazzling performance. His massive array of figures and his logical explanations were overwhelming. Like the trustees, the faculty was stunned into silence. How could they respond when they had seen nothing on paper, nothing concrete to ponder and nothing to analyze? Wagner permitted no questions, but even if he had, the faculty probably would have been unprepared for queries. They understood the desperate financial situation, but so many questions remained unanswered. Who developed the "mathematical formula?" What did the criteria for dismissal mean? Who, in fact, could remember those criteria? In this condition of uncertainty and confusion, each faculty member undoubtedly searched for and found reasons to believe he or she did not fit the predetermined formula. At the Monday meeting, Wagner had promised to issue letters of dismissal immediately. But the first letter was not forthcoming until late Wednesday afternoon, and the majority of them did not appear until Thursday. In the interim, faculty members hovered before their mailboxes in extreme personal anxiety. As Royal France later expressed it: "For two breathless days the axe hung suspended over faculty heads, no one knowing who was to be decapitated and soon anger rose alongside fear."[17]

The axe fell on Thursday, March 8, and the thudding of heads falling reverberated throughout the community. Initially, the sheer numbers startled everyone. The dismissals totaled 19 full-time and four part-time faculty members, one-third of the entire faculty. As names became known, the shock and anger deepened. Thirteen of those dismissed had earned tenure, and most had served Rollins for 15 to 20 years. The president had dismissed the only two men who could teach German and Calculus, both courses required for pre-medical majors. Dismissals included all faculty members in education and business, thereby abolishing those departments. Five of the seven full-time English professors received dismissal notices, which left the department with two full-time professors and two part-time instructors to teach required English composition to 400 students. Included in the English group was Professor

Nathan Starr, perhaps Rollins' most distinguished scholar and one of its most popular teachers at the time. In addition, those dismissed also included Paul Vestal, a Harvard Ph.D. in Biology and an outstanding teacher; Rudolf Fisher, a talented professor who taught German and also violin in the Music Conservatory; and both intercollegiate coaches, Joseph Justice and John McDowell. As an alumnus wrote to one of the trustees, Wagner may have gotten away with a few select dismissals of weak faculty members, but the sheer number and quality of the terminations showed a "lack of wisdom." Even those who received notices of reappointment did not feel secure because they were given only one-year contracts. Gloom and dread hovered heavily over the campus by the end of that "black Thursday."[18]

That afternoon, on March 8, the local AAUP called a meeting at the Art Studio where the faculty began discussing alternatives for avoiding the cuts in their numbers. Wagner appeared in their midst, turned the gathering into an official faculty meeting and gave them another lecture on the necessity of making tough-minded decisions. The president agreed to hold another faculty meeting on Sunday, May 11, to listen to any new practical suggestions for solving the imminent financial situation.[17] If Wagner had made such an effort several months earlier, it may have produced less contentious results. By this time, a bewildered, enraged faculty was in no mood to listen. Wagner's imperious style of governance had become all too obvious to them.[19]

The news of the dismissals spread like brushfire throughout the college community. On Friday, March 9, students gathered for the first of a series of spontaneous reactions to the rumors of so many faculty cuts. A group met in the dean's and the treasurer's offices on Friday morning to discuss the ways they could help save money. Suggestions included student participation without pay in maintenance, dormitory and dining room work. The following Saturday morning another large group of students gathered in the student center to discuss the dismissal issue. At this meeting the student mood, originally positive and optimistic, turned sour when a delegation returned from the president's home with the news that Wagner would not see the students because he was still interviewing dismissed faculty members. The gathering broke up after the student leaders pledged to persuade the president to attend a meeting on Sunday evening. On that Saturday afternoon and Sunday morning, the campus boiled with activity. Small groups of students and faculty met informally and spontaneously here and there on the campus, seeking to find out what was happening and what could be done about it.[20]

By mid-Sunday afternoon, the time set for a pre-arranged faculty meeting, the mood of the college community had shifted from a mixture of shock, fear and uncertainty to one of anger and resentment. Those feelings predictably began to center on the president himself. Students felt he was consciously snubbing their efforts to open a dialogue on the dismissal problem. They saw his unwillingness to meet with them in the student center as typical of his tendency to ignore the college's most important constituency. A student letter to the editor a year earlier concerning the football issue had revealed some latent student concern and discontent: "Dr. Wagner, you probably need not be told that you are being talked about in terms varying from four letter adjectives to their intellectual equivalents. This situation will continue until the student body has at least an idea of the aims and policies of the college. The unrest over dropping football lies in the fact that it manifests a more general concern about the future of Rollins. Could this be cleared up? How about a consumer's report?" No report was forthcoming. Nor, over the next months, did the president attempt to close the communication gap that was obviously creating uncertainty on the campus. The arbitrary firing of such a large number of popular faculty brought a simmering student discontent to the surface. The students learned of the cuts in bits and pieces, from second and third hand sources. By Sunday, they were in an ugly mood.[21]

Much the same emotions swept over the faculty. Despite initially dazed and shocked, they grew angry and resentful. They had been given no role in a decision that would drastically affect their lives and radically reshape the college's future. They felt they had been handed a decree without the opportunity to discuss its worth or to determine its validity. Hadn't Wagner told them there would be no debate and no revision of this proposal? What had happened to the democratic community that was so much a part of the college's tradition, so loudly intoned in the college literature and so reverently proclaimed by Wagner himself? At a faculty gathering in the chapel on Sunday, March 11, a large group openly attacked the president and his proposal for the first time. As the time for the 3:00 p.m. scheduled meeting approached, they were primed for action.

At the meeting, the faculty unanimously passed a motion

demanding, "the president right here and now rescind the dismissals and begin work with the faculty and students on alternative proposals." The president quietly remarked that he had no authority to revoke a decision made by the Board of Trustees. The faculty then elected a special faculty committee to confer with the board "on the whole problem and to resolve the situation." Then the faculty asked the president to leave the meeting. After the president left, Professor Nathan Starr introduced a motion, which stated: "The faculty feels that the present situation within the college has been handled improperly and could have been avoided. Our confidence in the Presidential leadership has been irreparably damaged." No vote was taken on 'no confidence' resolution that evening but they agreed to reconvene "without the president" on Tuesday, March 13.[22]

As the faculty filed out of Dyer Hall, the president was meeting with several hundred students in the student center. In retrospect, this gathering proved critical for the future of the Wagner administration. Wagner undoubtedly sensed the significance of this meeting because he brought along the board's executive committee. (Frances Warren, Louis Orr, Eugene Smith, Raymond Greene and Webber Haines). For reasons not quite clear, he also invited the mayor of Winter Park, William McCauly. It was perhaps Wagner's last opportunity to keep the dismissal problem from boiling over into a full-fledged revolt.

Student President Kenneth Horton opened the meeting with a plea for calm and restraint. "Nothing constructive," he cautioned, "could be achieved through emotional upheaval." Other student leaders echoed Horton's plea for a rational discussion, but one student, Hal Suit, a veteran of World War II who had lost a leg at the Battle of the Bulge, began asking obviously hostile questions. The dismissals, Suit stated bluntly, lowered the quality of education at Rollins College and in effect "broke student contracts." Trustee Eugene Smith, rather than the president, attempted to answer Suit. To the contrary, Smith answered, the president and the board were upholding college standards by forestalling financial bankruptcy. Smith insinuated the students ought to be thankful for Wagner's wise leadership in these difficult times. But Suit would not be put off. If the college was in such desperate financial straits, Suit asked Wagner, why was so much money spent on decorating the president's office and in furnishing the president's home with expensive furniture? Wagner, who to this point had remained silent, told Suit that the board wanted constructive discussion not insulting questions. A groan from the audience enticed Wagner to irritably respond he had made serious cuts in administrative services during the last two years. Before the president could resume his seat, another student asked why he had refused to accept faculty offers to teach without financial compensation. When the president replied no one had made such an offer, the student brandished a list of five faculty names. "Let me see those names," Wagner demanded, but the student refused. At that point, Wagner suddenly turned on his heels, and, along with the trustees, walked out of the meeting.

The president had missed perhaps his last opportunity to defuse a deteriorating situation. The students wanted to discuss their own proposal for saving money, but the president never heard them because he left before they could present it. Wagner's behavior united faculty and students into a solid core of opposition and, in turn, drove an unbridgeable wedge between him and the college community. Both sides were now edging the college to the brink of a major crisis that would leave a residue of hate and resentment for several decades afterward.[23]

A combat analogy is by no means an exaggerated way to describe what became known as the "Wagner affair." After the student meeting on Sunday, March 11, the opposing lines formed: the president, his staff, the executive committee and later a coalition of Winter Park citizens on one side and the faculty, students, a majority of the Board of Trustees and the alumni on the other. Retiring to their appropriate redoubts, they gathered ammunition for their causes and then began hurling accusations, resolutions and press releases at each other.[24]

The faculty initiated its first skirmish on Tuesday, March 13. They listened politely, but with no sympathy, to impassioned speeches by the president's staff that professed loyalty to the president and faith in "his honesty, sincerity and integrity." After they had finished, the faculty passed a statement lauding the president and the trustees' "tireless efforts" but also criticizing specific aspects of those efforts, to wit, the faculty should have been previously advised of the retrenchment policy, and the president should have asked for suggestions before taking such a drastic step. The statement argued that the dismissals represented a violation of Rollins' democratic traditions and of its rules on academic tenure. The new policies, they predicted, would lower Rollins' educational standards. The statement ended with a pointed criticism of the presidential leadership: "We deplore the failure to take advantage of student sentiment. The shock to the student body was profound. With youthful idealism the students are asking for guidance and advice as to how and where they can help and will be bitterly disappointed if it be not forthcoming."[25]

On the same day, almost simultaneously, the executive committee prepared its own statement. Present economic conditions, they argued, had led to the "difficult task of organizing a small college." It was unfortunate, the committee declared, that the "natural distress over the loss of valued members had led to insinuation and charges of personal vindictiveness" toward the president. He simply had followed trustee instructions. "The existence of this college is at stake. Personal considerations and personal feelings, important as they may be, must under such circumstances be subordinated to the preservation of an institution in the value of which we so strongly believe."[23] Both the faculty and the trustee statements were circumspect in language, but each revealed some hardening positions. In the following days both sides met frequently, but there was no meeting of the minds. Neither side was willing to move from its original position.[26]

In the following weeks, both elements tore the campus asunder as they attempted to force the surrender of the other. Through the public relations office, the president issued to local newspapers news releases supportive of his cause. A student committee began meeting with a faculty counterpart almost daily in the student center. *The Sandspur* editor, expressing student attitudes through his weekly editorials, accused Wagner of breaking his word and of taking Rollins "down the rocky road of ruin."[35] Then, on March 16, the alumni executive committee headed by Howard Showalter issued a damning public statement. The committee announced it had lost confidence in the president's "judgment and leadership" and called upon the Board of Trustees to remove Wagner. On the same day, Winthrop Bancroft, chairman of the board, took an action that would lead ultimately to the end of Wagner's presidency. He appointed trustee George Carrison to head a special committee to investigate the campus upheaval.[27]

The Rollins row began to dominate local news, and by mid-March it had been picked up by the national wire services. In its March 12 issue, *The Christian Science Monitor* carried a story about the faculty cuts and discontentment with the administration. A few days later, *The New York Times* cited the Rollins incident in an article on the effect of the Korean War on higher education. One week later, the two leading national news magazines, *Time* and *Life,* carried the news of the Wagner affair, both placing it in the context of a national educational malaise. Some aspect of the affair appeared almost daily on the front page of the *Orlando Sentinel.*[28]

The Carrison committee convened on March 21, and spent the day listening to all the major constituents. The next morning, the committee received a group of 34 faculty members. One of members, Art Professor Hugh McKean, spoke for the faculty: "We are some of the members of the faculty who think that Mr. Wagner should resign as president. We do not wish to take up your time with conversation, we just wish to show ourselves and make this statement." Carrison asked that everyone who concurred raise his hand. All 34 responded. Several reported they held proxies of others who could not attend. The unanimous agreement among the faculty greatly affected the trustees. Eldridge Haynes, whom Wagner had insisted be appointed to the committee, began to waver in his original support of the president.

Later that day, Carrison and his colleagues heard Wagner read several letters from students, faculty and alumni supporting him as president. He then delivered a lengthy speech accusing his opposition of using "communist and fascist tactics." The committee departed much disturbed by the president's erratic behavior. At 1 p.m. on Friday they met again with the president and the executive committee, where Eldridge Haynes presented the committee's findings and recommendations. The overwhelming evidence, Haynes told them, proved Wagner could not continue as president of Rollins College under the prevailing conditions. Haynes then spelled out the committee's recommendations: "The president should immediately call a meeting of all faculty members, students and alumni and tell them in his best manner that he and the board had misjudged the tremendous response that was made by the Rollins family and that he would use this response as a way of solving the college problems. He should say that in response to such a display he would accept the challenge and recommend that the Board reverse itself and also accept the challenge. He would say that all faculty would be reinstated; that we would gamble on our ability to get students, to raise money and keep Rollins as we know it. He would say further that he would get out on the firing line to do what he could do which was raise money." Wagner burst into a long, agitated speech claiming the recommendations were "character assassination" and condemning the persecution he had to endure. Pressed for a reply, he promised to give an answer in a few days. The committee spent the next few days preparing its report to a special Board of Trustees meeting called by Chairman Bancroft. Meanwhile, they waited for Wagner's answer. It never came.[29]

A few days later, Wagner's cause suffered a severe blow. On April 10, Hamilton Holt wrote his young successor that, as far as he could tell from a distance of a thousand miles, the president's cause seemed hopeless. Holt said he understood Wagner's sincerity, but the young president must look realistically at the fact he had lost the support of the faculty and the students. No president, he declared, could succeed without these two constituencies. Holt advised Wagner to resign. When the President resisted this suggestion, Holt sent his letter to the *Orlando Sentinel*, which published it on April 12 as a front-page headline. It was one of Holt's last acts on behalf of the college. He died a few days later.[31]

Tension and drama abounded when Winthrop Bancroft opened the special trustee meeting on Friday, April 14. One member presented detailed evidence his committee had gathered from the college community and then solemnly recommended the president's dismissal. After a brief silence, the room erupted into a cacophony of heated accusations and unstructured debate. As one trustee later remembered: "Everyone was furious. Everyone was shouting. Ray Maguire (college attorney) was pacing up and down, shouting things no one had asked him to say and no one was listening to." Some were calling for adjournment, others protesting they were leaving town that evening. Finally, after Bancroft restored order, the board agreed to adjourn until the following morning, hoping to resume deliberations with calmer nerves and less intense emotions.[32]

That night both pro and anti-Wagner forces prepared strategies for the Saturday morning meeting. When Bancroft called the meeting to order, two members simultaneously asked to be recognized. By prearrangement, Bancroft recognized Miller Walton who proceeded to move to adjourn until the board could reconvene on April 27 in New York City. Throughout Walton's reading of the motion, Wagner was shouting "Point of order, Point of order." He wanted a debate, but the chairman ruled the motion not debatable. Bancroft broke a seven-seven tie in favor of the motion to adjourn. Ignoring the college lawyer's argument the vote violated parliamentary rules, Bancroft declared the meeting adjourned and, with the other trustees, left the room.[34]

Although neither President Wagner nor the executive committee members appeared at the April 27 meeting in New York, a bare quorum of 11 trustees did assemble. By the start of the meeting, several trustees had already worked out a face-saving plan. If Wagner would resign the presidency of Rollins College, the trustees would place Wagner at the head of a "Commission To Study the Financial Problems of Liberal Arts Colleges" across the nation. They gave Wagner until May 3 to accept or reject the offer. In the event he failed to resign by that date, they authorized a group of Winter Park trustees to issue an order of dismissal. After an "exhaustive discussion" regarding "possible persons who might be able to save the college from ruin," the trustees elected Hugh McKean as acting president.[35]

Eldridge Haynes assumed the responsibility of reporting the board's proposal to the beleaguered Wagner who was in New York at the time. Wagner seemed genuinely interested in the prospects of heading such a commission; yet, he kept repeating to Haynes, once with tears in his eyes, he wanted more than anything else to be president of Rollins College. Haynes could not convince him of the impossibility of that alternative. When the exhausted trustee left in the early morning hours, Wagner had agreed only to give the matter serious thought.

One week later, on the May 3 deadline, Wagner still had not given an answer. McKean automatically became acting president, but, because Wagner still occupied the president's office in Warren Hall, McKean set up shop in Morse Art Gallery. Rollins now had two presidents! One was determined to resist ouster and the other held office with dubious legitimacy. In the meantime, Wagner's supporters undertook measures which looked as if they intended to keep him in office for a long time. Louis Orr, a local trustee, publicly announced his unwavering support for Wagner. The *Orlando Sentinel* reported that Mrs. Frances Warren wanted the college community to reunite behind Wagner and a group of local supporters, called the Citizens Committee for Rollins College, placed a full-page advertisement in the newspaper asking everyone to rally to Wagner's side in these times of crisis.

Despite these efforts in support of Wagner, his authority began to crumble. On May 10, a majority of the students
walked out of classes and refused to return until Wagner
resigned. Wagner called a faculty meeting the following day
to determine "what action the faculty wished to take toward
the student strike." Never had a president faced a more
hostile faculty. Following a motion to refer the problem to a
special committee, the faculty adjourned. The meeting had
lasted 15 minutes. Two days later all the deans announced
that "in order to restore harmony," they would begin working with McKean rather than Wagner.[36]

Finally, a group of trustees headed by George Carrison
gathered in Winter Park on May 13 prepared to serve Wagner
an ultimatum and end the intolerable divisive upheaval.
Along with Trustees Arthur Schultz and Jeannette McKean,
Carrison arranged a face-to-face meeting with Wagner at
the Winter Park home of Trustee Eugene Smith, a member
of the executive committee. Carrison later recalled in great
detail the pitiful demise of the Wagner presidency. He told
the beleaguered president if he would resign he would be
financially compensated and could leave the college with
"personal dignity." Wagner continued to resist arguing
he could still carry on effectively. "Paul," Carrison told
him, "this is getting us nowhere. The time has come when
we cannot negotiate any further." Carrison then handed
Wagner a letter of dismissal, left the meeting and, as he
later wrote, "went to the Morse Gallery of Art, where a press
conference had been arranged and a rather sizable group of
faculty, students, and alumni and the press was assembled."

At the meeting he announced that "Hugh McKean had been appointed acting president of Rollins College."

The next day, McKean called an all college meeting where he, Treasurer John Tiedtke and Carrison gave victory speeches to an applauding audience. When they emerged from the Annie Russell Theatre, the students spontaneously lifted Hugh McKean on their shoulders and walked with him through the campus shouting cheers of victory. This gesture left a deep imprint on the McKean presidency.[37]

On May 15, all students returned to classes eager to restore normal conditions. The Wagner affair should have receded mercifully into the past, but the executive committee, Wagner and his local friends would not concede defeat. On May 16, The *Orlando Sentinel's* front-page headline proclaimed "Wagner Says Still President." The deposed president, the paper reported, refused to recognize as legal the decision of the April 27 trustee meeting and the later attempts to oust him. The executive committee held a special Board of Trustees meeting to discuss the matter but failed to secure a quorum. The pro-Wagner local citizens committee, after holding a large meeting in the Winter Park Country Club on May 14, began publishing a series of advertisements in Orlando papers questioning the legal authority to fire Wagner. The first, entitled "Who Owns Rollins College?" listed the names of those trustees who attended the New York meeting and implied that they had acted illegally. A second, entitled "Fair Play The American Way," accused the trustees of defaulting on their promise to back Wagner after the February 1951 decision. An anti-Wagner group responded with its own full-page advertisement, entitled "What Rollins Is Trying To Achieve." On May 21, Wagner filed a $500,000 suit against the eleven trustees who had voted for his dismissal.[38]

This disruptive newspaper and legal war suddenly took a serious and dangerous turn. On May 24, the campus received the startling news that the Florida Legislature had passed a bill ousting all out-of-state members from the Rollins Board of Trustees. Local representatives had introduced the measure at the request of the pro-Wagner citizens committee. They argued the trustees were hopelessly deadlocked and out-of-state trustees would not take time to attend meetings. The only solution was to create a Board of Trustees willing to devote time to the college. It is the duty of the Legislature "to remove this valuable asset of the state from the grasp of a small group of selfish and irresponsible men from other states and their rabble-rousing followers on the campus and put it under the control of open minded capable people close to the situation and aware of the interests of Central Florida and the whole state."[39]

The news of the bill threw the recently subdued campus into turmoil once again. A hastily called general meeting of faculty, students and townspeople created the Friends of the College Committee, which began organizing opposition to the bill. On May 24, over 200 people left by buses and motorcade for Tallahassee to persuade the governor not to sign the legislation. In the meantime, important townspeople, trustees and college officials began exerting pressure on Central Florida representatives in the legislature. In addition, indignant protests against the legislature's unprecedented and potentially dangerous interference in

the internal affairs of a private institution of higher learning erupted throughout the state. In the face of mounting
pressure, representatives of the Florida Legislature asked
the governor to return the bill for a second consideration.
On May 28, both houses unanimously rescinded their original legislation.[40]

The following day, May 29, the trustees held their regularly scheduled, and now critically important, commencement meeting. The vote here would either reconfirm or
reverse the special New York meeting's decision. When
the members arrived at their usual meeting place, the
conference room of Knowles Memorial Chapel, they found
Paul Wagner and his attorneys already seated. Chairman
Bancroft gaveled the meeting to order, called the roll (15
members present) and then declared a recess. The Chairman then asked Wagner and his attorneys to leave the
meeting, but they remained firmly seated in their chairs.
Bancroft then called the meeting to order again, declared
an adjournment to Morse Art Gallery and barred Wagner
and his attorneys from the building "unless they used
force to enter." Wagner made no effort to follow the trustees to Morse Gallery. Raymond Greene, Louis Orr, Eugene
Smith and Raymond Maguire all resigned from the Board
of Trustees. Reconstituted, the trustees moved quickly to
affirm the decisions and resolutions of the April 27 meeting
and formally removed Wagner as president of the college,
"effective instantly." They also reconfirmed Hugh McKean
as acting president and, in addition, elected Alfred J. Hanna
as first vice-president and John Tiedtke as second vice-president and treasurer of the college.[41]

Still Wagner continued his suit against the New York trustees and hovered around the campus for a few days following the May 29 meeting. He watched Rollins commencement exercises from a distance. The diplomas were signed by Acting President Hugh McKean. Under pressure from college attorneys, Wagner finally relinquished the keys to the president's office on Friday, June 8. Five days later, Hugh McKean for the first time entered the office in the administration building as acting-president of Rollins College.[42]

The Wagner affair had mercifully come to a close. However, the hostile memories engendered by the episode forever poisoned friendships. Individuals in Winter Park who were on opposite sides never spoke to each other again. The college was so embarrassed by the virulence of the disagreements it attempted to conceal most of the documents connected with the incident. When I began researching the chapter on the Wagner presidency, I was puzzled by the scarcity of archival evidence. After a long search I discovered a rusting file cabinet hidden in a dark corner of Mills Library's basement. The cabinet was simply labeled as "Wagner." Everything pertaining to the Wagner Affair had been locked and sealed with an iron bar and stowed in a dark corner of the basement. The securely locked file cabinet's shadowy location is symbolic of the college's resolve to bury from sight and memory one of the most ignominious episodes of its history.

Paul Wagner's demise was tragic in the sense that his good intentions were doomed by the man's own hubris. He brought plight upon an institution he was trying to guide into a new era of educational change. His downfall left the college with a deep awareness of what might have been. He deprived Rollins of his exceptional insight into the future of higher education and the opportunity of placing itself in the forefront of the coming 21st century technological innovations in education. Wagner, and Wagner alone, was responsible for squandering that opportunity. He fell into the same trap as his predecessor. Instead of defusing a growing crisis, Wagner, like Holt, fueled it. Rather than mediating the crises, both chose to assert their personal authority. Both claimed they were acting in the best interest of the college. The tragedy is they were blind to the fact their arbitrary behavior was actually damaging it.

The Wagner Affair left the entire college in a state of exhaustion, with a deep desire to experience some peace and harmony. As a result, the college community began to look backward to the perceived harmonious past of Hamilton Holt rather than forward to an exciting, unpredictable and innovative future beyond the Holt era. That unrealized future was the goal of Paul Wagner. His failure resulted in the appointment of Hugh McKean who, as a committed protégé of the deceased Hamilton Holt, tended to see Rollins' future from the perspective of the past. Thus, "Mister Rollins College" would continue to cast a long shadow, and Hugh McKean would prove to be his last legacy.

1. Trustee Minutes, May 31, 1950. For Wagner's background, I have used material from the biographical file in the Wagner Papers, Rollins Archives and from Hartzell Spence, "Education's Boy Wonder," *Colliers* (January 13, 1951).

2. Spence, "Boy Wonder"; *Newsweek* (August 8, 1949); *New York Times*, June 8, 1949.

3. Faculty Minutes, January 7, 1950; *Sandspur*, January 18, 1950.

4. *Sandspur*, October 10, 1950; Trustee Minutes, October, 1950.

5. Faculty Minutes, April 10, 1950; Enyart Statement Concerning the Wagner Affair <no date>. Rollins Archives. I believe I was the first person to see these records since they were placed in the basement of Mills library.

6. Inaugural Address, February 8, 1950.

7. Memorandum to the Faculty, July 15, 1950; Wendell Stone and Nathan Starr Statements. Wagner Affair Records.

8. Faculty Minutes, September 25, l950; Trustee Minutes, October 1950. For the national problem see "Crisis in the Colleges," *Time* (June 29, 1950).

9. Faculty Minutes, October 30, 1950.

10. Wagner to Stone, December 15, 1950; Trustee Minutes, February, 1951.

11. I have reconstructed Wagner's performance from several trustee depositions located in the Wagner Affair Records.

12. Trustee Minutes, February 27-29, 1951.

13. *Ibid.*

14. *Ibid.*

15. Depositions Wagner Affair

16. Faculty Minutes, March 5, 1951.

17. Depositions

18. *Ibid.*

19. *Ibid.* This and the following discussion of faculty activity is reconstructed from several faculty statements in the Wagner Affair Records.

20. Sandspur, March 10, 1951; Kay Lehman to George Carrison, March 15, 1951.

21. *Sandspur*, March, 1951.

22. Faculty Minutes, March 11, 1951. For faculty sentiment see Statement by Flora Magoon, Wagner Affair Records.

23. My account of this meeting is reconstructed from statements by students, faculty and trustees in the Wagner Affair Records, and a special issue of the *Sandspur*, March 12, 1951.

24. Trustee Minutes, March 14, 1951.

25. Faculty Minutes, March 13, 1951; Faculty statements in the Wagner Affair

Records.

26. Trustee Minutes, March 16, 1951.

27. Public Relations News Release, March 17, 1951; Stone Survey, February 1, 1951.

28. See *Orlando Sentinel*, March 12-20, 1951 for almost daily coverage of crisis; *Sandspur*, March 17, 1951; Alumni statements in the Wagner Affair Records; Bancroft and Carrison in the Wagner Affair Records. TIME, March 19, 1951; *Life*, March 26, 1951.

29. Carrison Statement.

30. Trustee Minutes, March 29, 1951. 31. Holt to Wagner, April 10, 1951; *Orlando Sentinel*, April 12, 1951.

32. Trustee Minutes, April 14, 1951; Statements by Trustees in Wagner Affair Records.

33. *Ibid.*

34. *Sandspur*, April 15, 1951; Trustee Minutes, April 16, 1951; Visiting Committee Report, May 9, 1951; *Orlando Sentinel*L, April 26, 1951.

35. Trustee Minutes, April 27, 1951; Trustee Statements in Wagner Affair Records.

36. *Sandspur*, May 10, 1951.

37. Reconstructed from Statement by George Carrison in Wagner Affair Records.

38. *Ibid.*, and statements by faculty and trustees in Wagner Affair Records.

39. Trustee Minutes, May 15,17, 22, 1951; *Orlando Sentinel*, May 17, 20, 1951.

40. Telegram to Florida House of Representatives, May 24, 1951; *Orlando Sentinel*, "Central Floridians to Run Rollins," May 25, 1951.

For statewide protest see for example *Tampa Tribune*, May 27, 1951.

41. Trustee, April 27, 1951.

42. Wagner to McKean, June 7, 1951.

Paul Wagner settled in New York after leaving Rollins and entered the public relations business. He rose to Senior Executive of Hill and Knowlton, a renowned global public relations firm. In the 1970s he founded his own public relations business which concentrated on serving not for profit organizations. In 1999, he and his wife Jeannette, Vice Chairman of Estee Lauder Companies, formed a pro bono group—Nulli Seconds Associates—devoted to aiding global not for profit companies with strategies to achieve success. Wagner died in December, 2015.

Chapter 9

—

RESTORING THE HOLT LEGACY: THE MCKEAN ERA 1951–1968

SHORTLY AFTER ASSUMING the title of acting president, Hugh McKean admitted with refreshing, but troubling, candor: "As a college president, I am a rank amateur. I have the additional handicap of being almost an unwilling one. I taught art at Rollins for twenty years and that is what I should be doing now."[1] No one who knew McKean would have quarreled with this self-assessment. The question then is: why, from all the administrators and faculty at Rollins College, the anti-Wagner trustees singled out this inexperienced, self-effacing artist to bring stability back to a college in disarray? There is nothing in the copious Rollins archival records of this period that would even suggest an answer. In all his years at Rollins, McKean had not been a leader of the faculty nor had he shown any interest in administration. His main accomplishment was as an artist, and in that field he achieved moderate success. His paintings were shown in a few reputable galleries and, at least one time, a studio featured his collection. His files contain no evidence suggesting he was an exceptional teacher. Thus, with scant indications of the trustees motives, inferences are our only recourse.

The trustees knew Hugh McKean well because his wife Jeannette was an active member of the board. She was also the granddaughter of wealthy industrialist/philanthropist Charles Hosmer Morse, an influential Winter Park citizen who owned large tracts of land in Winter Park and who had served on the Rollins Board of Trustees from 1901 until his death in 1921. The Morse wealth could not have been far from the trustees' minds when they named McKean acting president. The young professor's close relationship with Hamilton Holt was another possible motive guiding their decision. Reaction to the Wagner affair caused the entire college community to suddenly develop a romantic vision of the Holt era as a period of sweet harmony and peace. Exhausted by the recent turmoil, the community seemed almost excessively eager to restore what seemed in retrospect to be a period of equanimity. No one embodied that vision more than Hugh McKean. During McKean's undergraduate years at Rollins, he and Holt developed a father/son attachment and that bond continued when McKean returned to the college as an art professor. Holt served as McKean's counselor when the young professor struggled through personal issues. In his retirement, Holt wrote Hugh and Jeannette with genuine affection: "I am sure I need not tell you that no one was closer to my thoughts and heart than you two souls." Thus, as one alumnus wrote, McKean was the perfect candidate because of his "knowledge and under-standing of the principles of Hamilton Holt."[2]

However, the person most familiar with the college's past and by far the most qualified to restore the Holt tradition was Alfred Jackson Hanna. By the 1950s, Hanna's career at the college, which spanned almost four decades, was already legendary. After graduating from Rollins in 1918 he was named registrar of the Business School and president of the Rollins Alumni Association. During the Blackman admin-istration, he held the office of secretary and advisor to the president. Hamilton Holt retained him as his chief advi-sor and also named him assistant treasurer. He was Holt's constant companion on the president's many fund raising trips. Throughout this period, Hanna had been studying Florida history and in 1928 persuaded Holt to appoint him instructor in the History Department. Within ten years he had risen to a full professor position and was appointed chairman of the History Department. By then he had estab-lished a reputation as a serious scholar who had written several books dealing with Florida and Latin America. He was a popular teacher, a recognized scholar and an experi-enced administrator, who was respected by the faculty and well known to the Board of Trustees. He should have been the obvious choice for acting president.[3]

So why wasn't he chosen? The answer seems to lie with Hanna's personality. He was more comfortable in the role of an eminence grise, someone who preferred to exercise influence behind the scenes. Over the years, except for his scholarly and academic endeavors, Hanna chose to remain quietly inconspicuous. In photographs where he appears with Holt, he is always standing in the background, observing the proceedings with a penetrating gaze. Nevertheless, there is sufficient evidence in the records to show that Holt found him indispensable as an advisor, seeking and accepting Hanna's guidance on all college matters. Naming Hanna vice president of the college was both an indication the trsutees were unsure about McKean's capabilities as a leader and a conviction Hanna could mentor him though difficulties. For good measure they appointed Holt's Treasurer John Tiedke as a second vice president, forming a kind of triumvirate they hoped would collaborate to stabilize the college community. Thus, the trustees had installed three Holt disciples to govern the college. They, and apparently the college community, seemed determined to reestablish continuity with the Holt tradition.

In appearance and demeanor, Hugh McKean seemed to be someone who could calm the turbulent waters of the previous spring and summer. A soft-spoken, gentle and artistic man with a penchant for philosophizing on any subject—from the art of fishing to the meaning of art—McKean seemed an especially appropriate appointment in the post-Wagner years. There was a certain romantic appeal about the picture of an uncomplicated man who happily taught art suddenly thrust into the presidency due to an urgent mission of wresting his alma mater from the throes of deep crisis. His modest candor about his lack of experience and his inability to mesure up to the responsibilities conferred on him was somehow seen as a virtue. *The Sandspur* editor spoke for the entire community when he noted in the first issue of the 1952–1953 academic year: "Our new administrators have brought peace and harmony with simple sincerity and courage."[4]

However, other than restoring harmony to the college, the most pressing issue facing the McKean administration was a development foreseen by Paul Wagner: the transformation in American education between 1945 and 1970. "Cautious egalitarianism" represented the most important of these developments. The Commission on Higher Education, appointed by President Harry Truman, concluded in 1947 that approximately 50 percent of the American population possessed "the mental ability" to succeed in college if society would remove economic, geographic, religious and racial obstacles barring their way. Through the creation of more schools, increased scholarship funds and the process of desegregation, many of these barriers were eliminated or at least lowered by 1970. The first massive wave of increased enrollment was initially stimulated by the passage of the Serviceman's Readjustment Act, commonly known as the G. I. Bill of Rights, in 1944. The act was responsible for sending more than 2.5 million veterans to over 2,000 institutions of higher learning. Veteran enrollment lagged after 1955 and, along with the Korean War draft, brought on an economic recession in higher education. Then in the early 1960s, the children of the war and postwar "baby boomers" came pouring into colleges, again creating unprecedented enrollment increases. Prior to World War II, 40 percent of those in "college age" went to college, but by 1945 that figure had risen to 60 percent. Between 1955 and 1968, student enrollment doubled from just over 3 million to 6.5 million.

The flood of students drastically altered American higher education. With greatly increased numbers of applications, stable colleges could raise their requirements for entrance. Prestigious institutions, and even those with less prestige, demanded higher and higher scores on the Scholastic Aptitude Test (SAT) and higher class rankings. The federal government, along with private educational foundations, began providing funds for higher education so institutions could enlarge their physical plants to meet the burgeoning demand. This growth also accelerated a process of faculty specialization that had been underway since the turn of the century. By the mid-1960s, a Ph.D. qualification had become an essential preparation for college teaching, and colleges soon found themselves in intense competition for faculty with certified doctorates. Moreover, this generation of faculty began to demand and receive more responsibility in college governance. The presidents remained a dominant figure in their institution, but without the authority characteristic of the pre-World War II academic world. More and more the college president was forced to share authority with other staff and faculty members and, in many cases, to abdicate academic authority entirely in favor of administrative deans and faculty committees.[5]

This sudden broadening of responsibility and authority in American higher education proved a mixed blessing for the academic world. A large group of institutions, perhaps even a majority, comprehended the nature of the changes taking place, and, seizing upon this development, sought and secured aggressive admissions and development officers and deans, who then drastically raised the quality of

TOP Dean Enyart and Students

MIDDLE Holt and Mary Bethune, Holt and Students at Home

BOTTOM Faculty 1932

TOP Holt, Faculty and President
Roosevelt

BOTTOM Holt and President
Truman, Holt's Commencement

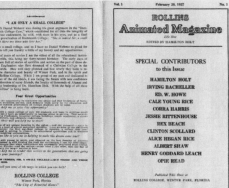

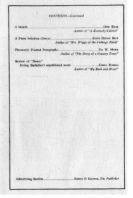

TOP Theatre/Chapel Complex

MIDDLE Animated Magzine Contents

BOTTOM Holt Welcoming Paul Wagner

TOP John Tiedtke

BOTTOM Student Center
c.1950

TOP Campus Overview,
c. 1970

BOTTOM Fred Hanna,
President McKean

Alberta Haynes

Anita Thomas

Tony Layng

Earl White

Laurence Martinez

black students at rollins
by TONY LAYNG

EDITOR'S NOTE: This ... presented to Alumni as a ... tive story, and is not nec... flect the opinions of the ... Alumni Association, or the ... There are nineteen black... currently enrolled in the ... graduate full time day p...

If you graduated from Roll... than four years ago, and ... previously been back for ... brief tour of the campus m... change in the student ... occurred here. Although ... fewer than twenty black ... student body, what is ... is that five years ago th... none. Fortunately, Rolli... content with token integra... President Critchfield and ... are aware of the need fo... meaningful black-white re... student body, and they ... cerned about developing ... of making it financially fe... more blacks to come to R...

As a former Rollins' ... was naturally interested in ... about this new dimensio... returned to campus this ... first thing that became e... me was the active and cre... the black students are a ... Rollins. But what is most ... to perceive, and perhaps ... vealing to those of us no... terested in learning abou... black students, is the fo... cerns they have about Ro... following interview is in ... the interest of identifyin... these concerns.

Laurence Martinez, our leading scorer on the basketball team, is a Chapel reader and a member of Lambda Chi Alpha fraternity. He has also served on the Homecoming Committee and the Steering Committee of College Preparation Week. He has recently been nominated to be included in the 1969 edition of OUTSTANDING COLLEGE ATHLETES OF AMERICA. Laurence comes from Ft. Lauderdale.

Earl White, known to most of Rollins as E.G., is a resident of Gainesville. He has been on the staff of the Rollins SANDSPUR and is now president of the recently established organization of Rollins' black students. He also served as a discussion leader during College Preparation Week.

Anita Thomas, is from Atlanta. An active member of the Rollins Players, she was also a member of the Steering Committee of College Preparation Week, serving as a discussion leader. She is now a member of the newly formed Community Action Board.

Alberta Haynes, from St. Petersburg, was elected by the Behavioral Science majors this year to be one of their four participant representatives at all departmental meetings. A Dean's List student, she finds time for working on the Films Committee and playing intramural basketball. As a member of the staff of the Office of Student Affairs, she is a counselor and resident advisor in one of the girl's dormitories.

Professor Tony Layng, a former Rollins student '54-'57, received his M.A. degree from Indiana University where he is continuing work on his Ph.D. Prior to joining Rollins in 1969 as Assistant Professor of Anthropology, he taught at Washington College and Tougaloo College, a black school in Alabama.

TOP Campus Overview, 1985

MIDDLE, LEFT TO RIGHT Three Presidents, Seymour's Inauguration; President Critchfield; President Seymour

BOTTOM, LEFT TO RIGHT Olin Library, 1985; Sandspur, 1975

the educational programs and sought the necessary funds to support them. They improved the quality of the faculty and students and they reformed and improved the academic programs; but when the "revolution" was over in the late 1970s, they had been strengthened but not transformed. Rollins College was among this group.

The McKean administration sensed the impending changes in the academic world almost from the beginning. In response to the increase of military personnel in the Central Florida area, the college contracted with Patrick Air Force Base in Cocoa Beach to create a college program on the base. Rollins professors began conducting college credit classes for service personnel and their families. During the first semester, 168 students enrolled in the seven courses offered, and by 1970, enrollment had grown three-fold and had blossomed into a full-fledged branch campus program. For the cash-starved college, the program meant thousands of dollars in uncommitted income. In addition, in 1954, the administration inaugurated an adult education program in Winter Park that mushroomed into several thousand students by 1970. As with the Patrick program, adult education provided the college with more uncommitted income.[6]

In response to the growing academic professionalization, and more likely in reaction to Wagner's imperious governing style, the administration introduced democratic procedures in college governance. In his first faculty meeting, McKean called for a revision of the faculty bylaws to provide more governing responsibility to the faculty. The change, passed in December 1951, gave each department responsibility for its new appointments and reappointments. The faculty as a whole was made solely responsible for "devising and administering curriculum studies" required for graduation, crafting the academic calendar and maintaining "good order and discipline." The faculty also acquired the authority to "devise and revise salary scales and systems of promotion in rank," to be consulted in matters "involving the possible freeze or lowering of salaries" and "to study the facts before a final decision is made by the President to the Board of Trustees." The revision of bylaws reiterated the college's commitment to the principles of tenure outlined by the 1940 statement of the AAUP, a move intended to avoid unexpected and unexamined policy decisions of the sort that led to Wagner's dismissal.[7]

Although by the end of the first term the college seemed well on its way to recovering from the spring's upheaval, uncertainty about the future leadership still hung over the community. The trustees had appointed each of the triumvirate for only one year. In an early act of abnegation, McKean submitted his resignation to be effective on or before commencement. The board, in response, appointed an all-college search committee, but by October the committee had submitted only the names of several "possible candidates," and at the end of the spring term, it had made not a single formal suggestion. Meanwhile, the triumvirate reported the college was now "restored to its former thriving condition." They therefore requested "an early release from administrative duties." Citing their "experience as members of the faculty for many years and as interim administrators for nine months," the triumvirate stated they were in a position to propose a list of qualities the "new leader should possess." Included in this list were a sympathy with the conference plan of teaching, the humility of "well-informed and wise men," a known support for quality education and a capacity for satisfaction derived from helping young people. Notably, the triumvirate proposed the new president should be "an educator with *adequate* training and experience as teacher and administrator and he must be prepared *to go to work immediately.*" (emphasis added) The triumvirate "wished to point out that the present condition of Rollins achieved by the cooperation [among] an artist, a historian and a farmer is an indication that the task of finding a president should not be as difficult as many might suppose."[8] It must have been obvious even to the most uninformed observer the statement described the acting president himself. Yet, during the fall term, McKean had refused every effort to make himself a candidate, a refusal puzzlingly contrary to his comportment as acting president. Then word was passed to the trustees that while McKean would not offer himself as a *candidate*, he might readily accept the presidency if asked.[9] In the February 1952 meeting, the trustees "in recognition of his overall general knowledge of the college and its problems" unanimously voted to name Hugh McKean the 10th president of Rollins College.

Now secure in his office, McKean turned his thoughts to Rollins' future. His annual reports for the next 10 years show a president struggling to make sense of the coming academic revolution. In his 1955 report he told the trustees that "within four or five years there will be tremendous pressure on all of us to increase the size of the college." He predicted a "groundswell of applications" that would shape the college's future for years to come. Serious scholars would avoid Rollins, he warned, if the college acquired the reputation of "taking weak students," and good students would not stay if the academic departments were weak. Therefore, he predicted, "the admission picture is clearly related to the quality of the faculty."[10]

A few years later, however, McKean's philosophical emphasis changed. The academic explosion had created "impersonal education," making grades and test scores the major criteria for student selections. Professors using "loudspeakers and television screens" simply provided students with information. Rollins, McKean admonished, should "stand against this trend, should maintain its small size with a continuing concern for the individual," seeking "both average students and those with highest scores" but demanding superior personal qualities.[11]

With much insight, McKean peered prophetically into the future of American education, and tried to envision Rollins' place in that future. He pictured "a complex of institutions" with the undergraduate college at the center. For the liberal arts college he made no specific predictions, but, for the other areas of the institution, McKean offered incisive ideas. An early proponent of "non-traditional" education, McKean called for an "external college," a new institution designed to offer varied and rich educational programs to anyone within academic reach of the college. Through communication techniques—"radio, television, learning tapes, etc."—the college would confer "external bachelor degrees on any candidate who qualified by passing a very complete written examination." The traditional practice of satisfying the nation's educational needs by educating only teenagers, McKean wrote with prescience, "is a relic of another era." Colleges no longer would be entrusted to educate only young people or those with special privileges. "This country must have continuous high level education for everyone all of the time. The day is past when an education is completed."[12] Ironically, it was an education program with which Paul Wagner would have had little quarrel.

This was Hugh McKean at his best, a philosopher-president reminding the college of the wider scope of its educational responsibilities. But the most profound philosophy could not solve the serious problems the triumvirate had inherited, nor was it a substitute for meaningful, aggressive admission strategies and faculty recruitment policies. In order to prepare for this growth, the institution needed above all a well-constructed professional development policy that would accumulate the funds necessary for creating a relevant, high-quality institution. In a period of high faculty demand and rapidly rising faculty salaries, the college could attract and hold first-rate faculty only if it paid salaries competitive with other institutions and, in some cases, competitive with those of government and business. In a period when public institutions provided both excellent education and low tuition costs, Rollins could only grow if it offered an attractive educational program supplemented by scholarship funds to attract quality students. Clearly, the key to success depended on the college's ability to attract necessary funding.

McKean strove mightily to meet these challenges, and

after a decade and half, the president and his colleagues were able to look back with justifiable pride at their 15 years of service to the college. The institution was not faced with a perennial financial crisis as it had been in the 30s and 40s. Under the triumvirate, Rollins had weathered the debilitating Wagner affair with an even stronger sense of community and had attempted to address many of the issues raised by the academic revolution. They had increased the size of its physical plant to meet the needs of a burgeoning student population (by 1966 total enrollment exceeded 1,000), and even more importantly, under the leadership of Dean of Admissions Spencer Lane, they had significantly improved the academic quality of students.[13]

Students during the McKean era provided the college with much excitement in almost every field of endeavor. Theater majors Bill McNulty, Bill Millard, Nancy Yardlow, Ray Edwards and others presented four years of outstanding plays. *The Sandspur* editor Mark Billson produced quality newspaper journalism in what many considered the best ever printed at Rollins. Fred Giddes and Al Holland gave the college community intelligent and imaginative leadership in student government. An increasingly large number of students continued in graduate study, six receiving Woodrow Wilson Fellowships and one, Norman Friedland, receiving the prestigious Root-Tilden Scholarship to study at New York University. Star college golfer Jane Blalock ('67), a scholar/athlete history major, soared even higher as a pro in the LPGA. Her list of accomplishments—from being named LGPA Rookie of the Year in 1969 to being inducted into the Legends Hall of Fame in 2014—established Blalock as one of the greatest golfers of all time. In addition, she started her own business, the Jane Black Company, worked as a periodic golf commentator on NBC, organized and served as director of Legends of Golf and wrote two books. Gilbert Klein, also a history major and editor of *The Sandspur,* made a very successful career in journalism. He started as a reporter for the *Tampa Tribune* before going to Washington as a national correspondent for the Media News Service. In 1994, he was named President of the National Press Club and later wrote the organization's history. These alumni clearly revealed the college's potential for attracting talented students. These students in turn had launched the college into a new era of accomplishments.

Fox Day typified, perhaps even symbolized, McKean's informal, personal and sensitive style and recreated the relaxed aura of most of the Holt years. In 1956, the president created a full day of celebration centered on a statue owned by the college since 1934. Holt had convinced Senator Murray Sam of New Smyrna to donate two statues—a fox and a cat—for display on the campus. For years they sat on the walkway leading to the Recreation Hall. When a student prank damaged the cat, Holt stored the fox for safekeeping. For years it was assumed lost. McKean, claiming to have found it, secretly brought the fox from hiding, placed it on the horseshoe lawn and announced that the fox had decided to emerge and to proclaim "Fox Day." Classes were dismissed, and the Rollins family would "just take it easy," going to the beach or participating in organized activities. The celebration would culminate with an all-college picnic and a special commemorative meeting in the chapel. For years afterward, Fox Day brought together the college family in an informal and relaxed way, nurturing a community spirit that might have been threatened by the greatly increased size of the college. McKean's Fox Day proclamations, poetically melding the college's natural beauty with the joy of learning, created nostalgic memories for students and invariably captured the essence of the day. He always began the proclamations with poetic musings. May 2, 1963: "The auguries and the winds foretell that May the second will be a day of sunlight and beauty"; May 6,1964: "Tradewinds now add softness to the nights and freshness to the days; and phlox, that glorious flower of May, is ablaze in the Parsonage garden; and mocking birds are adding special magic to it all"; May 7 1966: "Florida's skies are blue and filled with winds and clouds, and spring is here, a time when chuck-wills' widows call their name at night for reasons known alone to them, but good, no doubt, and jasmine stars give fragrant beauty to the evening air." In this realm Hugh McKean truly seemed to be the protégé of Hamilton Holt.[14]

In the financial domain, the McKean administration was a product of the Holt era's influence as well. Consciously or unconsciously, the McKean administration tried to either emulate or to avoid Holt's methods in fund raising. Like Holt, the president would be the principal fundraiser—but he also wanted to change the perception left by Holt that the Rollins College president was always "begging for contributions." McKean presented his initial ideas on development in his first report to the trustees. It included a broad statement that set the tone for his future development philosophy. The administration, he wrote, was considering "a 7-year plan designed to present the aims of Rollins College to thoughtful persons with such clarity and force that they will wish to give it the financial support it must have." One year later McKean declared further: "When I became President I said that I would ask no one to contribute to support the college but that if the facts about the college were good and reasonable and if they were presented to the friends of the college in a way that they could be thoroughly understood, it was my opinion that the college could win its own support." In 1955, after he assumed personal responsibility for fundraising, he admitted with characteristic self-effacement some uncertainty in this field. "I do not know if I will succeed but I will try," he told the Trustees. "My policy will continue to be that of speaking frankly about the college and making no direct requests for funds."[15]

Convinced the merits of the college would suffice to attract the necessary funds to assure its future, McKean made no further development plans. He ignored the trustees's suggestion to hire a development officer who could construct a systematic fundraising policy. After eight years, McKean felt constrained to admit that his program "had not been a great success." He had predicted that by 1960 the college would require annual income, gifts and funds of 10 million dollars. But in that year, he was able to report only half of that amount raised. It was not, he conceded, "a dazzling record," but he hastened to add, it had "been accomplished without high pressured solicitation and without a development officer."[16]

In the face of the college's slow financial growth, the

trustees began pressing for a management study that would, as one of them argued, "help set goals and point out areas for improvement." In response, McKean included a long section in his 1961 annual report entitled "Appraising Rollins' Development Program." He admitted his philosophy and methods differed from "the more or less standard methods" and his plan contained no provisions for development professionals. His administration had purposely "employed no development officer ...[set] no goals, [had] no solicitation, no teams." McKean warned the trustees that if they engaged a fundraising firm, the consultants "would expect them to contribute at least fifty percent of the goal on the theory that the Trustees who are at the college cannot expect others to contribute if they do not lead the way." In evaluating his own program, the president reported: "We did not expect to have raised the funds in the usual sense of the word," expecting that the bulk would come in wills and trusts. In an attempt to change the image created in the Holt era that Rollins was "always begging and always spending more than its income," he had constructed a development program based on "winning support rather than solicitation," even though such an approach might take a long time to show results.[17]

Finally conceding in 1962 that his "development program was lagging," the president reluctantly accepted the management study that was suggested in the previous year. In the past spring semester, the trustees signed a contract with the American Institute of Management, a New York firm that had recently completed an impressive audit of a college in Pennsylvania. A representative arrived at Rollins in September 1962, completed his study by December and submitted a report in January 1963.

The report began by praising several aspects of the McKean administration's efforts. Its academic goals were correct; it was defining and redefining the educational philosophy of Hamilton Holt, it was improving the quality of students and teachers and it was relating the college to its own geographical area. The report particularly praised McKean's efforts to create a new community role for the college through the General Studies Program, through the Patrick Air Force Base Program and through a proposed research institute in space science. It further praised the administration for holding these programs to a secondary function, leaving the liberal arts program at the center. It did recommend the college appoint a dean of community programs and it suggested these programs be tied more closely to the college by using its own faculty and buildings and by bringing the standards of the program to the college's level. These recommendations almost precisely paralleled those of a planning committee some 15 years later. The AIM report suggested that the college give serious thought to these problems.[18]

The investigators felt the most pressing administrative problem was the absence of a development program. They suggested appointing a permanent development officer with the status of a vice president whose sole function would be to organize and direct the development effort of the college. They recommended short-term (three to five years) and long-term (10 to 15 years) plans that would provide the college with a sense of direction. The development officer would construct a program based on plans that would involve all possible sources of support: alumni, trustees, local business and industry, national business and foundations, the community, parents and friends of the college.

The investigators focused their attention on the alumni contributions, a source of support that possessed little to praise. The problems, they reported, came from the Rollins Alumni Corporation. The organization responsible for alumni affairs and contributions remained an *independent* entity with its own board of directors and executive director. The AIM's report was direct in its analysis and suggestion: "The continued independence of the Alumni organization today is anachronistic, purposeless and damaging. Certainly the Alumni organization can have no reason for existence except support of the College. Yet its separateness denies it the benefit of direct guidance by the administration and Trustees that could improve its support of the College." The report suggested the trustees should change "this awkward arrangement" and reunite "their organization with the college it was founded to serve." It was the responsibility of the alumni association, the institute report lectured, to "convince the alumni that their education was in great part subsidized; that their schooling had been underwritten by friends of the college through contributed funds, and by teachers willing to teach without adequate compensation, and by administrators and staff who worked for low wages." AIM ended its study with an optimistic prediction for Rollins' future—if the college moved forcefully to deal with its quite manageable problems.

The institute presented the college with a challenging

analysis and evaluation, one that could have served, had McKean chosen to use it, as the basis for a planning document. But the administration neither requested nor desired the audit and therefore did not embrace enthusiastically a report full of implicit criticisms. After a few polite bows to the report's suggestions, the administration shelved the document, deeming the criticisms unwarranted and unspecific. Besides, it argued, the Southern Association of Colleges and Schools (SACS) had just directed a self-study evaluation that already outlined the college's problems and needs.

The problem with this argument is normally the SACS studies are designed to make certain a college has maintained its accreditation standards. It rarely ever probes deeply a college's administration issues. The association's study merely noted that the president's "high degree of informal" administration created uncertain lines of responsibility and communication; it suggested the creation of higher standards in the college's peripheral programs, but primarily, it lauded the college's "personalized education," its improved science program and its beautiful campus. Understandably, in the eyes of the administration, the Southern Association of Colleges and Schools report described the college's "true condition."[19]

One of the "true conditions" the administration was most proud was its annually balanced budget. After all, after years of deficit financing during the Holt era, the achievement was not an inconsequential one. Unfortunately, this balanced budget did not allow the college to pay faculty competitive salaries in comparison to similar institutions. This factor led to some faculty discontent and probably contributed to high faculty attrition. Each annual report of the president contained a section entitled, "Serious Losses to the College," wherein he listed talented faculty and staff who had left for more lucrative positions. In 1963, for example, he cited a typical case of a faculty member with a salary of $5,700 who left Rollins for a position which paid him $3,000 more. The president reported faculty complained that astronomical raises elsewhere in academia were not being matched at Rollins.[20]

Ironically one of the administration's successes—improvement in quality faculty—led to serious problems in late 1960s. In the decade between 1960 and 1970, many of the older professors began to retire and to be replaced by a large group of young, activist professors with doctorates. Looking to respond to the changes taking place in academia throughout the nation, and eager to assume responsibility of the college in the next decades, this young faculty cohort began to pressure the administration for changes in leadership. In combination with an assertive student body, this faculty inevitably turned critical eyes on an administration they felt was lagging behind the times. Steeped in the values and mores of pre-World War II America, McKean and his staff uneasily faced the Vietnam generation and its world of drugs, mini-skirts, long hair, sexual freedom, political activism and anti-establishment attitudes. Efforts by the administration to resist these new modes of behavior brought only derision. An editorial in the January 19, 1968, issue of *The Sandspur* denounced the administration's over-protective *in loco parentis* policies. A small infraction "of general conformity in appearance," wrote the editor, "brought letters of protest to the students' parents." Frequently, parents of several male students received letters from the dean's office "complaining about the length of their son's hair." A new generation of students eager to break down the administration's paternalist attitude and a group of aggressive, young faculty discouraged by low salaries and disappointed with the administration's failures to fully realize the college's academic potential began exerting tremendous pressure on McKean for some sense of direction. When the trustees arrived for the 1968 commencement meeting, they found the campus in mild turmoil. Just prior to the end of the spring term, the community was shaken by the firing of three popular faculty members for improper personal conduct. Although most of the college community supported the dismissals, many of the faculty attributed the dismissals to a lack of leadership. Even earlier, McKean seemed to sense the growing of serious discontent. He frankly admitted in his 1969 annual report that the faculty believed his administration to be "ineffective and that was the college's chief problem." In May 1969, as several trustees arrived for the commencement meeting, a faculty group expressed a loss of confidence in the president's leadership. Sensing an impending crisis, the trustees began negotiations with McKean for his resignation. They seized upon the beleaguered president's suggestion in his February report for a college reorganization that would create the position of a chancellor responsible for endowment development. The trustee negotiators offered that position to McKean, and he agreed.

Thus, despite his significant achievements, McKean's presidency ended amid a sense of frustration. Although most of the faculty admired McKean's sense of humanity and his genuine sensitivity to faculty and student needs, they were also deeply disappointed with his impressionistic administrative style and with his inability to give more purposeful leadership to the college. The president's last annual report revealed his own sense of frustration. In the report he proclaimed he, as well as the faculty, knew that Rollins College *should be* standing alongside the nation's best small liberal arts colleges. He, as well as the faculty, knew the college was worthy of the same financial support that had helped make other colleges great. Thus, eighteen years after he assumed the presidency, Hugh McKean was still searching for the kind of breakthroughs that would advance the college beyond the Holt years. He could depict the vision in poetic language, but it always seemed just out of his grasp. It was a story of good intentions, missed chances and lost opportunities. While many small liberal arts colleges took advantage of the all too brief period of a cornucopia educational abundance, Rollins made only moderate advances. Under McKean, the college had held its own as a *good* liberal arts college, but the important elements of the community never considered that sufficient. In a situation maddeningly familiar to Rollins supporters, the college seemed perpetually poised on the edge of greatness.

With stoic reluctance, the aging president stepped down. He had been associated with the college for almost four decades and the length of his presidency was exceeded only by his idol. His ability to restore the Holt patrimony and to bring harmony and hope back to a dispirited college was his greatest accomplishment. But restoration of that patrimony may have also been the source of his most salient weakness. In a period of dramatic educational change, McKean seemed stuck in the past, unable to move beyond the world of his most cherished memories. Ironically, like Wagner, McKean was a captive of the Holt era.

After retirement, McKean devoted his time to planning a museum that would house his impressive Tiffany stained glass collection. His professional life had come full circle. At the beginning, he had told the trustees he was an artist who should be teaching instead of undertaking the role of president. He had taught art for 20 years, he told them, and that is what he should be doing. However, McKean relished serving as president of Rollins College; that early assessment of his own abilities was as much an insightful self-perception as it was an act of modesty.

1. McKean to Lester Sutler, January 24, 1952. For more details on McKean's background and a good discussion of his painting career see Randy Noles, "The Hugh We Never Knew," *Winter Park Magazine,* Winter 2016.

2. Alcott Deming to McKean, June 5, 1951

Charles Hosmer Morse first visited Winter Park in the early 1880s and was enamored by its natural beauty. He purchased property on Lake Osceola and soon became involved in the development of the city of Winter Park. By 1904, he had become the largest landowner in the area. His land donations to the city, many of them made anonymously, are sites of such prominent city facilities as City Hall, the Woman's Club, the municipal golf course and Central Park. By 1915, Charles Hosmer Morse retired to Winter Park permanently. In 1920, just one year before he died, he acquired land situated between Lakes Virginia, Berry and Mizell. On this site, he planted citrus groves and carved a scenic road that would later become a local attraction: Winter Park's treasured Genius Drive.

Jeannette Genius McKean was the granddaughter of Charles Hosmer Morse. She was born in 1909 into an atmosphere of refined tastes and talents. Both the Morse and Genius families were collectors of fine art. Jeannette's mother, Elizabeth Morse Genius, loved to paint, and passed this artistic bent onto her daughter. In college, Jeannette studied art and interior design. She had an affinity for designing "vignettes," or themed rooms. Jeannette became an acclaimed painter, heavily influenced by the natural world. In 1936, Jeannette's parents, Elizabeth Morse and Richard Genius, built a Spanish renaissance-style home on Lake Virginia in Winter Park across from Rollins College. Eventually, Jeannette and her husband, Hugh McKean, inherited Wind Song and the surrounding land. Hugh and Jeannette often entertained the faculty at Wind Song during the years of his presidency.

3. Biographical information drawn from the Hanna Papers, Archive. In addition to his immeasurable contributions to Rollins College, Fred Hanna was perhaps its most prolific scholar.

4. S*andspur*, September 27, 1951.

5. The national educational account was reconstructed from Christopher Jencks and David Reisman, *The Academic Revolution* (1962), 28-50. Report of the Presidents Commission on Higher Education, 1947, 41-51; Frederick Rudolph, *Curriculum*, 282-285.

6. President's Annual Report, 1954.

7. Faculty Minutes, January 7, 1952.

8. Trustee Minutes, July 11, 1951; Report to the Trustees, February, 1952. Emphasis added.

9. Trustee Minutes, February 23, 1952.

10. President's Annual Report, 1955; 1956.

11. *Ibid.*, 1965.

12. *Ibid.,* 1953, 1954, 1955.

13. Ibid. Mckean added several buildings the campus: five new dormitories, Rex Beach Hall, Elizabeth Hall, McKean Hall, Holt Hall, and Ward Hall. He also raised money to fund a classroom building for Crummer Business School and to build the Bush Science Center.

14. Copies of McKean proclamations in his Archive papers.

President Hamilton Holt had admired the pieces for years; in 1929 he wrote his friend that they "have long appealed to my antique sense" and he believed they would be "fittingly enshrined" at Rollins.

In 1959 Genevieve Sams, the wife of the Senator, visited the campus and asked about the statues. By then, the Cat had been destroyed (the location of its remains is unknown), and the Fox appeared only on the College's annual holiday. Royle Howard, secretary to the Archives, wrote to update Mrs. Sams: "The poor cat has met with a fatal accident, but the Fox is a treasured possession of the College, and when he comes out of hiding, an occasion of much joy!" Mrs. Sams gave the Archives as much background information on the statues as she could. They originally came from France, she said, and although it was "hearsay," she had been told that these were satirical pieces, depicting "the Populace (Cat) making his sweeping bow in hypocritical salute to the Papacy (Fox)."

15. President's Annual Report, 1968.

16.. President's Report, 1963

17. Faculty Minutes, 1963.

18. Report of William Reich for the American Institution of Management, January, 1963.

19. *Ibid.*

20. *Trustee Minutes, May, 1969; December, 1969*

Chapter 10

———

TO THE CENTENNIAL,
1978 – 1985

THE CHOICE OF Jack Critchfield to replace Hugh McKean came after a search that lasted through the summer of 1968. When he accepted the call to Rollins, Critchfield was serving as associate provost at the University of Pittsburgh. That office was his sole administrative experience. He had received a B.S. in Education from Slippery Rock State University, a small former normal state school in Pennsylvania. Subsequently he earned a M.A. and in 1968, an Ed.D. from the University of Pittsburgh. For the 11th time, the college entrusted its future to a person with no collegiate presidential experience, no fund raising experience and a meager administrative background. As with the others, he was forced to learn how to govern while he was governing. He did possess promising personal qualities: he was young (36), bright and afable, and he approached this new challenge with a youthful enthusiasm and a style reminiscent of an early Paul Wagner. While McKean governed somewhat impressionistically, believing quality would speak for itself, Critchfield set about governing with a management outlook. After the intensely personal and paternalistic style of President McKean, community members believed they saw in Critchfiled a more objective, predictable and professional management approach to college governance.

True to this perception, one of Critchfield's first endeavors was to lead the faculty in a college governance restructuring process. He spearheaded a revision that led to the creation of a College Senate headed by a faculty president, vice president and secretary. The revision also created the new office of Provost that, along with the faculty senate structure, placed academic affairs completely in the hands of the faculty. This represented a major shift in the college's traditional governing arrangements. Traditionally, the president assumed the role of academic leader, presiding at faculty meetings and keeping enough involvement with academic affairs to intelligently represent the college's academic program. The direction of the new governance, which tended to separate the president from academic affairs, undoubtedly came from Critchfield's university experience. On the other hand, placing more authority with the faculty was probably another reaction to Wagner's overbearing leadership style. It remained to be seen whether or not it was wise to isolate the president from the essential academic core of the college community.

Four years before Critchfield arrived, the faculty had already set in motion a major curriculum revision. The Hourglass Curriculum provided a course of study that required students to begin with broad foundation and to concentrate on particular interests, related fields and directed studies in their middle years. In their senior year, students would draw upon the foundation courses and major interests to integrate their knowledge though a Senior Synoptic Course. Finally, passing a comprehensive examination would be the last requirement for graduation. The new curriculum owed its guiding principles to the college's progressive student-centered patrimony. "Inherent in the new plan," the catalog explained, "is the philosophy that each student should move from a passive absorption of knowledge to self-motivated learning." In a statement Hamilton Holt would have found familiar, the catalog made clear the "final responsibility for each student's academic progress rests with the student."[1]

Students responded with enthusiasm to these new progressive initiatives, creating their own alternative programs. Within the academic realm, the students initiated the Holt House, a program in which they chose "dons" to serve as "a faculty advisors." The student and the don designed a personalized program of study, which they formalized with contracts. In the social realm, students pushed for alternative housing choices and special interest groups, like the Holt House, the Fine Arts House, the Student Center for Social Concerns and the Environmental Conservation Organization.

Coincidentally with the new curriculum reforms, social pressures calling for more diversity began to reshape the college community. More than a decade after the Supreme

Court's desegregation decision, Rollins still remained an all-white college. Responding to demands for change, the college admitted its first African American student in 1968. By the mid-1970s a larger enrollment of African American students led to the creation of the Black Student Union. Founded in 1972 to serve an ever-increasing population of black students, the BSU aimed to "bring together students who are interested in, passionate about, or members of the black community." Almost immediately the BSU began to make the college aware of the nation's African American heritage. The organization's Black Awareness Week was its successful cultural diversity contribution. In its first years, this annual event attracted activist speakers such as Dick Gregory and Jesse Jackson. The first Black Awareness Week also focused on "An African Happening" and a "soul luncheon." In later years, the latter morphed into an annual event called Soul Food Sunday, a "semi-formal, catered dinner of traditional African-American cuisine celebrating Black History Month." Soul Food Sunday, declared a BSU proclamation, "embodies everything that the BSU stands for—community, inclusivity and connection."[2]

By the mid-1970s, the numbers of black students still remained just a trickle. Concerned with this slow pace of recruitment, the BSU issued a public petition in 1975 for a policy of affirmative action. It "demanded" the college increase black students to numbers "no less than ten percent of the total student body." The BSU called for the college to provide "more financial aid for black students," to appoint a BSU faculty adviser "familiar with problems peculiar to black students," to add more courses in the curriculum and more books in the library "dealing the history, sociology and literature of black people." The petition was followed by a faculty appeal, initiated by Professor of English Maurice O'Sullivan, asking the trustees and President Critchfield to act quickly to meet the demands of the black students. Citing the 1977–1978 Handbook stating the college's "commitment to understand and value other cultures and to identify and correct deficiencies in the social structure," the faculty petition called on the administration to "increase the minority population of the total college community with all deliberate speed" and "for President Critchfield to report to the faculty in the May faculty meeting on the progress being made." By the Rollins' centennial, enough black students had enrolled to allow for the creation of an academic minor in Africa and African American Studies.[3]

Within a few years of the introduction of the Hourglass Curriculum, the faculty had made so many revisions to the program it hardly resembled its original course of study. Therefore, in 1978, a curriculum committee headed by philosopher Bruce Wavell and historian Jack Lane proposed yet another major curriculum reform. The new curriculum was based on Benjamin Bloom's taxonomy, a set of hierarchical learning domains used to classify educational learning objectives into levels of complexity and mastery. The new curriculum's three domains were: skills acquisition, cognitive and affective developments. Written composition and value skills were assigned to courses throughout the departments. A grant from the National Endowment for Humanities allowed the faculty to attend training workshops in each area.[4]

By drawing upon Bloom's taxonomy, the new curriculum was at the cutting-edge of educational thought at the time. It was constructed in part to meet the demands of "academic accountability," a movement that gained even more steam in the years ahead. Lane and Wavell had explored the possibility of creating a revised core curriculum more in tune with Rollins' past traditions, but found little enthusiasm among the faculty. The recently arrived faculty resisted another program that required teaching interdisciplinary courses. Bloom's taxonomy allowed for a rational, sequential approach to learning without ignoring the growing trend among the faculty toward emphasizing departmental concerns. What bothered both Lane and Wavell and other faculty members was the loss of interdepartmental cooperation. The taxonomy compromise brought more order to the curriculum, but it left unanswered the question of the how it contributed to a liberal education.

Several faculty members, concerned the college was drifting away from its progressive roots, created a new innovative program called the Community of Learners (COL). The COL was composed of a small group of students and a Master Learner, a faculty member who took a term away from teaching to join the community. Together, the learners attended the same classes, participated in special seminars, maintained diaries and offered each other support. The COL student members formed a cohesive small community where members shared learning experiences and the Master Learner gained a fresh perspective on education from the students' point of view.[5]

Two programs that for several decades had coexisted

with the Arts and Sciences College realized substantial growth. The Roy E. Crummer Graduate School of Business, established a night program leading to the M.B.A as well as a special M.B.A. program for local business executives. In 1985, the Crummer School won AACSB accreditation, joining schools like Harvard and the University of Chicago as colleges with M.B.A. programs but not undergraduate majors in business. The continuing education evening school showed growth and development as well. In 1972, the school's name was changed from the Central Florida School for Continuing Studies to the Rollins School of Continuing Education. More alterations to its structure were implemented in the following years. In addition to creating a graduate degree in education, the school offered Associate of Arts (A.A.), Bachelor of General Studies (B.G.S.), and B.S. degrees. Later the school was then divided into the Division of Continuing Education (DCE) and the Division of Non-Credit Programs, which encompassed the School of Creative Arts. With these overall structural changes, the evening program enrollment increased 11 percent in one year.

Throughout these early years, although not directly involved, Critchfield actively supported the new academic and social changes taking place on the campus. With his academic responsibility diminished by the new governance structure, he was able to devote a large portion of his time to administering the college's multiple programs and to fund-raising. He created the college's first functioning development office, but failed to appoint a professional director. He tended to hire officers with training and experiences in fields other than development, one of whom was a retired general. As with former presidents, the bulk of fundraising fell on his shoulders. Critchfield's greatest virtue in this area was his talent for establishing relationships with local businessmen to a degree that had eluded other presidents. He made many new contacts that would serve the college well in the future. Perhaps his most important contribution to the financial future of Rollins College was the establishment of a relationship with the Harold Alfond family and the Alfond Foundation. The Alfonds' son Ted and his wife Barbara graduated from Rollins in 1968 and immediately became fervent supporters of the college.

In 1967, the family provided the funds for the Alfond Athletic Scholarship. Later the family's gift allowed the college to build the Alfond Pool, its first swimming facility. Over the decades, Lake Virginia had provided the only opportunity for recreational swimming and intercollegiate swim tournaments. By the 1950s, however, the water in the lake had become too polluted for swimming. Therefore, the Alfond Pool, completed in 1973 and located on the shores of Lake Virginia, became a perfect facility for aquatic sports and a favorite space for student recreation.

A year later, Hauck Hall, home of the Foreign Language Department, was built next to Casa Iberia thanks to a gift from Frederick A. Hauck, a legendary benefactor from Cincinnati who had retired in Winter Park. The Music Department moved into the newly constructed R. D. Keene Hall later that year. In 1978, thanks to a gift from George D. and Harriet W. Cornell, the Art Department and the Rollins College Museum of Art found a new home in the Cornell Fine

Arts Center. To Critchfield's great credit, these necessary buildings—all constructed in Rollins' traditional Spanish Mediterranean style—added a new dimension to the physical plant.

Consistent with a familiar pattern of deception, Critchfield was led to believe the college had balanced its budget throughout the McKean years. Thus, the new president was shocked to learn he would be required to raise an additional $100,000 to balance the budget in his first year. He later found that the college had operated in the red for the past decade with a secret "angel" making up the difference with a single gift at the end of the each year. Such a bestowal was unavailable to Critchfield. At the Board of Trustee's insistence he balanced the budget, Critichfield began selling offsite property owned by the college to make up any deficit. The first to be sold was the Pelican Beach House on New Smyrna Beach. Built in the 1920s as a conference center for the Presbyterian Church USA, Rollins had received it as a gift in 1931, and Hamilton Holt turned it into a recreational beach house for the college community. The college sold the ocean front lot for $150,000; the building was demolished and replaced by a 150-unit condominium. Critchfield also sold Martin Hall, a gift of John and Prestonia Martin, located across from the college on Lake Virginia. John Martin who was a specialist in international affairs, served as visiting professor at the college during the 1930s. His wife Prestonia Mann, was a popular writer, who focused on feminist and poverty themes. The building had housed the Music Department until the construction of Keene Hall in 1974. The two pieces of extremely valuable property were sold for what many thought were bargain prices.

From the beginning of his tenure, Critchfield indicated he would serve no more than 10 years. True to his promise, he announced in 1977 he would retire at the end of the 1978 academic year to assume the post of CEO of the Florida Power Company.

Students dedicated their 1977–1978 yearbook, the *Tomokan*, to President Critchfield "in grateful thanks for his years of dedication to Rollins College." The issue contained tributes from several members of the community. One was particularly perceptive. "Jack brought to the presidency a realism of what could and could not be accomplished. He was a pragmatic, tolerant leader with an ability to generate the best in people. He compensated for his lack of academic experience with insight and good common sense." Perhaps these qualities were exactly the ones most needed to sustain the college in the post McKean years.

The announcement sparked a presidential search that ended with the appointment of Thaddeus Seymour as Rollins' 12th president. For the first time since the Blackman era, the trustees appointed a man with a long and successful background in academia, and for the first time, the college would be guided by a person with previous experience as president of a college. After receiving an undergraduate degree from the University of California, Berkeley, Seymour was awarded a master's and a doctorate degree in literature from the University of North Carolina. His first teaching position was at Dartmouth where, in 1959, he was appointed dean of the college. Ten years later he accepted a call to the presidency of Wabash College in Indiana, where he remained until coming to Rollins.

Seymour found the college in a state of disquiet. Members of the liberal arts faculty indicated to him that the college was losing its focus. A major cause, they argued, was the addition over several decades of piecemeal peripheral programs extending the college far beyond its central liberal arts mission. They cited the creation of a business progam as an example. The trustees created a School of Business early in the McKean administration, and McKean then appointed a dean. The purpose of the school, McKean told the faculty, was to encourage more males to apply for admission. The business school limped along until 1964, when Roy E. Crummer, a successful Florida businessman, donated a million dollars to build a new facility to house the program. From this point on, the Crummer School of Business made consistent growth. After several months of preparation under the deanship of Dr. Martin Schatz, the graduate school received accreditation from the American Assembly of Collegiate Schools of Business. By 1980, one-third of the undergraduate students (mostly male) were majoring in business, requiring a large increase in the size of business faculty. According to the Arts and Sciences faculty, this enlargement of the undergraduate major threatened to turn the college into a business school with a liberal arts college attached. For years the liberal arts faculty attempted to deal with this problem with little success.[6]

Another program peripheral to the liberal arts college was created after World War II when Rollins was asked to offer adult education courses for service personal at Patrick Air Force Base. The program was so successful (at least financially) that in 1960 the Board of Trustees authorized extending the program to the Winter Park campus. In order to distinguish it from the liberal arts college, the Institute for General Studies awarded the program a General Studies degree. As mentioned earlier, the program under President Critchfield began offering additional Bachelor of Arts and Bachelor of Science degrees. The year Critchfield announced his retirement, continuing education added a Master's Degree in Guidance and Counseling. Many of the courses in the program were taught in overloads by Rollins faculty. This condition raised the issue of whether the SCE was sapping the resources of the liberal arts college. These coexisting programs raised an even more fundamental question: Where and how did these programs fit into the liberal education mission of the college?

Seymour's experience at Dartmouth and Wabash left him deeply committed to traditional liberal arts education. After listening to the liberal arts faculty, President Seymour reset the direction of the college. In his first major speech, he urged Rollins to "return to its roots. Our aim is to know ourselves and to be known by others as the finest small liberal arts college in the Southeast, standing among the finest colleges in the country. The future destiny of Rollins College depends upon its excellence—the quality of the educational experience, the quality of the students and faculty, the quality of individual performance and the quality of our life and work together."

In one of his first acts, President Seymour initiated the process that pointed the college toward that goal. At his suggestion, the trustees established a College Planning

Committee, charging it with "the responsibility to organize and implement a comprehensive planning effort which will engage the participation of all elements of a college community." In particular the charge asked the committee to:

1. Articulate the institutional mission of the college
2. Propose an institutional structure and program which reflect this mission
3. Develop appropriate objectives for each division of the college
4. Recommend allocation of funds, physical resources and personnel
5. Determine the needs and goals of a development effort to coincide with the college Centennial.

THE COMMITTEE, UNDER the chairmanship of Dr. Daniel R. DeNicola, professor of philosophy, presented a mission statement that set the tone for the college's expectations: "For nearly a century the primary mission of Rollins has been to provide excellent liberal arts education for students of ability and promise. It is and should remain a small independent co-educational institution serving a national constituency."

After 18 months of exacting labor, the committee produced a detailed study of this "set of imposing tasks," including recommendations for their implementation. With the publication of the Planning Report, a wave of optimism and expectation swept the campus. Upon recommendation of the report, the business major became a minor. A communications major was placed in the same category. The initial apprehension that turning business and communications majors into minors would cause a drop in enrollment proved unfounded. For the next few years, enrollment remained steady and, in some years, it significantly increased. Thus, one of the chief issues facing Seymour when he arrived had been resolved without serious damage. As Seymour noted during the debate, "if you say you are a liberal arts college, then you have to be a liberal arts college."[7]

Other changes added emphasis to restoration of the college's traditional roots. In 1980, the college revived its dormant Classics Department, complete with an endowed chair funded through the National Endowment for the Humanities' grant. The second change was symbolic but nonetheless significant: Rollins diplomas were once again written in Latin. When Seymour learned of the Fox Day tradition and that it had been discontinued during the previous administration, he immediately reinstated it. Liberal education, he noted, was supposed to be fun as well as serious. In the spring of 1978, after 8 years in seclusion, the fox reappeared on the horseshoe lawn to announce the resumption of a venerable tradition.[8]

President Seymour hired two new administration officers who would make significant contributions to securing the future of the college. In 1984, he called David Erdmann to serve as dean of admissions. A graduate of Colby College, Erdmann came to Rollins with a deep appreciation for the importance of a liberal education. During his almost 30 years as dean, Erdmann created a professional approach to the Rollins' admission process that consistently attracted highly qualified students to the college. Seymour's other addition to the administration was Treasurer Jesse Morgan. He had persuaded Morgan to come to Rollins from his position of vice president/treasurer at Tulane University. Under Mr. Morgan's guidance, the school eliminated operating deficits and overhauled its bill collection and investment procedures. President Seymour later said "persuading Jesse to come over from Tulane was the best thing I have had a hand in here at Rollins."

Having brought some stability to the college's finances, Seymour turned his attention to the need for a new library. Mills Memorial Library, the last building constructed during the Holt administration, was proving woefully inadequate to meet the needs of a college growing in numbers of students and faculty. Olin Library, dedicated in 1985 and funded by a F.W. Olin Foundation gift, had a capacity two times that of Mills Library. Gamble Rogers's design was consistent with the college's traditional Spanish Mediterranean architectural style, with the addition of a few Gothic and Roman features. The state-of-the-art library followed prevailing trends in library design with open floor space that mingled reading stations and bookshelves. Olin Library instantly became the center of campus academic life.

Sadly, the historic Knowles Hall II was demolished to make a space for the library. At one time Knowles was considered the most beautiful building on campus, and its demolition meant the loss of another physical reminder of the college's early history. Fortunately, Chase and Carnegie Halls, built in styles similar to Knowles II, provided some reminders of the college community's rich architectural past. As the college's oldest structure, Pinehurst was in a special category. As part of the centennial celebration,

President Seymour ordered the renovation of Pinehurst in a way that would return it to its original state. The building was stripped of layer upon layer of paint then repainted according to the instructions found in the original plans. To ensure that the college's only remaining wooden building would survive the wrecking ball, Pinehurst was placed on the Winter Park Register of Historic Places. One of Seymour's last contributions to the Rollins' physical landscape was to secure funds for the construction of a home for the social science division, which had been displaced by the demolition of Knowles II. The college's most generous benefactors, George and Harriet Cornell, both 1939 Rollins graduates, provided the funds. Built in a style resembling a Spanish villa, the Cornell Hall for the Social Sciences was constructed with the distinctive feature of having a community open space in its center. A tiled logia containing permanent benches, wooden tables and a deli cafe nearby became a central gathering space for students and faculty. An engraved "schoolhouse stone" was set as a main feature of the courtyard. The slab was cut from the Silurian formation near Central Valley School in New York, a school founded by George Cornell's grandfather.

The years of the Seymour presidency proved to be a turning point in Rollins' history. At a time when the college community was somewhat adrift—or at best standing still—Seymour instilled a revived enthusiasm, provided a sense of continuity and gave Rollins a new sense of direction. By the end of his tenure, the college had firmly established that its identity and its future rested with its historical liberal education mission. It was left for future presidents to determine how the additional programs and the liberal arts fit the overall liberal education mission. Perhaps John Phillips, president of the National Association of Independent College and Universities, best summarized what he called Seymour's remarkable accomplishments: "He's gone against the trends of others saying whatever people want, let's provide it. Seymour had never veered from his purpose of establishing a high-quality liberal arts institution in a place that's associated in the public's mind with Disney World and fun in the sun."

At the same time as the Rollins community was reclaiming its roots, the college was also fortuitously nearing its 100th anniversary. In 1985, in addition to an elaborate ceremony on Founder's Day (which included a revival of the Animated Magazine and a colorful fireworks display), the centennial allowed the college to emphasize and reflect on its venerable liberal education heritage. During that century, the little school, founded in a tiny village on the fringes of the Florida frontier, had been transformed into a preeminent liberal arts college. As a proof of its success, starting in 2004, *US News and World Report* annually ranked the college number one in academic quality in the Southeast.

The 100-year journey had not been without its of highs and lows or its exhilarating successes and dispiriting failures. Rollins often found itself teetering on the edge of financial disaster or suffering from self-inflicted wounds; however, at the last moment, a group of intrepid souls had emerged to save the little college from oblivion. The single most meaningful phrase to describe the vicissitudes of college's 100-year journey would be: "Rollins College Persevered." Perhaps the insight of the great scientist Louis Pasteur explains the resolute character of Rollins College. "It may be necessary to encounter defeats," Pasteur once observed, "so you can know who you are, what you can rise from, how you can still come out of it."

In spite of every obstacle thrown in their paths, year after year, decade after decade, committed presidents, administrators, faculty, students and staff expended their love and labor in creating and passing on to the next generation a well grounded liberal arts college. The intrepid little band of 19th century Congregationalists had dreamed of a college, "with her broad foundations wisely laid" and with "fair halls clustering in their quiet shade by the blue lake," that would grow to become an exceptional institution of higher learning. One hundred years later, that vision had finally come to fruition. However, no one participating in the centennial commemoration thought the college had reached its possibilities. In true progressive tradition, they were passing on to future generations a liberal arts institution that was prepared for even more changes and transformations. A committed belief in transformative change is probably the most revealing and enduring legacy of the college's 100-year history.

No one understood the significance of this progressive tradition better than Hamilton Holt. In 1927, he wrote in the first Animated Magazine brochure—with prophetic insight—a clever introduction that portrayed Rollins College as a school that spoke for itself. Drawing inspiration from Daniel Webster's plea that Dartmouth was small but still loved, the "College" then proclaimed:

I am only a small college and as I have no Daniel Webster to plead for me, I want to tell you frankly of my history. In point of years I am the oldest of all educational institutions in Florida. The earliest years are of stories and service on the part of those devoted New Englanders who dreamed of a college in Central Florida. How well they planned and how wisely they built is revealed in the spirit and purpose of Rollins College. While I am proud of my past and dedicated to a continuance of the old ideals, I am facing the future with new confidence born of the devotion of many friends, the loyalty of thousands of Alumni and the dedication of the faculty and my new president. With the help of all these the "New Rollins" is being built.

He later added an even more prescient coda to that last sentence: "Rollins College is a daring dream in the process of fulfillment. It has not "arrived"—and we hope it never will." Almost a century after Holt penned these words, the vision of a "New Rollins" rooted in past liberal education traditions and in the process of fulfillment, remains the college's central ideal and its main source of identity. To paraphrase the psalmist, after 100 years of striving, the lines had finally fallen in pleasant places and the college's "goodly heritage" would serve as a solid foundation for future generations.

FIAT LUX

1.Rollins College Catalog, 1965

2. See article in *Rollins 360, January, 2016*, entitled "Black Student Union," by Rob Humphreys.

3. See Critchfield Papers for copy of petition.

4. For a fuller description of the Hourglass Curriculum see Rollins College 1965-1966.

5. Brochures about the COL program in Rollins Archives. I created the program so some of the description comes from my experience.

6. The following discussion of early Seymour comes from documents in the Archives and from my own personal experience.

7. Keith Henderson, "How Thad Seymour Led a College Back to its Academic Roots," *Christian Science Monitor*, March 10, 1986.

8. Jay Hamburg, "The Day They Saved Fox Day," *Rollins 360*, March 23 2015.

ACKNOWLEDGMENTS

RESEARCHING AND WRITING HISTORY is a lonely endeavor. Still, every historian understands the finished product is the result of a cooperative effort. Therefore, with deep appreciation, I acknowledge the many friends and colleagues who helped make this book possible.

I want to express my appreciation to President Thaddeus Seymour for appointing me college historian and thus trusting that I had the wherewithal to undertake the college's centennial history. I was greatly buoyed by his confidence in me.

I want to give special consideration to Head of Archives and Special Collections Wenxian Zhang and Archival Specialists Darla Moore and Rachel Walton. Together, they have taken the archives to a new level. Their help and encouragement has been invaluable.

Thanks also to: President Grant Cornwell, who drew me back to the past by suggesting that I revive the dormant manuscript; Professor Maurice O'Sullivan, Kenneth Curry professor of English, a comrade in several collaborations, closet historian, and academic compatriot; Bob Morris, president and publisher of Story Farm; copy editor Marcela Oliveira; and designer Jason Farmand.

Finally, I would like to thank Janne, my wife, my soul mate and a dedicated grammarian. She laboriously read and edited every single page of the manuscript twice, preventing many embarrassing errors from creeping into the finished book. In this sense she has been a true collaborator.

INDEX

Morgan, Jesse, 310–311
Morse, Charles Hosmer, 118, 272
Morse, Oliver C., 98
Morton, Annie, 26, 52–53
Mt. Dora, FL, 12, 14, 18–19

N

Normal program, 40, 83
northern *vs.* southern identity
    of Rollins College, 9–10,
    23–24, 69–70, 112–113

O

Oldham, Cecil, 183
Olin Library, 311
O'Neal, William, 98, 209–210
Orange City, FL, 12, 14, 18–20

P

Patrick Air Force Base college
    program, 277, 307–308
Pattee, Fred, 160
Pearsons, Daniel K., 97–100
Pelican Beach House, 305
Perpente, Frances, 205
Phillips, John, 313
Pinehurst, 43–45, 311–312
Preparatory Department, 39–40
Pritchett, Henry S., 102–104
progressive culture of Rollins
    College, 162–163, 175
progressive education, 134–155
property sales to balance the
    annual budget, 305–306

R

racial tensions, 72–73, 106–107,
    162
Rand, George, 25
religion
    attacks on Christianity by John
      Rice, 170–172
    Congregational Church
      Association, 6–13, 171

Presbyterian and
    Congregational
    Association partnership,
    120
    requirements for students, 48,
      50
    requirements for trustees and
      faculty, 22–23
    role in college foundings
      throughout America,
      3–4
Rice, John A., 160–161, 168–192
Robbins, Margaret Drier, 186–187
Robinson, John Harvey, 152
Rockefeller Foundation, General
    Education Board of the,
    112–114
Rollins, Alonzo, 17
Rollins, George, 25
Root, Eva J., 47, 53
rules of behavior for students,
    48–51
Russell, Annie, 205

S

science education, 47
Seymour, Thaddeus, 306–313
Short, William, 207–209
Slosson, Edwin, 135–136
Smith, Eugene, 254
socialization, 48–49
Southern Association of Colleges
    and Schools (SACS), 289
sports, organized, 109–110, 234–
    235, 237
Sprague, Robert, 118–122
Starr, Nathan, 253
Stetson University, 113–114
Stone, Wendell, 236–238, 240–242,
    245
Student Center, 215
student sentiment about campus
    policies, 250–252
Suit, Hal, 254
"super-president," search for a,
    119–120

T

teachers' college. *See* Normal
program
Tiedtke, John M., 224–225, 238,
242, 244–245, 265–266, 274
Tollefson, Horace ("Tolly"), 236
The Tomokan, 306
Tory, Allan, 183
Training Department, 40–41
train travel, 43
transportation. *See* train travel
tuition, 41–42, 218–220
two-hour conference plan, 134–147,
165–167
Tyler, H. W., 177

V

Vietnam generation, difficulties
during the, 290–291

W

Waddell, George Edward "Rube,"
110
Wagner, Paul
arbitrary decision making,
236–238, 240
cancellation of the football
program, 234–235, 237
increased power and authority
at the expense of faculty,
245–250
legacy, 266–267
opposition to, 250–265
refusal to resign the presidency,
262–266
theatrical audio-visual
presentations, 232–233,
242–244
"Wagner affair" battle between
staff and students,
255–266
youthful demeanor, 233–234
Walton, Miller, 260
war, effects of, 220–222, 238–239
Ward, Emma Sprague, 85–86
Ward, George Morgan, 76–90, 116,
117–118

Warren, Frances Knowles, 86, 214,
261
Watson, Goodwin, 149–150
Wattles, Willard, 160, 199
Wavell, Bruce, 301–302
Weir, William Clarence ("W. C."),
121–122
Wilson, Kenneth, 211–212
Winter Park, FL, 1–2, 9. *See also*
Florida
advantages over other cities, 14
community pledges for Rollins
College, 17–18
land development, 15–16
skepticism about, 20–21
victory celebration at initial
announcement, 1–2
Wunsch, Robert, 184